KEEPING THE FAITHS

RELIGION AND IDEOLOGY
IN THE SOVIET UNION

KEEPING THE FAITHS

RELIGION AND IDEOLOGY
IN THE SOVIET UNION

Paul D. Steeves

From the Series Beyond The Kremlin

A publication of the Committee for National Security

HM

Holmes & Meier
New York ■ London

Published in the United States of America 1989 by
Holmes & Meier Publishers, Inc.
30 Irving Place
New York, N.Y. 10003

93   92   91   90   89   5   4   3   2   1

Library of Congress Cataloging-in-Publication Data

Steves, Paul D.
    Keeping the faiths: religion and ideology in the Soviet Union/
Paul D. Steeves.
      p. cm.
    ISBN 0-8419-1203-3 (pbk.: alk. paper).
    1. Soviet Union — Religion — 1917-   2. Ideology — Soviet Union —
History — 20th century.   I. Title.
    BL940.S65S73   1988
    291'.0947 — dc 19   88-39630
                                                      CIP

Paul D. Steeves is Professor of History and Director of Russian Studies at Stetson University in Deland, Florida, where he has taught since 1972. Educated at Washington University and the University of Kansas, Professor Steeves is a specialist in the history of Protestantism in Russia and the Soviet Union. He is the editor of *The Modern Encyclopedia of Religions of Russia and the Soviet Union*.

Designed by Meadows & Wiser, Washington, DC

Cover illustration by Matt Mahurin.

Composed in Century Expanded and Franklin Gothic by
General Typographers, Inc., Washington, DC

This book was manufactured in the United States of America and has been printed on acid free paper.

THE COMMITTEE FOR NATIONAL SECURITY

A national organization with headquarters in Washington, DC, the Committee for National Security (CNS) informs Americans about U.S. — Soviet relations, national security, and arms control issues and encourages active citizen participation in the ongoing debate over U.S. foreign policy. The Committee was founded in 1980 and currently has eleven full-time professional staff. The membership of the Committee is composed of prominent citizens concerned about our nation's drift toward excessive reliance on military power to resolve complex foreign policy problems. The Committee is a nonprofit and tax-exempt organization located at 1601 Connecticut Avenue, N.W., Suite 301, Washington, DC 20009; (202) 745-2450.

ACKNOWLEDGEMENTS AND EDITORIAL NOTES

The preparation of this volume would not have been possible without the assistance of a diverse group of dedicated scholars, artists and photographers, student interns, and financial contributors.

We first express particular gratitude to the officers and directors of the following foundations for their essential financial support: the Carnegie Corporation of New York, the General Services Foundation, the John D. and Catherine T. MacArthur Foundation, and the Topsfield Foundation.

We solicited and received valuable advice and suggestions from numerous people with extensive knowledge of religious affairs in the Soviet Union. We are particularly indebted to the following individuals for finding time on their overfull calendars to read and respond thoughtfully to an early draft of this volume: Susan Alexander, Anne Cahn, Robert Donaldson, Fred Eustis, William C. Fletcher, Nancy Ignatius, Lawrence Kaagan, Don Nead, Pedro Ramet, Michael Roshak, Robert Schmidt, Zeesy Schnur, Anne Shirk, and Robert Smylie.

Many other individuals provided us with guidance on issues as broad as overall structure and as narrow as identification of particular Russian icons. We thus thank Martin Bailey, Steve Batalden, Evelyn Musser, Mary Catherine Shambour, Richard Singleton, David Snelbecker, and Lynn Wildman. For his commitment and generosity, we express special thanks to Matt Mahurin for creating a powerful and captivating painting for the book's cover.

The preparation of this book would not have been possible without the permissions CNS was granted to reprint copyrighted textual and graphic materials, and we are especially grateful to those who granted such permission without charge.

Finally, we acknowledge the enormous amount of talent, energy, and scholarship that our author brought to this project. Paul Steeves's knowledge and insight, patience, and flexible yet determined character made possible the creation of this book. Working with him has been a pleasurable and enriching endeavor.

A few brief editorial observations are required to avoid confusing readers. First, inconsistencies in the spelling of Russian names exist because the authors of various excerpts used different systems of transliteration. Second, short quotations from official Communist Party documents and speeches — available in primary sources and in numerous reprinted forms — are not footnoted. Sources for basic primary documents, however, are listed as part of the Suggested Readings in the last section of the book. Finally, excerpts and quotations from Russian newspapers, journals, and official documents were translated by Paul Steeves unless otherwise noted.

Despite the good advice we received throughout this collaborative effort, errors may remain; they are solely the fault of the author and the Committee for National Security.

JJH
Washington, DC, 1989

BEYOND THE KREMLIN

SERIES INTRODUCTION

We have been on a blind date with the Soviet Union for decades. Although skeptical about our compatibility, we have been unable, often unwilling, to end the relationship. We fear what might happen.

We have tried working things out. We have challenged each other, "eyeball to eyeball," in Cuba and Berlin. We have signed documents, held meetings, and consulted with friends about what to do. We have tried to cooperate and build on common interests. But still we remain unsure, ambivalent, worried about how to handle this troubled relationship. What should we do? Can we learn to live with the Soviet Union? Can we afford not to?

Even to begin tackling these questions, we need to know more about the Union of Soviet Socialist Republics, and that is the goal of this series: to enable Americans to assess more accurately the Soviet Union — its policies, goals, people, culture, and problems. There are, however, numerous obstacles. Language is a problem. Travel is restricted. The Soviets make it difficult for journalists and scholars to prepare books and articles accurately portraying the state of affairs in their country. This penchant for secrecy and distortion is part of the dark, menacing side of the Soviet Union: its controlled press, its limited freedoms, its lack of what our Declaration of Independence calls "unalienable rights."

In addition, educating ourselves about the Soviet Union is difficult because we are now adversaries. We treat each other as such, competing for power, access to resources, and influence around the globe — from Poland to Nicaragua and the Philippines. Our leaders point at each other, posturing for their audiences. Being enemies in the nuclear age carries enormous risks; the stakes could not get much higher. Fears are heightened, time for reflection and judgment is shortened, and reasoned discourse can be (and often is) replaced by anxious rhetoric. Ideological differences present yet another obstacle. We believe in and live by different sets of principles. Communism and democracy represent alternative ways of organizing society, and they embody powerfully contrasting views about the role of individuals in politics and society.

One of the greatest strengths of democratic nations is that they preserve for their citizens the right to know and learn and talk about systems of government and ideologies that differ from their own. By exercising this right, we can help ourselves and our nation. We need to know more about the Soviet Union, a country that is so important but with which we have had such a stormy relationship. There are expansive political, even philosophical, questions crying out for our attention. What really makes the Soviets tick? What does the withdrawal from Afghanistan mean? Is Gorbachev really going to be different? Can religion survive in a Communist state? And there are small, even simple, questions too — but questions we also need to address before we can know what the Soviet Union is all about. What do the people eat? What do they read and do for pleasure and wear? Do they watch TV? What are Soviet schools like? Do children go to summer camp? What is the divorce rate? Do mothers work?

The books in this series are organized topically and address both broad political questions and precise factual ones. Each book can be read by itself or in conjunction with others in the series. A list of the other books planned for the *Beyond the Kremlin* series is in the Reader's Guide.

As you begin to probe the complexity of the Soviet Union by thinking about the readings in *Beyond the Kremlin*, you will almost certainly imagine more questions than we have been able to ask or answer. The Reader's Guide, which includes an annotated reading list, suggests some ways in which you might pursue your questions. The Reader's Guide offers suggestions on how to organize discussion groups, how to lead discussions, and some questions to consider. It also briefly describes other educational activities that might complement or flow from participation in a discussion group. Although a discussion group is not essential to enjoying and benefiting from the material, its give and take may be stimulating and helpful in trying to understand the U.S.S.R.

The relationship in which we are enmeshed with the Soviet Union is complex, confusing, and sometimes frightening. It is, however, a relationship, and the Soviet Union is a nation we need to know more about. The cost of remaining uninformed is high. By its very nature, a blind date does not last forever.

CONTENTS

INTRODUCTION

What does the typical American think about religion in the Soviet Union? If we put this question to a handful of "typical" Americans, it is likely that we would get as many different answers as the number of persons we asked. Some Americans seem to assume that the religious situation in the U.S.S.R. is ordinary and routine, although they may not think much about what that would mean. Others think that there probably is little religious activity, at least that is legal. Still others may imagine that Russian religion is a bit exotic because Russians seem rather Asiatic instead of European.

It is not surprising that we would get so many different answers; conflicting reports and impressions about religion in the Soviet Union abound. Images of "Godless Communists," of the mass destruction of churches during Josef Stalin's rule, and of present day Jews protesting the denial of their right to emigrate conflict with recent accounts of vigorous religious activity in the Soviet Union. Indeed, during the 1988 celebration of the millenium of Christianity in Russia, Americans learned of monasteries being returned to the church and saw pictures of worshippers crowding into recently renovated churches. On April 30, newspapers across the United States ran front page pictures of General Secretary Gorbachev and Russian Orthodox Patriarch Pimen exchanging smiles and a warm, friendly handshake.

A first step toward understanding religion in the Soviet Union is to recognize the dimensions of religious life in this vast country. Today, the Soviet population includes as many as seventy million Orthodox Christians, approximately forty million Muslims, three million Eastern Rite Catholics in Ukraine, over two million Roman Catholics, and many thousands of Baptists, Lutherans, Jews, Evangelical Protestants, and a variety of other religious denominations.

Second, it is essential to understand the role of the Orthodox church in

How are political ideology and religious belief related — in the Soviet Union today and in ancient Russia centuries ago?

From *Moscow: Monuments of Architecture of the 14th-17th Centuries,*
Courtesy of the USSR Embassy, Washington, DC.

■ 13

Russian history. Until the twentieth century, a large majority of the Russian Empire's population professed Orthodox belief. Now, while somewhat more than half the Soviet population claims no formal religious affiliation, Orthodoxy remains the largest single religion in the Soviet Union. At least one sixth of the population maintains some sort of identification with it. But more than sheer numbers make Orthodoxy important. To a large extent, the coming of Christianity to ancient Kievan Rus in 988 determined the course of Russian history and shaped the nature of Russian culture. Even Konstantin Kharchev, chairman of the Soviet Council for Religious Affairs — the government office that oversees religious activity — notes this fact. "It would be a mistake," he says "to deny the positive role of Orthodoxy in the expansion of political and cultural ties of Rus with the West and the development of literacy, architecture, and painting. The church played its role in the establishment of centralized government, and the service of its representatives in patriotic matters is beyond question" (quoted in an interview in "Guarantees of Freedom," *Nauka i religiia*, no. 11, 1987, p. 22–23).

As Kharchev implies, the Orthodox church's importance derives, in part, from its close affiliation with the state; the two have always been closely tied. Both when the ruler was required by law to be of Orthodox faith and for most of the time since the rulers have been of the atheist Communist Party, the civil government has subjected the church to its control. The church, for its part, has accepted its subordinate position, receiving in exchange a modicum of privilege and support. Subjection to state control has been the norm even for religions other than Orthodoxy. To be sure, there have been instances when people resisted this subordination, especially when a religion had newly appeared in Russian society as a result either of territorial expansion or of a sectarian breakaway from an established church. But continued resistance has generally been an anomaly in Russian religious history; resistors have usually reconciled themselves to the state system.

Similarly, Orthodox religious belief has always been equated with patriotism. From the thirteenth century when monks fought to protect the state from the Mongol Hordes to World War II when the church created, at its own expense, the Alexander Nevsky aircraft squadron and the Dimitry Donskoy tank column, the church has always committed itself to defending the nation. Indeed, at the onset of World War II when Stalin needed to stir the Soviet citizenry to take up arms and fight, he invoked images of Orthodox Mother Russia, not of the socialist Soviet Union.

Ironically, many characteristics of Orthodoxy not only survived the Bolshevik revolution, but helped to shape the athiest Union of Soviet Socialist Republics. The Communist emphasis on community rather than the individual, for example, reflects Russian Orthodox tradition. In Orthodox Christianity, the importance of individual interests is minimized. Religious organizations consistently — if not always successfully

— sought to elevate the good of the community above the rights of the individual. Likewise, Communist ideology and Orthodoxy share an intolerance of ideological and doctrinal diversity.

Orthodox and Communist Russia share, further, an emphasis on ritual. In Orthodoxy, worship is far more important than theology; the emotional has taken precedence over the intellectual. In today's Soviet Union, the power of ceremony to move and motivate people has not only been a factor behind religion's persistence, but it has also become a part of socialist life. Religion's secular opponents have devised surrogate ceremonies as alternatives to religious ceremonies in an attempt to channel this Russian emotion for their own purposes.

Understanding the state of religion in the Soviet Union today is a complex task. It cannot be summed up simply, either by labelling the populace "Godless Communists" or by considering only the abundant religious activity we have witnessed during the celebration of the millenium. However, there is no doubt that religious life continues in the Soviet Union. As Michael Bourdeaux, the director of Keston College's Center for the Study of Religion and Communism writes, "Wherever we look beneath the surface in a Communist country, there is evidence of great religious vitality. . . . The Soviet press cannot disguise the fact that more and more young people are returning to the fold of the church in a way that hasn't happened in Russia in over a hundred years" (quoted in an editorial in *America*, July 28, 1984, p. 21).

In discussing both the history of religion and its place in society, *Keeping the Faiths* explores how Russian religion has developed and continues to develop as it adapts and perseveres in changing circumstances.

RELIGIOUS TRADITION:

FROM KIEVAN RUS TO A TSARIST EMPIRE

All people feel a sense of the spiritual. Not satisfied with meeting just their physical needs, they search for meaning in life and order in the surrounding world. For many, religion satisfies these spiritual longings and provides a structure for celebrating life's milestones — birth, marriage, death—and an outlet for the most intense emotions—love and happiness, grief and guilt. While there are clearly many similarities in how people express their religious aspirations, there are also marked national differences. With some effort, it is possible to find out what these differences are and to answer questions such as, What is "Russian religion" like? or What makes up the Russian soul? Indeed, this chapter will be devoted to that effort.

Through an evolutionary process, religious expression in a particular nation takes on distinctive characteristics, and these mold the values and world outlook of the people. Even when large numbers of a population abandon the regular practice of formal religion, as they have in the Soviet Union, the influence of their religious tradition lives on.

It is not possible to understand the present moral, spiritual, and ideological values found in the Soviet Union without knowing something about its religious tradition. What are the distinctive features of religion as it has been practiced in what is now the U.S.S.R.? In seeking to answer that question, this chapter focuses mainly on the Russian people, even though the U.S.S.R. now includes a large minority of ethnic groups with their own particular religious traditions. The 140 million Russians of the U.S.S.R. make up just over half of the population; sharing a common religious and cultural heritage with the Russians are 50 million Ukrainians and Belorussians. These three groups, which trace their religious roots to the baptism of the people of Kiev in 988, make up 70 percent of the population. Because this group has been culturally dominant for centuries, its religious tradition, Eastern Orthodoxy, has

"To understand the present moral, spiritual, and ideological values found in the Soviet Union it is first necessary to know its religious tradition."

17

had a powerful impact, even upon Jews and Muslims, not to speak of the Christian Protestants and Catholics.

What the Russians came to consider good and true and beautiful we find in the story of the Russian past. That is what the values of a nation are about — what a people declares to be right and worthy of their allegiance. We find these values in the legends they treasure and the heroes they honor. We find them in the causes for which they are willing to lay down their lives and in the ordeals they endure. We find them in their religious ceremonies and in the way they express joy and sorrow. These are the things we shall look for as we scan almost one thousand years of Russian history.

A tale from the Russian treasury of the past that is told over and over again is the story of how Prince Vladimir (Volodymyr in Ukrainian) of Kiev chose Byzantine Christianity as the religion for his people. Tradition says that happened in the year 988, one millennium ago.

In 988, Kiev was the chief city of a loosely united federation of tribes and urban trading centers which bore the name Rus. Vladimir claimed to be a descendant of the Viking princes who had asserted political control in the late 800s over the native Slavic inhabitants of the land of Kievan Rus, a geographical area roughly equivalent to the present-day regions of Ukraine, Belorussia, and northwestern Russia. Little is known of the religion of the tribes of tenth century Rus. Apparently it was animistic, with a multitude of deities and spirits associated with the meadows and woodlands. Each tribe honored those spirits which inhabited the locale where tribe members lived. In the course of the 900s, Rus emerged as a thriving commercial region, profiting from vigorous trade with two great empires to the south, those of Byzantium and Baghdad.

For a short time around the middle of the 900s, a woman, Princess Olga (Olha in Ukrainian) ruled the Rus confederation. (Olga had taken over as chief after her husband was killed in a rebellion.) She acted quickly and firmly to restore order in Rus and to consolidate her control, which she maintained until 962 when she turned power over to her son, Vladimir's father. In about 955, Olga became a Christian and was baptized in Constantinople. For the next five years, she tried unsuccessfully to promote Christianity as a religion for all her subjects but failed to persuade even her son to become a Christian.

After Vladimir became prince of Kiev in 978, he tried to impose a uniform religious system upon the people of Rus, with gods modeled after those worshipped by the Vikings. The chief god, for example, was Perun, who was much like Thor, the Viking god of thunder and war. Vladimir set up a shrine in Kiev with images of the gods he wanted his subjects to respect. It appears, however, that Vladimir's pantheon failed to replace the tribal animism of his subjects.

In the aftermath of this failure, Vladimir turned to Christianity and ordered his subjects baptized into Eastern Orthodoxy. The timing of

Portrayed in thousands of images over many centuries, the baptism of Prince Vladimir forever altered the course of Russian history.

From the *Radziwill* Manuscript.

Vladimir's conversion suggests that he adopted the new religion to serve his political interests, thus beginning a tradition that has run virtually unbroken throughout the history of the Russian Orthodox Church. The church has generally been willing to serve the interests of the government, even when the government has infringed upon the interests of the church. That precedent has continued to the present, even with a government fostering an atheistic ideology that views the traditional principles of the church as socially harmful.

The story of Vladimir's conversion, recounted below, need not be read as a literal account. In fact, the story was not even written down until almost 100 years after Vladimir's death, and we cannot be certain that any single detail of it is precisely true. National legends are easily changed and embellished in oral retelling, and Nestor, the Christian monk who authored the first written version, obviously let his Christianity bias his report. We cannot tell whether Vladimir's consideration of what religion to pick for his people involved events even remotely like the ones in the story.

But the power of this tale for the Russians lies not in the details of what actually happened but in the way the national memory has preserved it. This is the case with great folk legends; they enshrine the qualities which people value most, as Romans praised chastity in the figure of Lucretia and selfless patriotism in Cincinnatus, and Americans lifted up honesty in the young George Washington.

The significance of the following legend about how Vladimir chose Orthodoxy from among several alternatives lies in what it reveals about his perceptions of the desirable and undesirable features of different religions. The desirable values were love of the beautiful, maintenance of tradition, the quest for national security, and even a certain hedonism and emotionalism. These could be contrasted with values esteemed by other traditions, perhaps our own, such as rationality, discipline, temperance, and virtue.

" At this time (A.D. 983) the Russes were ignorant pagans. The devil rejoiced thereat, for he did not know that his ruin was approaching. . . . Vladimir was visited by Bulgars of Mohammedan faith, who said, "Though you are a wise and prudent prince, you have no religion. Adopt our faith, and revere Mahomet." Vladimir inquired what was the nature of their religion. They replied that they believed in God, and that Mahomet instructed them to practice circumcision, to eat no pork, to drink no wine, and, after death, promised them complete fulfillment of their carnal desires. . . . They also spoke other false things which out of modesty may not be written down. Vladimir listened to them for he was fond of women and indulgence, regarding which he heard with pleasure. But circumcision and abstinence from pork and wine were disagreeable to him.

Samuel H. Cross and Olgerd P. Sherbowitz-Wetzor, eds. and trans., *The Russian Primary Chronicle* (Cambridge, MA: Harvard University Press, 1953), pp. 96, 97, 110, 111, 116, 117.

"Drinking," said he, "is the joy of the Russes. We cannot exist without that pleasure."

Then came the Germans, asserting that they were come as emissaries of the Pope. They added, "Thus says the Pope: 'Your country is like our country, but your faith is not as ours. For our faith is the light. We worship God, who has made heaven and earth, the stars, the moon, and every creature, while your gods are only wood.'" Vladimir inquired what their teaching was. They replied, "Fasting according to one's strength. But whatever one eats or drinks is all to the glory of God, as our teacher Paul has said." Then Vladimir answered, "Depart hence; our fathers accepted no such principle."

The Jewish Khazars heard of these missions, and came themselves saying, "We have learned that Bulgars and Christians came hither to instruct you in their faiths. The Christians believe in him whom we crucified, but we believe in the one God of Abraham, Isaac, and Jacob." Then Vladimir inquired what their religion was. They replied that its tenets included circumcision, not eating pork or hare, and observing the Sabbath. The Prince then asked where their native land was, and they replied that it was in Jerusalem. When Vladimir inquired where that was, they made answer, "God was angry at our forefathers, and scattered us among the gentiles on account of our sins. Our land was then given to the Christians." The Prince then demanded, "How can you hope to teach others while you yourselves are cast out and scattered abroad by the hand of God? If God loved you and your faith, you would not be thus dispersed in foreign lands. Do you expect us to accept this fate also?" . . .

(A.D. 987). Vladimir summoned together his boyars and the city elders and said to them, "Behold, the Bulgars came before me urging me to accept their religion. Then came the Germans and praised their own faith; and after them came the Jews. Finally the Greeks appeared, criticizing all other faiths but commending their own, and they spoke at length, telling the history of the whole world from its beginning. Their words were artful, and it was wondrous to listen and pleasant to hear them. They preached the existence of another world. 'Whoever adopts our religion and then dies shall arise and live forever. But whosoever embraces another faith, shall be consumed with fire in the next world.' What is your opinion on this subject, and what do you answer?" The boyars and the elders replied, "You know, oh Prince, that no man condemns his own possessions, but praises them instead. If you desire to make certain, you have servants at your disposal. Send them to inquire about the ritual of each and how he worships God."

Their counsel pleased the prince and all the people, so that they chose good and wise men to the number of ten, and directed them to go first among the Bulgars and inspect their faith. The emissaries went their way. . . .

[Later] they returned to their own country, and the Prince . . .

> "The power of Vladimir's conversion for Russians lies not in the details of what actually happened, but in the way national memory has preserved the tale."

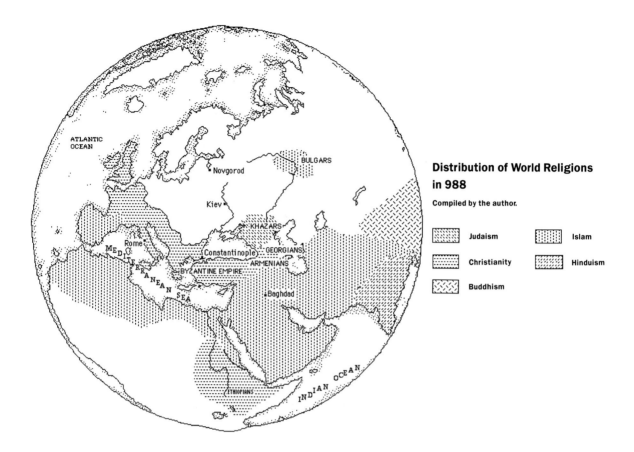

Distribution of World Religions in 988

Compiled by the author.

- Judaism
- Christianity
- Buddhism
- Islam
- Hinduism

(labeled on map: ATLANTIC OCEAN, BULGARS, Novgorod, Kiev, KHAZARS, Rome, MEDITERRANEAN SEA, Constantinople, GEORGIANS, ARMENIANS, BYZANTINE EMPIRE, Baghdad, ETHIOPIANS, INDIAN OCEAN)

commanded them to speak out before his retinue. The envoys reported, "When we journeyed among the Bulgars, we beheld how they worship in their temple, called a mosque, while they stand ungirt. The Bulgar bows, sits down, looks hither and thither like one possessed, and there is no happiness among them, but instead only sorrow and a dreadful stench. Their religion is not good.

Then we went among the Germans, and saw them performing many ceremonies in their temples; but we beheld no glory there.

Then we went to Greece, and the Greeks led us to the [Greek Orthodox] edifices where they worship their God, and we knew not whether we were in heaven or on earth. For on earth there is no such splendor or such beauty, and we are at a loss how to describe it. We only know that God dwells there among men, and their service is fairer than the ceremonies of other nations. For we cannot forget that beauty. Every man, after tasting something sweet, is afterward unwilling to accept that which is bitter, and therefore we cannot dwell longer here."

Then the boyars spoke and said, "If the Greek faith were evil, it would not have been adopted by your grandmother Olga who was wiser than all other men. . . ."

(A.D. 988). Thereafter Vladimir sent heralds throughout the whole city to proclaim that if any inhabitant, rich or poor, did not betake

What do the very beginnings of Orthodoxy in tenth century Kiev reveal about early Russian society and its values?

CHRONOLOGY OF EVENTS

955	Princess Olga of Kiev baptized in Constantinople
988	Baptism of Prince Vladimir and the people of Rus; Orthodoxy becomes Russian national religion
1015	Deaths of Princes Boris and Gleb, first native saints of Russian Orthodox Church
1019–54	Reign of Yaroslav the Wise, builder of Cathedral of Holy Wisdom and Monastery of the Caves
1155	Prince Andrei moves icon of Virgin of Vladimir from Kiev to Vladimir as symbol of that center of political power has shifted
1240	Prince Alexander defeats Swedes at Neva River; Mongol conquest of Russians
1388	Prince Dmitry Donskoy defeats Mongols at Kulikovo Field with blessing of St. Sergius
1395	Prince Vasily moves icon of Virgin of Vladimir to Dormition Cathedral in Moscow Kremlin
1411	Andrei Rublev paints icon of Old Testament Trinity
1505	Monk Philotheus states ideology of Moscow the Third Rome
1551	Council of the Hundred Chapters identifies distinguishing characteristics of Russian national Orthodoxy
1552	Moscow conquers Kazan and begins incorporating Muslims within Russian rule; Ivan the Terrible builds St. Basil's Cathedral on Moscow's Red Square to commemorate victory
1589	First Orthodox Patriarch of Moscow elected
1596	Union of Brest creates Eastern Rite Greek Catholic Church

himself to the river, he would risk the Prince's displeasure. When the people heard these words, they wept for joy, and exclaimed in their enthusiasm, "If this were not good, the Prince and his boyars would not have accepted it." On the morrow, the Prince went forth . . . with the priests . . . to the Dnieper [the river which flows past the city of Kiev] . . . and a countless multitude assembled. They all went into the water: some stood up to their necks, others to their breasts, and the younger near the bank, some of them holding children in their arms, while the adults waded farther out. The priests stood by and offered prayers.

When the people were baptized, they returned each to his own abode. Vladimir . . . ordained that wooden churches should be built and established where pagan idols had previously stood. He thus founded the Church of St. Basil on the hill where the idol of Perun and the other images had been set, and where the prince and the people had offered their sacrifices. He began to found churches and to assign priests throughout the cities. . . . He took the children of the best families, and sent them for instruction in book learning.

1652	Patriarch Nikon decrees reform of Orthodox liturgical practices which begins Schism of Old Believers
1666–67	Church Council approves Nikonian reforms and condemns both schismatics and Nikon
1701	Death of last Patriarch of Moscow before the twentieth century
1721	Peter the Great issues Spiritual Regulation, making Orthodox Church a department of state
1762–65	Monastery lands confiscated by orders of Emperor Peter III and Empress Catherine the Great
1772	First incorporation under Russian rule of a substantial body of Jews when Catherine the Great annexes a part of Poland
1839	Synod of Polotsk unites Eastern Rite Catholics within empire with Russian Orthodox Church, suppressing "Uniate" church.
1871	Wave of anti-Jewish pogroms begins
1876	First publication of entire Bible in Russian
1884	Formation of Russian Baptist Union; Procurator General of Holy Synod declares Russian Baptists illegal
1903	Kishinev pogrom against Jews; first appearance of fraudulent anti-Semitic Protocols of the Elders of Zion
1905	Nicholas II declares religious toleration for all religions except "socially dangerous" sects; proselytization of Orthodox by non-Orthodox forbidden
1911	United States abrogates commercial treaty with Russia in protest against anti-Jewish pogroms

The people receiving mass baptism probably understood little about their new religion, and it seems unlikely that they rejoiced as enthusiastically as the chronicle reports, especially in light of their stubborn resistance to Olga's and Vladimir's earlier attempts to change their religion. But by this time the might of the state must have proved decisive, and when the legend was recorded, Vladimir's chosen religion had penetrated Kievan society. The Christian chronicler therefore naturally assumed that the people would have rejoiced.

The new religion that Vladimir adopted from the Greeks is known as Eastern Orthodoxy or Greek Orthodoxy, as distinct from Western Christianity or Roman Catholicism. When Vladimir had his people baptized, the division of medieval Christendom into these two branches, which occurred gradually over several centuries, was not yet formalized. (The conventional date for the formal rupture is 1054.) As the legend makes clear, aesthetic values, rather than intellectual or ethical ones, made Orthodoxy appealing. But in making that point the chronicler was again reading later conditions back into Vladimir's time.

The Orthodoxy that Vladimir brought to his people claimed to be doctrinally complete. Orthodoxy calls itself "the Church of the Seven Councils." This label refers to seven meetings of leaders of churches, representing most of the Christians in the world at the time. These "ecumenical councils" met between the years 325 and 787 A.D. In Orthodoxy's view, these councils defined the theological, liturgical, and ethical norms which Christians were to follow. Any addition to these norms could be made only by another ecumenical council, and Orthodox belief holds that such a council has not convened since 787.

The Russians' perception that their religion was doctrinally complete and not open to theological development determined their religious behavior. They immersed themselves in the experience of ritual and developed an artistic culture and historical sense which enshrined the values of Orthodoxy, as the following excerpt explains.

James H. Billington, *The Icon and the Axe* (New York: Random House, 1966), pp. 6–9.

"Kiev accepted more unreservedly than Byzantium itself the claim that Orthodox Christianity had solved all the basic problems of belief and worship. All that was needed was "right praising" (the literal translation of *pravoslavie*, the Russian version of the Greek *orthodoxos*) through the forms of worship handed down by the Apostolic Church and defined for all time by its seven ecumenical councils. Changes in dogma or even sacred phraseology could not be tolerated, for there was but one answer to any controversy. The Eastern Church first broke with Rome in the late ninth century. . . . Nowhere was the traditional Eastern formula defended with greater zeal than in Russia. As if compensating for the relative lateness of their conversion, Russian Orthodoxy tended to accept unquestioningly Orthodox definitions of truth and Byzantine forms of art. . . .

Working within this ornate and stylized Byzantine heritage, Kievan Russia developed two distinctive attitudes which gave an all-important initial sense of direction to Russian culture. First was a direct sense of beauty, a passion for seeing spiritual truth in concrete forms. The beauty of Constantinople and of its places and forms of worship was responsible for the conversion of Vladimir. . . . The Kievan princes sought to recreate this experience of beauty in the Byzantine-style cathedrals that sprang up in every important city of Eastern Slavdom. The panoply of heaven was represented by the composed central dome; its interior was embellished with the awesome image of the Pantokrator [the Almighty], the Divine Creator of both heaven and earth. Prominent among the other mosaic and frescoed figures that beautified the interior walls and domes was the Theotokos, the "God-bearing" Virgin. The cathedrals provided a center of beauty and a source of sanctification for the surrounding region. . . .

Concrete beauty rather than abstract ideas conveyed the essence of the Christian message to the early Russians, and inspired a fresh flowering of Byzantine art and letters on Russian soil. Man's function was not to analyze that which has been resolved or to explain that which is mysterious, but lovingly and humbly to embellish the inherited forms of praise and worship. . . . The early Russians were drawn to Christianity by the aesthetic appeal of its liturgy, not the rational shape of its theology. . . .

The same desire to see spiritual truth in tangible form accounts for the extraordinary sense of history that is a second distinguishing feature of early Russian culture. As with many simple warrior people, religious truth tended to be verified by the concrete test of ability to inspire victory. The miraculous pretensions of Christianity were not unique among world religions; but Orthodox Christianity offered a particularly close identification of charismatic power with historical tradition.

> **"Concrete beauty rather than abstract ideas conveyed the essence of the Christian message to early Russians."**

Another feature of the Byzantine heritage concerns church-state relations. As the following excerpt explains, the way that Byzantium defined the relationship between religion and politics greatly influenced Russian culture. In Russia, the church generally has taken a subservient position in relationship to the state, while in the frequent confrontations between church and state in the west — among Catholics and Protestants alike — the church has repeatedly emerged as independent from the state and often somewhat dominant over it.

O f the many elements of this intricate [Byzantine] civilization that were influential among the Russes, perhaps the most important for politics were their ideas of harmony and of kingship, which include the relations between church and state.

The first of these goes back to the shadowy figure of Pythagoras in the sixth century B.C., who expressed a conception of the universe of which the essence was the order of number and proportion. All things in heaven and earth were made to fit together, to work in harmony, each in its proper sphere. . . .

When [the church father] Eusebius, in the fourth century, undertook to explain the position of the Christian emperor, Constantine, he found the well-established pagan theory to be quite acceptable. It was necessary only to regard the emperor, not as a god, but as the vicegerent of God; all the rest of the old explanation remained intact. The earthly empire was a copy of the heavenly, just as the pagans had said. As in heaven there was one God and one divine law, so on earth there could be only one emperor in a universal empire, centralized and autocratic, yet ruling by one law. . . .

Thornton Anderson, *Russian Political Thought* (Ithaca, NY: Cornell University Press, 1967), pp. 23–26.

The onion domes of Russia's cathedrals were designed to shed snow easily as well as to fulfill the spiritual desire to reach up reverently toward heaven.

Courtesy of Lynn Wildman.

With the world conceived as partaking in the celestial harmony, and the emperor in the role of the good shepherd, the relations of church and state were also conceived to be harmonious. Further, the purposes of the two were not viewed as being distinct or separate but rather mutual and united. The doctrine of the separation of church and state, developed in the West by Ambrose [fourth century] and Gelasius [fifth century], had few adherents in the East. In Constantinople the church had never exercised authority over secular affairs as it had in Italy when the temporal power collapsed during the barbarian invasions. . . . The Eastern Church developed the theory of symphonia, a theory of judicious consultation and mutual respect that did not separate but rather combined the two powers in the apostolic task of conducting the people to salvation, on earth and in heaven.

This old and well-tried theory the bishops brought and applied to Rus, even though conditions there required that it rest upon somewhat modified bases. . . . The scales in Rus may have tipped a bit in favor of the princes, as compared with Byzantium, but . . . the symphonia in Rus retained its primary quality of cooperation between prelates and princes. **"**

The writer of this excerpt uses the term "symphonia" to describe the pattern of church-state relations which Russia acquired from Byzantium, expressing the theoretical ideal of those relations. The way those relations actually developed in practice for Eastern Orthodoxy, first in Byzantium and later in Russia, is more accurately described as "caesaropapism," the control of the church by the state. The history of relations between Russian rulers and the church, which are traced in this book, shows how the state repeatedly asserted its control over the religious experience and institutions of the people. This is a theme of Russian history which continues to echo today in the Soviet Union.

After his conversion, Prince Vladimir spent much of his life building churches and introducing Byzantine culture into Rus. He is one of the great saints of Russian Orthodoxy, a religion in which the veneration of saints plays an essential role. The Orthodox calendar assigns to each day of the year the names of several saints to whom the day is dedicated. When infants or adults are baptized as Orthodox Christians, they are given the name of a saint, usually one designated for that day. The saint for whom a believer is named has special significance for that believer: he or she prays daily to that saint, and the date assigned for honoring the saint is the believer's "name day," which has more significance for the believer than the birthday.

Many of the saints the Russians honor lived in the early centuries of Christianity, and the Russians' respect for them is shared with Christians throughout the world. Other saints were Russians who had no significance for most Christians elsewhere but who won special places in the hearts and national memory of the Russians. These "Russian saints" became religiously significant for Russia because of that distinctive sense of history which was previously mentioned in the excerpt of James Billington; they demonstrated charismatic power in events that formed the Russian people. The stories which the Russians tell about their saints vividly illustrate what kind of behavior the Russians consider worthy of praise. Episodes from the stories of four beloved Russian saints are included as excerpts below. The four are heroes of the Russian nation: Saints Boris, Gleb, Alexander Nevsky, and Sergius. The great deeds that made them saints served the welfare of the Russian nation and state. These saints are revered for qualities which other Christians seldom associate with sainthood. The typical Christian saint was beatified for spreading the gospel, or humbly serving the unfortunate, demonstrating extraordinary piety and self-discipline, or dying a martyr for the faith. These were not the kinds of deeds that promoted the chief saint-heroes of the Russians. It is significant that three of these four were princes; that is, they were political and military figures, as were an uncommonly large proportion of other Russian saints.

The following story tells of the martyrdom of the first Russian saints, Boris and Gleb. When Prince Vladimir died in 1015, a bloody conflict over who should ascend to the throne erupted among his sons. The Russian chronicle tells how Vladimir's retinue wanted Boris to become prince, but the oldest son, Sviatopolk, plotted to win the throne for himself.

"THE SEALED ANGEL"

In the eleventh century, Metropolitan Illarion described the city of Prince Vladimir's conversion as "a city glistening with the holy light of holy icons, fragrant with incense, ringing with praise and holy, heavenly songs."

The mystical attraction that "glistening" icons still hold for Russian believers is revealed in the following story by Nikolai Leskov, a nineteenth-century writer unsurpassed in his portrayal of ordinary Russian peasants. In "The Sealed Angel" he tells how a group of itinerant workers lost their favorite icon and struggled to recover it. The worker who narrates the tale talks reverently about that icon of the angel.

Nikolai Leskov, "The Sealed Angel" in *Lady Macbeth of Mtsensk and Other Stories* (Middlesex: Penguin, 1987), pp. 180–181, 214.

"That angel was truly indescribable. His face — I can see it before me now — was so divinely radiant and so compassionate; his gaze was tender; there were thongs above his ears, a sign of his universal power of hearing; his raiment burned, mottled all over with gold pendants; his armor was like fishes' scales, and his shoulders were heavily girdled; at his breast he bore a round icon of the boy Emmanuel; in his right hand there was a cross, in his left a fiery sword. Wonderful! Wonderful! . . . You would look at [his] wings, and all your fear would vanish: "Protect me," you would pray, and in an instant you would grow calm, and peace would enter your soul. That was what kind of an icon it was! The icon went before us wherever our steps took us, as if the angel himself were preceding us. We would tramp from place to place through the steppes, always in search of new work. . . . Everything went swimmingly for us, and we had the most marvelous success in each and every one of our endeavors: we invariably found good work; harmony prevailed among us; and the news from those we had left at home put our minds at rest. For all this we blessed our angel who went before us, and I think we would have found it easier to surrender

But Sviatopolk was filled with lawlessness. Adopting the device of Cain, he sent messages to Boris that he desired to live at peace with him, and would increase the patrimony he had received from his father. But he plotted against him how he might kill him. So Sviatopolk came by night to Vyshegorod. After secretly summoning to his presence Putsha and the boyars of the town, he . . . commanded them to say nothing to any man, but to go and kill his brother Boris. . . .

These emissaries came to the Alta, and when they approached, they

Samuel H. Cross and Olgerd P. Sherbowitz-Wetzor, eds. and trans., *The Russian Primary Chronicle* (Cambridge, MA: Harvard University Press, 1953), pp. 126–130.

our very own lives than to part with this miraculous icon.

[Later in the story the narrator reports an encounter with an Englishman who found the Russians' devotion to icons puzzling from his Protestant point of view. To explain how icons taught piety to the believers the Russians described the iconostasis of the church of Holy Wisdom (Hagia Sophia) in Novgorod, a church for which Russians have especially great affection.]

I began telling him about the way the starry heavens are painted in Novgorod, . . . the seven-pronged candlestick, representing the gift of reason; the seven eyes representing the gift of wise counsel; the seven trumpets, representing the gift of strength; the right hand amidst the seven stars, representing the gift of vision; . . . "There," I said, "that's the kind of depiction that's uplifting!"

But the Englishman replied: "I'm sorry, old chap, but I don't understand why you consider all that uplifting."

"Because a depiction like that tells a man in no uncertain terms that the duty of Christians is to pray and yearn to be exalted from the earth to realms of unspoken glory."

"But anyone can understand from the Scriptures and the orthodox prayers."

"Certainly not," I replied. "It isn't given to everyone to understand the scriptures, and for those who don't understand, there are obscure passages in the prayers as well . . . But when he sees before him a depiction of heavenly glory, he thinks about the higher things of life and comes to understand how this goal [of heaven] may be reached, because here everything is simple and sensible: if a man prays first of all for the gift of the fear of God to enter his soul, that soul of his will immediately pass, made lighter, from stage to stage, appropriating with each new step a superabundance of higher gifts.

In what ways are the revered saints of Russia different from the saints worshipped by Christians in the West?

As illustrated in this depiction of Mongol Chief Chelibey combating a chaplain at the famed Kulikovo battle, Russian Orthodox clergy have fought to defend their monasteries as well as their country throughout history.

Sovfoto.

heard the sainted Boris singing vespers. For it was already known to him that they intended to take his life. . . . After finishing vespers, he prayed, gazing upon the icon, the image of the Lord, with these words: "Lord Jesus Christ, who in this image hast appeared on earth for our salvation, and who, having voluntarily suffered thy hands to be nailed to the cross, didst endure thy passion for our sins, so help me now to endure my passion. For I accept it not from those who are my enemies, but from the hand of my own brother. Hold it not against him as a sin, O Lord!"

After offering this prayer, he lay down upon his couch. Then they fell upon him like wild beasts about the tent, and overcame him by piercing him with lances. . . . Thus died the blessed Boris, receiving from the hand of Christ our God the crown among the righteous. He shall be numbered with the prophets and the Apostles, as he joins with the choirs of martyrs. . . .

The impious Sviatopolk then reflected: "Behold I have killed Boris; now how can I kill Gleb?" . . . Yaroslav [another son of Vladimir] sent word to Gleb that his brother had been murdered by Sviatopolk. Upon receiving these tidings, Gleb burst into tears. . . . He wept and prayed with lament: "Woe is me, O Lord! It were better for me to die with my brother than to live on in this world. . . ." While he was thus praying amid his tears, there suddenly arrived those sent by Sviatopolk for Gleb's destruction. . . . He was offered up as a sacrifice to God like an innocent lamb, a glorious offering amid the perfume of incense, and he received

the crown of glory. Entering the heavenly mansions, he beheld his long-desired and rejoiced with him. . . .

[The storyteller now addresses the glorified Boris and Gleb as patrons of the Russian nation.]

United thus in body and still more in soul, ye dwell with the Lord and King of all, in eternal joy, ineffable light, bestowing salutary gifts upon the land of Russia. . . . Ye are protectors of the land of Russia, shining forever like beacons and praying to the Lord in behalf of your countrymen. . . . Ye glorious ones, with the sacred drops of your blood ye have dyed a robe of purple which ye wear in beauty, and reign forevermore with Christ, interceding with him for his new Christian nation. ,,

Boris and Gleb personified an important Russian value. They are honored because they submitted meekly to unjust treatment by their brother and thereby saved the nation from bloodshed. Their suffering was a sacrifice with clear echoes of the crucifixion of Christ. For Russians, the lives of Boris and Gleb provide a model of submission (some might say fatalistic resignation) to life's difficulties and injustices.

In the aftermath of the murders of Boris and Gleb, Sviatopolk paid for his crime against his brothers. Yaroslav avenged their deaths by making war against him and driving him from Rus, for which Yaroslav was awarded the throne of Kiev. His reign brought great prosperity to Kiev, and he is remembered in Russian history as Yaroslav the Wise, a Russian counterpart of the Hebrew king Solomon.

Another type of Russian saint-hero is the warrior who saves the nation from foreign invaders. Alexander Nevsky and Dmitry Donskoy are the two most famous saints of this type. Alexander was the prince of Novgorod in 1240, at a time when the Mongols had already conquered most Russian lands and inflicted upon the people immense sufferings which are remembered with horror to this day. In the wake of the Mongol invasion, the Swedes attacked from the west in 1240 as did the German knights two years later. The Novgorodian army, led by Alexander, repulsed both these attacks in legendary battles. The first victory was on the river Neva, where the city of Leningrad now stands, and from it Alexander received his surname, "Nevsky," or "Alexander of the Neva." The second was the "Battle on the Ice" on Lake Chud, which is portrayed in the classic movie, *Alexander Nevsky*, filmed just before World War II by the pioneer Soviet film director, Sergei Eisenstein. Josef Stalin gave his special patronage to the making of that film with the clear interest of transferring Russian reverence for Alexander into patriotic support for the state, then threatened with invasion by Hitler's armies. Russians remember these Swedish and German invasions — which the pope declared to be crusades for the faith—as treachery by a Christian people against their brethren, who had been brought low by the Mogul invasion.

"Boris and Gleb are honored because they submitted to unjust treatment to save the nation from bloodshed."

Another well-known warrior saint, Dmitry Donskoy, was the prince of Moscow about 140 years after Alexander's victories. In all that time, the Russians had been under the domination of the Mongols — an era remembered as the "Mongol Yoke." They seldom put up any resistance to that domination because the Mongols retaliated with such cruelty, but in 1380 Dmitry mustered his countrymen to resist the conquerors in the Battle of Kulikovo Field, the first Russian victory over a Mongol army. For that act of heroism Dmitry was canonized by the Russian Orthodox Church.

According to legend, Dmitry found the courage to do battle with the Mongols because of the intervention of Sergius of Radonezh, another Russian saint. Saint Sergius represents the monk who devotes himself to prayer so that he can give sound advice to people and intercede with the Virgin Mary and the saints for the nation. The following story, which describes Sergius's accomplishments as a monk and as Dmitry's advisor, memorializes the role of the church in serving the interests of the state by using whatever resources it possesses on behalf of the rulers and for the good of the nation. That role is a constant theme in the Russian story from the time of Vladimir to the present.

Serge A. Zenkovsky, ed., *Medieval Russia's Epics, Chronicles and Tales* (New York: Dutton, 1974), pp. 262, 268–269, 284–285, trans. Nicholas Zernov.

"Our holy Father Sergius was born of noble, Orthodox, devout parents. His father was named Cyril and his mother Mary. They found favor with God; they were honorable in the sight of God and man, and abounded in those virtues which are well-pleasing unto God. . . .

Our saint was twenty-three years old when he joined the order of monks. Blessed Sergius, the newly tonsured monk, partook of the Holy Sacrament and received grace and the gift of the Holy Spirit. . . . Who can recount his labors? Who can number the trials he endured living alone in the wilderness? Under different forms and from time to time the devil wrestled with the saint, but the demons beset St. Sergius in vain; no matter what visions they evoked, they failed to overcome the firm and fearless spirit of the ascetic. At one moment it was Satan who laid his snares; at another, incursions of wild beasts took place, for many were the wild animals inhabiting this wilderness. . . . He diligently read the Holy Scripture to obtain a knowledge of all virtue, in his secret meditations training his mind in a longing for eternal bliss. Most wonderful of all, none knew the measure of his ascetic and godly life spent in solitude. God, the beholder of all hidden things, alone saw it. . . .

[After some time, Sergius built a monastery in the forest area to the north of Moscow called Radonezh (present day Zagorsk). That monastery, later known as the St. Sergius-Holy Trinity Monastery, has occupied an honored place in Russian history. In the twentieth century it has been the site of the headquarters of the Russian Orthodox Church, and the location of the Moscow Theological Academy. Although the

Orthodox Church is moving its headquarters to Moscow, the monastery will remain as a preeminent place of pilgrimage because Sergius's relics are kept there. The story of Sergius continues with the account of his role in the defeat of the Mongols.]

A rumor spread that [Mongol] Khan Mamai was raising a large army as a punishment for our sins and that with all his heathen Tatar hordes he would invade Russian soil. Very great fear prevailed among the people at this report. The puissant and reigning prince, who held the scepter of all Russia, great Dmitry, having a great faith in the saint, came to ask him if he counseled him to go against the heathen. The saint, bestowing on him his blessing, and strengthened by prayer, said to him: "It behooveth you, lord, to have a care for the lives of the flock

Founded by St. Sergius in 1340, the Trinity Monastery in Zagorsk has been one of the most important centers of Orthodoxy for centuries; it now houses the Moscow Ecclesiastical Academy.

AP/Wide World Photos.

committed to you by God. Go forth against the heathen; and upheld by the strong arm of God, conquer; and return to your country sound in health, and glorify God with loud praise. . . ."

And with the saint's blessing he hurriedly went on his way. Assembling all his armies, he marched against the heathen Tatars. . . . Dmitry and all his armies were filled with a spirit of temerity and went into battle against the pagans. They fought; many fell; but God was with them, and helped the great and invincible Dmitry, who vanquished the ungodly Tatars. In that same hour the saint was engaged with his brethren before God in prayer for victory over the pagans. Within an hour of the final defeat of the ungodly, the saint, who was a seer, announced to the brotherhood what had happened, the victory, the courage of the Grand Duke Dmitry, and the names, too, of those who had died at the hands of the pagans; and he made intercession for them to all-merciful God.

The Grand Duke Dmitry returned to his country with great joy in his heart, and hastened to visit holy, venerable Sergius. Rendering thanks for the prayers of the saint and of the brotherhood, he gave a rich offering to the monastery.

"

Russian Orthodoxy's respect for saints is closely related to its love for icons. The icon is the most distinctive, visible characteristic of Russian Orthodoxy. Indeed, Russia could be called "the land of icons," for the religious icon is the grandest artistic form developed by Russia in its premodern period. It is a tangible embodiment of Russia's religion and a ubiquitous presence in Russian society. Even in today's secularized Soviet society, icons are found in more than two-thirds of the homes of Ukrainians, Belorussians, and Russians. For the religious faithful, "these ever-present icons act as a point of meeting between the living members of the Church and those who have gone before. Icons help the Orthodox to look on the saints not as remote and legendary figures from the past, but as contemporaries and personal friends" (Timothy Ware, *The Orthodox Church* [Harmondsworth, Middlesex: Penguin, 1967], p. 261).

The typical icon is a painting of a religious subject made with tempera on wood. Such a simple physical description fails, however, to convey the deep religious significance of icons. The Orthodox believe that an icon has supernatural qualities, and therefore it has to be made in a prescribed way in order to be spiritually authentic. The rules for painting icons were established early in the medieval period. The painters of icons had to be spiritually pure, and for this reason they were usually monks or nuns. The standard icon was made by joining together several boards of non-resinous wood, which were covered with canvas that had been primed with a solution of chalk and glue, creating a smooth painting surface. The outline of the figures was sketched, following a pattern or copying another icon. The long-established rules for the representation of each subject curbed the artist's imagination. The artist made the paints from egg yolk, water, or kvas (a Russian fermented beverage), and mineral pigments from the soil. The use of local natural substances also carried a religious message, declaring the harmony of the created world with the uncreated eternal spiritual order which the icon depicted. The finished painting was sealed with olive or linseed oil.

To the Orthodox, an icon is not merely the representation of a holy subject. Rather it is a "holy painting," a vehicle that conveys a spiritual essence: it reveals divine truth; it transmits grace; it brings the worshipper nearer to heaven. An icon creates a mystical communion

Composed of numerous icons, reaching from floor to ceiling and separating the altar from the congregation, an iconostasis, like this one in the Kremlin's Cathedral of the Dormition, reinforces worshippers' belief that saints watch over and protect them.

between the worshippers and the spirit of the person or persons portrayed on it. In its religious meaning, an icon is not a work of art but a vision of spirituality. An icon makes visible that which is essentially invisible, namely a saint or the Virgin Mary or even the deity.

The style of painting reinforces the viewer's sense that the icon is not a mere picture of some material thing. Shapes of bodies may be distorted; the painting is flat and two-dimensional instead of giving an illusion of three-dimensionality; perspective may be reversed. This deliberate avoidance of a naturalistic style demonstrates Orthodox teaching that the physical is less real than the spiritual and that the spiritual transforms the physical.

Icons were ubiquitous in Russia until after the revolution in 1917. They surrounded the people in church. In front of the main altar, an entire wall of icons, called an iconostasis, provided the backdrop against which the drama of the liturgy unfolded. Other icons were placed throughout the church, thus proclaiming that the people of this world are constantly in the presence of the saints, as the apostle had written: "We are surrounded by a great cloud of witnesses." In the churches, Russians frequently showed their affection for icons by prostrating themselves in front of them and kissing them. Beyond the church walls, Russians encountered icons every day in their homes, where icons occupied the place of honor called "the red corner." (It was called the "red corner" because the Russian word for "red," *krasnyi*, originally meant "beautiful." Thus at first the corner was called the beautiful corner because of the presence of the icon. When *krasnyi* assumed the meaning "red" and a new word for "beautiful" appeared, the corner continued to be called "red." The same thing happened with the name of Red Square in Moscow.) Icons in public places, on the streets, and in officials' offices served as constant reminders that all of life is lived in the presence of God and his holy ones. Icons were carried to sick people, bringing them the healing power of the saints. Of special importance to believers were the icons depicting the saints for whom they were named. They knelt in prayer in front of them morning and evening.

These observations about icons prepare us for a theological discussion of their meaning by a Russian church scholar who examines in depth the spirituality of icons. This excerpt may be hard to grasp on first reading, but it will clarify the religious views of Russians.

> **"An icon is not just a work of art; it is a vision of spirituality."**

Leonid Ouspensky, *The Theology of the Icon* (Crestwood, NY: St. Vladimir's Seminary Press, 1978), pp. 191, 208, 211.

"The icon is an image not only of a living but also of a deified prototype. It does not represent the corruptible flesh, destined for decomposition, but transfigured flesh, illuminated by grace. . . .

The unusual details of appearance which we see in the icon — in particular in the sense organs: the eyes without brilliance, the ears which are sometimes strangely shaped — are represented in a non-naturalistic manner not because the iconographer was unable to do otherwise, but because their natural state was not what he wanted to represent. The icon's role is not to bring us closer to what we see in nature, but to show us a body which perceives what usually escapes man's perception, i.e., the perception of the spiritual world. . . . The non-naturalistic manner of representing the sense organs in icons conveys deafness, impassiveness, detachment from all excitation and, conversely, the receptiveness to the spiritual world by those who have attained holiness. The Orthodox icon is the expression in an image of this hymn: "Let all mortal flesh keep silent . . . pondering nothing earthly-minded". . . .

Thus the icon is both a means and a path to follow. It is itself a prayer. Visibly and directly, it reveals to us this freedom from passion about which the Fathers speak. It teaches us "to fast with our eyes," in the words of St. Dorotheus. And indeed, it is impossible "to fast with our eyes" before just any image, be it abstract, or even an ordinary painting. Only the icon can portray what it means "to fast with our eyes" and what this allows us to attain.

The goal of the icon is neither to provoke nor to exalt a natural human feeling. Its goal is to orient all of our feelings, as well as our intellect and all the other aspects of our nature, towards the transfiguration, stripping them of all emotional exaltation. It works like the Gospel, to which it corresponds. **"**

In addition to the essential forms of their artistic culture, Orthodoxy also gave the Russian people their way of viewing the meaning and purpose of their nation. The Russian perception of the world and of Russia's place in it was substantially summed up in the phrase "Moscow the Third Rome." Russian Messianism — the view that Russia had a unique mission to serve the rest of humanity and to promote its welfare —was an outgrowth of the Third Rome ideology. The monk Philotheus in the early sixteenth century stated this ideology most concisely: "All Christian realms will come to an end and will unite into one single realm of our sovereign, that is, into the Russian realm, according to the prophetic books. Both Romes fell, the third endures, and a fourth there will never be."

The legend of the White Cowl, which is excerpted below, was composed in Russia somewhat earlier than Philotheus's time in order to express in vivid story-form the historical view that his statement summarized. According to his interpretation of history, at one time Rome was the Christian capital city, but it lost God's favor by embracing false practices. The place of honor was then transferred to Constantinople. But Constantinople, too, betrayed Christian truth, and God showed his displeasure by allowing the "infidel" Turks to conquer the city in 1453. As the only Orthodox nation still under the rule of a Christian

Many orthodox believers keep icon corners similar to these in their homes. This peasant's icon corner, above right, is draped with a veil as a sign of respect while the candle symbolizes prayer.

Courtesy of Evelyn Musser (above).
Courtesy of Paul D. Steeves (above right).

prince after the Ottoman Turks had triumphed throughout the Christian East, the Russians became convinced that they stood in a special place — in God's favor as the final preserver of religious truth. The legend of the cowl is a parable of God's successive choices of "holy cities."

The legend, which takes place during the time that Christians were still suffering persecution in the Roman Empire, begins with the healing of the Emperor Constantine. Constantine fell sick, Pope Sylvester healed him, and in gratitude, Constantine ended the persecution and gave the cowl to the pope. This gift represented imperial confirmation that the pope exercised supreme spiritual authority in the realm. The popes in Rome retained possession of the cowl for several centuries, but they lost their right to it as they developed "Latin heresies" (for example, they amended the Nicene Creed to say that the Holy Spirit proceeds "from the son," they expressed weak appreciation for icons, and they asserted that the pope had individual authority to define and restate Christian truth). The excerpt begins at the point where God arranges the transfer of the cowl to Constantinople so that it can be sent from there to Russia as a demonstration of God's choice of Russia as the land of spiritual authority. In this story, the Russians assert their spiritual superiority as well as their virulent animosity for Western Catholicism.

" At that time [i.e., mid-1300s] the Patriarch of Constantinople was Philotheos, who was distinguished by his strict fasting and his virtuous ways. Once he had a vision in the night of a youth from whom emanated light and who told him: "Blessed teacher, in the olden times the Roman Emperor, Constantine, who, through the vision of the holy Apostles Peter and Paul, was enlightened by God, decided to give blessed Pope Sylvester the White Cowl to glorify the Holy Apostolic Church. Later, the unfaithful popes of the Latin heresies wanted to profane and destroy this cowl, but I appeared to the evil pope, and now this pope has sent this cowl to you. When the messengers arrive with it, you must accept it with all honors. Then send the White Cowl to the Russian land, to the city of Novgorod the Great with your written blessing. And there this cowl will be worn on the head of Vasily, Archbishop of Novgorod, so that he may glorify the Holy Apostolic Cathedral of Holy Wisdom and laud the Orthodox Faith. There, in that land, the faith of Christ is verily glorified. And the popes, because of their shamelessness, will receive the vengeance of God." And having spoken these words, the youth became invisible. . . .

After the White Cowl was sent from Rome, the evil pope, who was counseled by heretics, became angered against the Christian faith and was driven to a frenzy, extremely regretting his allowing the White Cowl to be sent to Constantinople. And he wrote an evil letter to the patriarch, in which he demanded the return of the White Cowl on the golden salver. The patriarch read this letter and, understanding the pope's evil and cunning design, sent him a letter in return that was based on Holy Scripture, and in it he called the pope both evil and godless, the apostate and precursor of the Antichrist. . . .

When the pope had read the letter and learned that the patriarch intended to send the White Cowl with great honor to the Russian land, to the city of Novgorod the Great, he uttered a roar. And his face changed and he fell ill, for he, the infidel, disliked the Russian land and could not even bear to hear of this land where the Christian faith was professed.

Patriarch Philotheos, having seen that the White Cowl was illumined with grace, began to ponder how he might keep it in Constantinople. . . . [But he had a vision in which a messenger said to him]: "Stop pondering your wearing of the White Cowl on your own head. If this were to be, Our Lord, Jesus Christ, would have so predestined it from the founding of this city. . . . The ancient city of Rome has broken away from the glory and faith of Christ because of its pride and ambition. In the new Rome, which has been the city of Constantinople, the Christian faith will also perish through the violence of the sons of Hagar [that is, the Turks; Russians viewed all Muslims as 'sons of Hagar,' the woman by whom the Hebrew patriarch Abraham fathered Ishmael]. In the third Rome, which will be the land of Russia, the Grace of the Holy Spirit will be revealed. Know then, Philotheos, that all Christians will finally unite into one Russian nation because of its Orthodoxy. . . . When you send it to

Serge A. Zenkovsky, ed. and trans., *Medieval Russia's Epics, Chronicles and Tales* (New York: Dutton, 1974), pp. 326–332.

How did Orthodoxy contribute to the Russians' historic sense that their nation had a special role to play in the world?

RELIGIOUS TRADITION

39

the Russian land, the cowl will be safe from seizure by the infidel sons of Hagar and from the intended profanation by the Latin pope, and the Orthodox Faith will be glorified." [The legend concludes with the arrival of the cowl in Novgorod.]

"

Eventually, the Third Rome ideology became widely accepted in Russia. Orthodoxy proclaimed itself as the one pure Christian church whose purity must be diligently preserved until the end of the world. This belief provided the foundation for two important events. The first was the establishment of a patriarchate in Moscow. In the first centuries of Russian Christianity, the Russian church had been under the administration of the Greek patriarch in Constantinople. Especially after the Turkish conquest of Constantinople, the Russian church gradually asserted its autonomy under its own chief bishop, for a time called a "metropolitan." Finally, in 1589 the Russian church showed its full

ICON OF THE VIRGIN OF VLADIMIR

The icon of the Virgin of Tenderness is the premier Russian Orthodox icon. This most venerated of ancient icons captures both the patriotic and the religious spirit of the Russian tradition. For centuries, the city which contained this portrayal of sublime maternal pathos served as the political center of the Russian nation. This icon arrived in Kiev when that city was the capital of Rus. In 1155, Prince Andrei moved the icon to the north. Legend reported that the horses which carried it halted at the town of Vladimir and refused to go further, thereby showing divine approval for Andrei's desire to locate the capital of the Russian nation there. Andrei put the icon in the Vladimir Church of the Dormition of the Virgin from which it gets its common name, "The Virgin of Vladimir."

According to tradition, the icon was painted by Saint Luke the gospel writer. Scholars conclude that it was produced in the twelfth century by an unidentified Byzantine painter.

The Byzantine artistic style appears in the almond-shaped eyes, long and narrow nose, and the thin lips and chin. But this painting shows none of the stern severity characteristic of Byzantine painting. It is intensely Russian in its portrayal of affection and sorrow. The child embraces the neck of the mother with his elongated arm, pressing his cheek against hers, as she extends her hand toward him in a gesture of love and prayer. Her eyes have a sorrowful cast as if she has a premonition of the tragic fate awaiting her son.

In 1395, when word reached the Russians that the dreaded Mongol conqueror Tamerlane was approaching Moscow, Prince Vasily

independence by naming its chief bishop a patriarch.

The second event took place in the mid-1600s in the aftermath of a decision by the Russian patriarch to change some Russian religious practices. This patriarch, named Nikon, had reached the conclusion, for reasons that are both complex and unclear, that the Russians had permitted errors to creep into their ways of worshipping. The response of many Russian people to Nikon's changes — illustrated in the following excerpt — demonstrates their fervent attachment to the traditional forms of religion.

Nikon ordered a series of changes in the wording, procedures, and actions used in church worship services. One of those changes became the symbol for them all. Nikon declared that when an Orthodox believer or priest made the sign of the cross, three fingers must be extended and two curled in the palm. One hundred years earlier, a church council in Moscow had declared: "The sign of the cross must be made according to the rules, . . . with the thumb and the two lower fingers joined together

From *Masters of World Painting: Andrei Rublev*

Courtesy of USSR Embassy, Washington, DC.

asked the head of the church to bring the Vladimir icon to Moscow. It reached its destination on August 26, the same day that Tamerlane ordered his troops to retreat. The story spread among the Russians that Tamerlane had been so frightened by a vision in the sky of a lady leading a large army to defend Moscow that he abandoned his attempt to conquer the Russians. From this the icon acquired its reputation as the protector of Russia and was given a place of honor to the right of the royal doors in the iconostasis in Dormition Cathedral in the Moscow Kremlin. It frequently appeared in civil processions and was used to bless Russian troops going to defend the motherland. Since the revolution, the icon has been part of the collection of the Tretyakov Art Gallery.

ICON OF THE OLD TESTAMENT TRINITY

The Old Testament Trinity is a preeminent example of the art form of Russian icon painting. The monk Andrei Rublev (1360–1430) painted this icon in memory of Sergius, about twenty years after Sergius's death, to hang in the church in present-day Zagorsk where the saint's body is venerated. (Sergius is the saint who defended Russia from the Mongols.) This portrayal of supreme tranquility constituted a perpetual prayer of the Russian people for respite from their enemies.

In this icon, it is fairly easy to see how icons present a visible revelation of the invisible supernatural realm. The historical and the eternal are combined in the simultaneous portrayal of two events. The historical event, the visit of three men to the Hebrew Patriarch Abraham described in Genesis 18, is suggested in the background — which shows the residence of Abraham and Sarah, the Oak of Mamre under which Abraham rested, and the hill on which Abraham intended to sacrifice his son Isaac — and by the table in the center at which he entertained his supernatural guests. The timeless event portrayed is the divine deliberation about human redemption, symbolized by the chalice containing an animal's head — representing the sacrifice of the Christ for the sins of the world. The Father, Son, and Holy Spirit solemnly contemplate the death of the Son, who reaches voluntarily for the cup of suffering while the other figures bless it.

From *Masters of World Painting: Andrei Rublev*

Courtesy of USSR Embassy, Washington, DC.

The Holy Trinity is portrayed symbolically by subtle variations on the theme of three elements united into one. The inclined heads of the right-hand and central figures draw the viewer's eye naturally into a counterclockwise motion which encloses the whole, forming the traditional symbol of the Trinity — a triangle inside a circle.

The lines defining the chairs and platforms at the bottom of the picture show an essential feature of icons. Since they converge at a point in front of the painting, they produce a reversed linear perspective which creates the illusion that the icon is a window opening onto the infinity of eternity.

[in the palm] and the extended index finger joined to the middle finger . . . [and] if anyone should fail to give his blessing with two fingers, as Christ did, or should fail to make the sign of the cross with two fingers, may he be accursed." Nikon had decreed that the Orthodox do precisely what the earlier council had said would eternally damn their souls. And therefore when his order appeared, many Russians responded just like the writer of the next document: their "hearts froze" and their "limbs shook."

Nikon's declaration came at a time when many Russians were already fearful that the apocalypse was at hand. They believed that when Moscow departed from Orthodoxy, the world would end. Independent fanciful calculations widely known in Muscovy predicted that the world would end a few decades after 1650, perhaps in 1666 (because of the apocalyptic number of the Antichrist). Therefore, it was easy for the writer of the next document to apply the label "Antichrist" to the church leaders who condemned him during the church council that met in 1660.

The following excerpt is from *The Life of Archpriest Avvakum by Himself*, a work that has earned a place of honor in the world's heritage of autobiographical literature. In his religious devotion, Archpriest Avvakum was typical of many Russian believers who endured many tribulations because they remained faithful to traditional forms.

" I was born in the Nizhny country, beyond the river Kudma, in the village of Grigorovo . . . At the age of twenty I was ordained deacon and, after two years, priest. When I had been a priest eight years, I was raised to the rank of archpriest by Orthodox bishops, and this was twenty years ago. . . .

In Lent (1653) [Patriarch Nikon] sent a pastoral letter to St. Basil's Church, to John Neronov. . . . "According to the tradition of the holy Apostles and the Fathers, it is not seemly to make obeisance in the church to the knee, it should be no lower than the girdle, and moreover it behooves you to sign yourselves with three fingers." We met together and took counsel. It was as if winter was of a mind to come; our hearts froze, our limbs shook. Neronov entrusted his church to me and shut himself up in the Miracle Monastery, and he spent a week praying in a cell, and one day a voice came from the icon of the Savior: "The hour of tribulation has come; it behooves you to suffer and be strong." And, weeping, he recounted these words to me and . . . to Daniel the archpriest of Kostroma. Together with Daniel I wrote out excerpts from the Fathers concerning the manner to be used in crossing oneself and making obeisances, and we gave them to the tsar. And many were the excerpts we had made. But he hid them, we know not where. . . .

And a little later Nikon seized Daniel in the monastery outside the Tver Gates and sheared him [as a] monk in the presence of the tsar. . . . And in the same way with the Archpriest John Neronov, Nikon took off

The Life of Archpriest Avvakum by Himself, trans. Jane Harrison and Hope Mirrlees, (London: Hogarth Press, 1924), as quoted in Serge A. Zenkovsky, ed., *Medieval Russia's Epics, Chronicles and Tales* (New York: Dutton, 1974), pp. 401–402, 407–408, 441–442, 445, 447).

his biretta [i.e., priest's cap] in church and had him confined in the monastery of Simon, and later banished him to Vologda, to the walled monastery of St. Savior's, then to the fortress of Kola, and in the end, after having suffered exceedingly, he recanted — poor soul; he signed himself with three fingers, and so died a heretic. Woe is me! Let every man stand firm and be ever on the watch lest his foot shall stumble. In the words of Scriptures, these are surely evil days when even the elect yield to the blandishments of Antichrist. It behooves us to be exceedingly strong in prayer to God, and he will save us and help us, for he is merciful and loves mankind.

And I, too, while I was celebrating vespers, was arrested . . . and fastened with a chain for the night in the patriarch's court. And when the Sabbath dawned they placed me in a cart and stretched out my arms and drove me from the patriarch's court to the monastery of Andronicus, and there they put chains on me and flung me into a black dungeon, dug into the earth, and there I lay for three days, and I had nothing to eat or to drink in the darkness. . . .

[Avvakum was exiled to Siberia where he lived for about ten years before returning to Moscow. Leaders of the church in Moscow tried to persuade him to be reconciled to the changes Nikon had introduced, but Avvakum remained adamant. After further punishment and exile, in 1667 he was placed on trial before a church council.]

They set me down in the Miracle Monastery, before the patriarchs of all Christendom, and the Russian Nikonites sat there like so many foxes. . . . The last word they spoke to me was this: "Why," said they, "art thou stubborn? The folk of Palestine, Serbia, Albania, the Wallachians, they of Rome and Poland, all these do cross themselves with three fingers, only thou standest out in thine obstinacy and dost cross thyself with two fingers; it is not seemly." And I answered them for Christ thus: "O you teachers of Christendom, Rome fell away long ago and lies prostrate, and the Poles fell in the like ruin with her, being to the end the enemies of the Christian. And among you Orthodoxy is of a mongrel breed. . . . By the gift of God among us there is autocracy; till the time of Nikon, the apostate, in our Russia under our pious princes and tsars the Orthodox Faith was pure and undefiled, and in the church was no sedition. Nikon, the wolf, together with the devil, ordained that men should cross themselves with three fingers, but our first shepherds made the sign of the cross and blessed men as of old with two fingers. . . ." Then louder than before they began to cry out against me: "Away with him, away with him; he hath outraged us all"; and they began to thrust at me and to beat me. And the patriarchs themselves threw themselves on me; about forty of them I think there must have been. Great was the army of Antichrist that gathered itself together.

[Avvakum was condemned formally by the council and exiled, with several associates, to Pustozersk. The punishment of the recalcitrant traditionalists became progressively more extreme.]

> "Nikon decreed that Orthodox believers should do precisely what an earlier church council had warned would eternally damn their souls."

The Old Believers depicted here in a 1957 Moscow procession continue to believe that they are the true keepers of pure Orthodox belief.

AP/Wide World Photos.

The rebellion of Avvakum and his associates split the Russian church and ended the virtually total unanimity on religious questions that had prevailed for centuries in Russia. For more than 600 years after the baptism of Rus under Vladimir, the Russian people had been united in a single Orthodox Church. Those who broke away from the church in the seventeenth century — and they were probably the majority of Russians — came to be called Old Ritualists (their name for themselves) or Schismatics (the church's name for them). In English, they are most frequently called Old Believers.

As Avvakum's account shows, officials of church and state employed violent measures in their attempts to quash the schism. But violence only served to persuade the Old Believers that their reasoning was correct: the Russian Church had deserted the true faith; therefore, the reign of Antichrist on earth must have begun and the end of the world must be imminent. In some cases, the response of the Old Believers was

What is the enduring political significance of Patriarch Nikon's seventeenth century decree altering Orthodox religious practices?

in the tradition of Saints Boris and Gleb, who were revered for their voluntary acceptance of death. In numerous bizarre incidents, groups of Old Believers committed mass suicide by gathering in wooden buildings and igniting them as troops sent by the government to arrest them approached. Perhaps as many as 20,000 died in this way in the half century after the schism.

By using force to suppress the Old Believers who sought to break free from state-approved forms of religion, the Russians were pursuing a policy not much different from Western Europeans who at that time had been engaged for over a century in bloody conflicts and persecutions in the aftermath of the Protestant Reformation. But some distinctively Russian dynamics were also at work. In the West the struggle led to the emergence of religious toleration and independence of the church, but in Russia, the Byzantine heritage in church-state relations expressed itself in the subordination of the church.

Patriarch Nikon suffered an ironic fate. He had decreed the reforms which the Old Believers rejected, bringing the force of the state down upon them. But he himself was then crushed by the powers of the state. He was deposed from the patriarchal throne because he tried to advance the church at the expense of the state's prerogatives. In his assertion of the church's superiority over the state, excerpted below, he used the analogy of the sun and the moon.

"Nikon's Refutation" in George Vernadsky, *et al.*, eds. and comps., *A Source Book for Russian History*, vol. 1, (New Haven: Yale University Press, 1972), p. 256.

"t is very clear that the tsar must be lower than the prelate and obedient to him, for I also say that the clergy are chosen people and are anointed by the Holy Ghost. And if all Christians owe obedience to the prelates, such obedience is owed still more by him who with his sword forces the insubordinate to obey the prelates. . . . When the Lord God Almighty created heaven and earth, he ordered the two luminaries, the sun and the moon, which move across [heaven], to shine upon the earth. The sun represents episcopal authority, while the moon represents the authority of the tsar; for the sun illuminates the day, as the prelate enlightens the soul, while the lesser luminary illuminates the night, which is the body. As the moon receives its light from the sun . . . so it is with the tsar. He is consecrated, anointed, and crowned by a prelate, from whom he must thereupon receive his perfect light, to wit, his most rightful power and authority. . . . The tsar's sword must be ready against the enemies of the Orthodox faith; if the prelates and all the clergy demand that he defend them from all unrighteousness and violence, then the civil [authority] must obey the spiritual [authority] . . . . In spiritual matters which are of concern to all, the supreme bishop [i.e., the patriarch] is higher than the tsar, and all the Orthodox owe obedience to the bishop because he is our father in the Orthodox faith and the Orthodox church is entrusted to him. . . . The clergy is a more honored and higher authority than the state itself. "

Nikon's views were much more in keeping with Western Catholic ideas than with the Byzantine tradition which Russia followed. It was, therefore, easy for the tsar to have Nikon condemned by the same church council of 1666 which condemned Avvakum. Although he was removed as patriarch, his ill-fated attempt to advance the church's position was not forgotten and soon led the state to encroach even further upon the power of the church.

The Old Believers schism weakened the church, and Peter the Great, who during his reign from 1682 to 1725 radically altered almost every aspect of Russian life, was able to force it to submit totally to the power of the state. When Patriarch Adrian, the fourth since Nikon, died in 1700, Peter prevented the church from electing a new patriarch. After twenty years, Peter issued a decree that formally abolished the office of patriarch and replaced it with a committee of churchmen overseen by a lay official appointed by the emperor. The committee was called the Holy Synod, and the lay supervisor, who functioned as "the eyes of the tsar," was called the procurator general of the Holy Synod.

The text of Peter's decree is remarkably long — approximately 100 book-length pages. It was a civil law that regulated many details of the life of the church and thus intruded into the religious sphere. Early in the decree, Peter explained that he had eliminated the office of the patriarch because it threatened the authority of the tsar: "The common people do not understand how the spiritual authority is distinguishable from the autocratic; but marveling at the dignity and glory of the Highest Pastor, they imagine that such an administrator is a second Sovereign, a power equal to that of the Autocrat, or even greater than he. . . . Wherefore simple hearts are misdirected by this notion, so that, in any kind of matter, they do not look so much to the Autocrat as to the Supreme Pastor" (Alexander V. Muller, ed. and trans., *The Spiritual Regulation of Peter the Great* [Seattle: University of Washington Press, 1972], pp. 10–11).

Peter's change in the way the church was administered at its highest level had the practical effect of turning it into a department of the government, thereby destroying the independence of the church. One regulation made priests into a virtual secret investigative network for the state: "If someone in confession informs his spiritual father of some illegality that has not been committed, but that he yet intends to commit, especially treason or mutiny against the Sovereign or against the state, or evil designs upon the honor or well-being of the sovereign and upon His Majesty's family, and in informing of such a great intended evil, he reveals himself as not repenting but considers himself in the right . . . then the confessor must not only not honor as valid the forgiveness and remission of the confessed sins, but he must expeditiously report concerning them. . . . Wherefore a confessor, in compliance with the provisions of [the] personal ukase of His Imperial Majesty, must immediately report, to whom it is appropriate, such a

In preparation for the millennium celebration, this specialist works to restore an icon which was taken from an abandoned monastery for placement in an iconostasis at the Danilovsky Monastery.

person who thus displays in confession his evil and unrepentant intention" (*Spiritual Regulation*, pp. 60–61). This requirement made the church even more the slave of the state and undermined the reputation of priests, who now seemed more like threatening police officials than comforting pastors.

A major theme of Peter's decree is the desirability of ideological uniformity. This is an enduring theme in Russian history, which was manifested until recently in the lack of toleration for diversity in thinking in the Soviet Union. Peter's decree required that priests identify those who were straying from Orthodoxy so that they could be turned back to the church, by forceful measures if necessary. If they could not be won back, as non-Orthodox they would be placed at a

> **"Peter the Great's decree had the practical effect of turning the church into a department of the government."**

St. Basil's Cathedral in Moscow is one of more than ten cathedrals built by Ivan the Terrible, a religious zealot who condemned all dissenting religions and subjugated the church to state rule by crowning himself "tsar," leader of both church and state.

AP/Wide World Photos.

considerable disadvantage in society. Their taxes would be higher, and they would be barred from holding any civil office.

But any hope for a return to the religious conformity of earlier times was futile. The trend was in the opposite direction. The Old Believers schism could not be eradicated, and throughout the eighteenth century other forms of religious dissent cropped up in Russian society. In some cases, the new sects (like Khlysty and Skoptsy) were founded by Russians who sought a mystical experience that the church, itself undergoing chaotic changes, was not providing. Other sects (Lutherans, Quakers, Freemasons) were based on imported notions, many brought by Europeans whom Peter himself had encouraged to settle in Russia to help modernize the country.

A more important reason for the breakdown in religious uniformity was the steady expansion of Russian territory. From the sixteenth century onward, more and more non-Russian people were incorporated under the Russian crown. These people adhered to non-Orthodox and non-Christian religions.

Muslims were the first to be incorporated in substantial numbers. This happened during the reign of Ivan the Terrible (1547–1584), who began the conquest of the Tatar regions to the south and east of Muscovy. Before the sixteenth century, the Christian Russian people had lived under Muslim domination for three centuries as the Mongols ruled the lands of the Russians from the Golden Horde, the Mongol capital, in the south. Russian resentment and intolerance transformed the Russian advance into Muslim territories into a virtual holy war. Only by converting to the Orthodox Church could Tatars become Russian subjects with full rights. The Russian attempt to enforce religious uniformity by assimilating the conquered Muslims is described in the following excerpt.

"The presence of Muslim Tatars a mere 200 miles east of Moscow was seen as an intolerable blight on the Orthodox landscape."

" From 1605 until the 1770s Russian influence over the Muslim territories of the Middle Volga, Urals, Western Siberia and Lower Volga–Caspian Sea area was steadily strengthened. Ironically the process was helped by waves of peasants fleeing serfdom in Central Russia to settle in the Muslim lands, thereby reducing the natives to the status of a minority threatened by a systematic policy of assimilation. The government in St. Petersburg meanwhile was encouraging the inflow of foreign specialists, and was prepared to accept them as equals among the Russian nobility during the first half of the eighteenth century, to the extent that "foreigners" virtually ran the state apparatus. While Russia allowed itself effectively to be governed by a foreign aristocracy of Catholic and Protestant persuasion, few of whom spoke Russian or considered themselves as anything more than servants of the Emperor, paradoxically the country was not seen by its rulers to be a multinational Empire but a Russian and

Alexandre Bennigsen and Marie Broxup, *The Islamic Threat to the Soviet State* (New York: St. Martin's Press, 1983), p. 16.

Orthodox "nation state." The presence of a large body of Muslim Tatars a mere 200 miles east of Moscow was seen as an intolerable blight on this landscape which had to be eliminated, and their conversion to Orthodoxy was seen as the best way of solving this "nationality problem." From the reign of the first Romanov, the Tsar Mikhail [1613], to that of Catherine II [1762], Islam was treated as an alien, hostile body and various measures were taken to liquidate it completely: mosques were closed or destroyed (between 1738 and 1755, 418 out of 536 mosques of the Kazan gubernia disappeared); "waqf" [i.e., religious] property was confiscated by the state; special schools were opened for the children of the converted Tatars; intense missionary activity was instituted while

PROTOCOLS OF THE ELDERS OF ZION

Out of the fierce hatred for Jews on the part of some Russian Orthodox came the *Protocols of the Learned Elders of Zion,* one of the most pernicious documents of the twentieth century. The *Protocols* purported to be documentary evidence of an international Jewish conspiracy to manipulate world finance and the press, promote atheism and revolution, destroy the moral fabric of society, and subject the entire world to the rule of a Jewish super-state.

The *Protocols* were fabricated by a Russian secret police agent in Paris "for the education of the tsar." They appeared in a St. Petersburg newspaper in 1903. Since then they have been published repeatedly in many languages. Russian monarchists who fled the revolution circulated the document in Europe to turn world opinion against the Bolshevik government, which they claimed was part of the alleged Jewish plot for world domination. In the United States, Henry Ford paid for the printing of 500,000 English copies. Adolph Hitler spread the *Protocols* throughout Germany to support his anti-Jewish program. They have been an important part of Arab propaganda since the creation of Israel, and in recent times their message has fueled Soviet anti-Semitism.

The fraudulent *Protocols* are in the form of notes from speeches supposedly delivered by a Jewish "elder" explaining the plot to achieve world domination. The following fragments give an idea of the message and tone of the *Protocols.*

Muslim counter-measures were punishable by death; Muslims were expelled from villages where groups of converts had been formed and deported to remote districts. The first half of the eighteenth century — the reigns of Peter the Great and his successors, especially that of the Tsarina Anna — could be compared in terms of the persecution of Muslims to the worst period of Stalin's anti-religious campaign in the 1930s.

Catherine II abandoned the attempt to convert Muslims to Orthodoxy, and her successors generally followed her example as the numbers of

Our power in the present tottering condition of all forms of power will be more invincible than any other, because it will remain invisible until the moment when it has gained such strength that no cunning can any longer undermine it.

Our triumph has been rendered easier by the fact that in our relations with the men whom we wanted we have always worked upon the most sensitive chords of the human mind, upon the cash account, upon the cupidity, upon the insatiability for material needs of man; and each one of these human weaknesses, taken alone, is sufficient to paralyse initiative, for it hands over the will of men to the disposition of him who has bought their activities . . . .

We appear on the scene as alleged saviours of the worker from oppression when we propose to him to enter the ranks of our fighting forces — socialists, anarchists, communists — to whom we always give support in accordance with an alleged brotherly rule (of the solidarity of all humanity) of our social masonry. The aristocracy, which enjoyed by law the labour of the workers, was interested in seeing that the workers were well fed, healthy, and strong. We are interested in just the opposite — in the diminution, the killing out of the *goyim* [non-Jews]. . . .

We have set one against another the personal and national reckonings of the *goyim*, religious and race hatreds, which we have fostered into a huge growth in the course of the past twenty centuries. This is the reason why there is not one State which would anywhere receive support if it were to raise its arm, for every one of them must bear in mind that any agreement against us would be unprofitable to itself. We are too strong — there is no evading our power. The nations cannot come to even an inconsiderable private agreement without our secretly having a hand in it.

V. E. Marsden, trans., *Protocols of the Meetings of the Learned Elders of Zion* (Los Angeles: Christian Nationalist Crusade, n.d.), pp. 13, 14, 15, 16, 19, 21, 27.

Muslims in the empire grew. Especially in the nineteenth century, the Russian conquest of the Caucasus and Central Asia brought into the empire a wide variety of tribes that embraced Islam. By the time of the revolution there were about 18 million Muslims in the empire. As long as the Muslims remained docile and were content to live on the fringes of the empire, the Russian government let them practice their religion in relative peace, generally despising them as mired in hopeless backwardness and ignorance. As an exception to the typical pattern, some of the intelligentsia of the Muslim nations voluntarily converted to Christianity in order to improve their social status.

Another religious population that expansion drew into the empire was the Jews. Russia included a substantial number of Jews for the first time in the eighteenth century when Catherine the Great annexed large tracts of territory ruled earlier by Poland. Before that time Russians possessed almost no accurate information about Jews, but that did not prevent them from indulging in hostility against Jews. After the fifteenth century, it was not uncommon for a Russian who expressed skepticism about some Orthodox belief to be branded with the epithet "Judaizing heretic."

Russian anti-Semitism existed despite the fact that for centuries, no more than a mere handful of Jews ever lived in Russia. They were not welcome, as is illustrated in a letter to the Polish king from Ivan the Terrible: "We will in no way permit Jews to enter our state; we do not wish to see their evil in our realm; we wish only that God permit my people to live in peace without any disturbances." Ivan said that the presence of Jews in Muscovy supposedly gave rise to "evil" and "disturbances" because Jews "lead our people from Christianity and import poisonous herbs [tobacco ?] into our state and deceive many of our people." The Russian attitude, which Ivan expressed, was pure prejudice.

A century after Ivan, as the empire expanded westward into Poland, for the first time Russians met Jews face-to-face. Small numbers of Jews lived in the newly acquired areas. The initial response of the Russian state to the first meeting with flesh and blood Jews was rejection. In the first half of the 1700s, Catherine I and Elizabeth decreed that all Jews who refused to convert to Orthodoxy be expelled from Russia. But by the latter part of the century, such decrees could not be effectively enforced, for approximately one million Jews were brought into the empire as the result of the partition of Poland.

Thereafter, the government ordered the Jews to remain in their former home areas; they were prohibited from moving into Orthodox Russia. This restriction created the Pale of Settlement, from which only a few Jewish merchants and intellectuals managed to escape. In the nineteenth century, until the assassination of the tsar in 1881, there were occasional incidents of violence against Jews. These episodes served as harbingers of a plague of pogroms that descended upon the Jews after

Alexander II's assassination, for which the Jewish population was unjustifiably blamed. Rampant violence showed clearly that anti-Jewish attitudes pervaded all levels of Russian society.

Toward the end of the nineteenth century, Americans became aware of the conditions under which Jews were living in Russia, and several American ambassadors tried to urge the Russian Foreign Ministry to create more humane conditions for them. Early American concern for the plight of Russia's Jews can be seen in the following excerpt from a report prepared in 1893 by the American ambassador to St. Petersburg, Andrew White.

"There are about 5,000,000 Israelites in Russia, forming, as it is claimed, more than half of the entire Jewish race, and these are packed together in the cities and villages of what was formerly Poland and adjacent governments, in a belt extending along the western borders from northwest to southeast, but which for some years past has been drawn back from the frontier about 40 miles, under the necessity, as it is claimed, imposed by the tendency of the Israelites in that region to conduct smuggling operations. In other parts of the Empire they have only been allowed to reside as a matter of exceptional favor. . . . Certain skilled artisans have also been allowed to reside in certain towns outside the Jewish pale, but their privileges are very uncertain, liable to revocation at any time, and have in recent years been greatly diminished. . . .

From time to time, and especially during the reign of Alexander II, who showed himself more kind to them than any other sovereign had ever been, many of them were allowed to leave this overcrowded territory, and, at least, were not hindered from coming into territory and towns which, strictly speaking, they were not considered entitled to enter; but for some time past this residence on sufferance has been rendered more and more difficult. . . . Not only is great severity exercised as regards the main body of Israelites here, but it is from time to time brought to bear with especial force upon those returning to Russia from abroad. . . .

The restrictions are by no means confined to residence; they extend into every field of activity. Even in the parts of the Empire where the Israelites are most free they are not allowed to hold property in land, or to take a mortgage on land, or to farm land, and of late they have even been, to a large extent, prevented from living on farms, and have been thrown back into the cities and villages. . . .

As to religious restrictions, the general policy pursued seems to an unprejudiced observer from any other country so illogical as to be incomprehensible. On the one hand great powers are given to Jewish rabbis and religious authorities. They are allowed in the districts where the Israelites mainly live to form a sort of state within the state, with

"Report of Minister Andrew D. White on the Jewish Situation in Russia," reprinted from *Foreign Relations*, 1984, pp. 525–535, in Cyrus Adler and Aaron Margalith, *With Firmness in the Right* (New York: American Jewish Committee, 1946), pp. 455–462.

These men were members of Ataman Struk's nationalistic Ukrainian gang, which carried out approximately forty violent pogroms against Jews — including one in Chernobyl that lasted for twenty-five days.

Tcherikower Collection, YIVO Institute for Jewish Research.

power to impose taxes upon their coreligionists and to give their regulations virtually the force of law. On the other hand, efforts of zealous Orthodox Christians to proselyte Israelites, which must provoke much bitterness, are allowed and even favored. The proselytes, once brought within the Orthodox Russian fold, no matter by what means, any resumption of the old religion by them is treated as a crime. Recent cases have occurred where Jews who have been thus converted and who have afterwards attended the synagogue have been brought before the courts. . . .

It is also urged against the Israelites in Russia that they are not patriotic, but in view of the policy pursued regarding them the wonder is that any human being should expect them to be patriotic. There is also frequent complaint against Jewish fanaticism, and recently collections of extracts from the Talmud have been published here as in western Europe, and even in the United States, to show that Israelites are educated in bitter and undying hate of Christians. . . . There is no need of argument, either in the light of history or of common sense, to prove that these millions of Israelites in Russia are not to be rendered less fanatical by the treatment to which they are at present subjected.

"

The hopes of sympathetic Americans such as Ambassador White were in vain. In the early years of the twentieth century, the situation became even more bloody. For example, the most brutal anti-Jewish violence erupted on Easter of 1903, the Kishinev pogrom. Unhappy with the failure of Russian officials to stop the persecution of the Jews, the U.S. Congress finally showed its disapproval by voting overwhelmingly to cancel the commercial treaty between America and Russia in 1911. This action foreshadowed the U.S. Senate's action in 1974 (the Jackson-Vanik Amendment) in which favorable commercial terms for the Soviet Union were made contingent upon the liberalization of its emigration regulations. The people who sought recognition of their right to emigrate in the 1970s include a substantial number of Armenians, Germans, and especially Jews.

Another religious minority brought within the empire's borders by Russian westward expansion in the late eighteenth century were Catholics, several million of whom resided in the sections of Poland that Catherine the Great had annexed. There were two kinds of Catholics. Lithuanians and Poles practiced Latin Rite Catholicism and were grudgingly tolerated by the state. The treatment of those who practiced Eastern Rite Catholicism was quite different. These Catholics followed religious forms virtually identical to those of the Orthodox Church, but, under an agreement sanctioned by the Union of Brest of 1598, they recognized the religious authority of the Roman pope. Commonly known as Uniates, a term of derision in the mouth of the Orthodox and one which the Eastern Rite Catholics themselves avoid, the Eastern Rite Catholics of the Russian Empire were deprived of the legal right to separate existence as a church. In 1839 they were incorporated formally into the Russian Orthodox Church. In practice, many believers continued to follow their religion clandestinely. This sequence of events was repeated in the aftermath of World War II, under a Soviet rather than a tsarist government.

During the nineteenth century, a small minority Christian Protestant group emerged and grew to become today the second largest countrywide Christian denomination in the Soviet Union. Arising in the 1860s in the south of Russia, in Ukraine, and the Caucasus, this Baptist

What was the impact of Russian expansion on religion? And conversely, how did Orthodoxy view state expansion?

THE KISHINEV POGROM

In the last three decades of the 1800s, Russia was gripped by a frenzy of violent outbursts against Jews. The first massive pogrom broke out in Odessa on Easter of 1871. From 1881 to 1883, 224 pogroms were reported.

The most notorious pogrom occurred on Easter 1903 in Kishinev, a city of about 100,000 in which Jews made up almost half of the population. Forty-seven Jews were killed and over 400 were injured. The following news account dates from April 14, 1903. The violence was precipitated by a rumor reported in the local newspaper that Jews had killed a Christian boy in order to use his blood in their Passover celebration.

From *Novosti*, reprinted in Gerard Israel, *The Jews in Russia* (New York: St. Martin's, 1975), pp. 65–66.

" During the two days of Easter, an enraged crowd of Christians, made up of both young people and adults, of workers and even of men in uniform, and of civil servants, pillaged and destroyed all of the Jewish houses, their shops and their stores, and killed and wounded many people, among them a number of women and children. The assassins simply threw the latter from heights of two or three stories onto the pavement below. Several synagogues have been looted, and the rolls of the Torah torn and defiled. In some synagogues when the beadles tried to resist the attackers, they were beaten into senselessness. All the streets are covered with a thick layer of feathers and down from torn quilts, and often the furniture of the looted houses has been broken into bits and pieces. Even the flooring, the stoves and the walls have not been spared, but have been destroyed as well. I was witness in 1882 to the looting in Kiev, but what I saw there is nothing compared to my observations here during these two days. "

movement spread rapidly across the empire. Although officials tried to suppress it, the denomination extended its reach throughout the empire. Persecution and exile seemed to make its adherents more fervent and to increase their number. Especially during the reign of Alexander III (1881–1894), when the government earnestly sought to impose religious uniformity, Baptists were hounded by officials of both state and church. The restrictions on the Baptists are described in the following recollection by one of their preachers, which was published in the magazine of the All-Union Council of Evangelical Christian-Baptists now headquartered in Moscow. The theme of the persecution was enunciated by the procurator general mentioned in this article: "There are and there can be no Russian Baptists."

> **T**he period from 1885 to 1905 was an especially severe period. The tsarist government and the procurator general of the Holy Synod, Konstantin Pobedonostsev, began a cruel struggle against sectarianism. The believers of that time had to endure horrible persecution and pass through a laborious path of many sorrows and tribulations. Services were conducted, in the main, at night. Doors of the houses where believers gathered for prayer were locked with strong bolts and the windows were covered from the inside with cushions since frequently rocks were thrown through the windows and besides the preaching and singing would be less audible outside. Baptisms were conducted at night, too, and in order to have a baptism believers went twenty to thirty versts (twelve to eighteen miles) from their village so that no one would know.
>
> Upon orders of Pobedonostsev, [Orthodox] missionaries were sent to all villages where there were sectarians in order to attempt to convert them back to Orthodoxy. Two missionaries were sent to Sofievka village where Lysenko lived to struggle against the sectarians. These missionaries began to conduct conversations and then, by force, they began to baptize all the unbaptized sectarian children. In 1887, the Sofievka congregation again was subjected to an ordeal. In November they arrested and tried brothers Lysenko, Golovchenko, Goshko, Shipsha, Bozhanov, Koriakov, Stoialov, and others. All were sentenced to varied terms in prison and several, including Stoialov, were exiled to Siberia.
>
> Other congregations were subjected to similar repression. In the village of Voloshsk several persons were sentenced and two were exiled, brothers Gury and Guslisty. They were exiled to Orenburg. . . . Trials and exiles continued until 1905 and even afterward they did not cease, but became more rare. Several prisoners and exiles died, while some returned, but generally not until 1917–18.

N. Mel'nikov, "Eighty Years of the Evangelical Baptist Movement in the Dnepropetrovsk Region," *Bratskii vestnik* (Fraternal Herald), no.5 (1955), p.65.

As noted in the excerpt above, by 1905 the "especially severe period" of persecution had ended. In that year, legal toleration for most religions was declared for the first time in Russia. For a short time, most non-Orthodox religions could act somewhat more freely than they had been able to before, although they were forbidden by law to try to convert an Orthodox person. And the law still declared: "The foremost and dominant faith in the Russian Empire is the Christian Orthodox Catholic Eastern Confession. The Emperor possessing the throne of All Russia may not profess any faith but Orthodoxy. The Emperor, as Christian Sovereign, is supreme defender and preserver of the dogmas of the ruling faith, and protector of the orthodoxy of belief and the decorum in the holy Church."

In the decade before the revolution which overthrew tsarism, a significant number of intellectuals turned to religion in what is often called the "Russian Religious Renaissance." Several of the leading figures of this revival, including Sergei Bulgakov and Nikolai Berdiaev, became Marxists as students and then left Marxism to move into the Orthodox Church. The long-term significance of this development will be apparent in the description in subsequent chapters of the Christian Seminar on Problems of the Religious Renaissance and the appearance of "god-seeking" motifs in contemporary Soviet culture. Both trends reflect the Russian Religious Renaissance of the early years of the twentieth century. In his account of the history of Russian Communism, Berdiaev attempts to answer fundamental questions about religion in Russia like those we posed at the beginning of this chapter: What is religion like in Russia? What is the Russian soul? In the following excerpt from his book, which serves here to summarize the major themes of this survey of Russian religious history, Berdiaev explains how the religious

BEFORE THE BAPTISM OF VLADIMIR

Two minority ethnic groups within the present-day Soviet Union — Armenians and Georgians — boast a much longer history of Christian devotion than the Russian people.

The Armenians have the longest Christian history of any nationality in the U.S.S.R. In the early fourth century, under the patronage of King Tiridates of Armenia whom he had won to Christianity, Saint Gregory the Illuminator led the people of his country to put aside pagan worship and embrace Christian practices. At the end of the fifth century, the Armenian church broke away from the main body of Orthodox Christendom. The Armenian Apostolic Church rejected the Orthodox Ecumenical Council of Chalcedon (451 A.D.) and affirmed Monophysite Christology—the belief that in Christ there was only one nature combining divine and human attributes instead of two natures "unconfused, unchanged, indivisible, and insepar-able" (as the Chalcedon council formulated the doctrine).

The chief bishop of the Armenian church is Catholicos Vazgen I. His headquarters are in the city of Echmiadzin to which Armenian Christians throughout the world look for religious leadership. Part of Armenia, including Echmiadzin, was incorporated into the Russian Empire in 1828, ending almost a thousand years of Muslim rule over the Armenian church.

The Georgians became a Christian nation about two decades later than the Armenians, around 330 A.D., when a slave girl, later to be revered as Saint Nina, converted the queen and king of ancient Georgia who, in turn, ordered the baptism of the entire nation. The Georgian church which resulted remained united with the Armenian church until the seventh century, when the Georgians renounced the Monophysite doctrine and affirmed Orthodox Christology.

When Russia annexed Georgia

experience of the Russian people has molded their national character, and he draws some significant parallels between the Russian past and the Soviet present which suggest that there are strong elements of continuity between them.

" The inconsistency of the Russian spirit is due to the complexity of Russian history, to the conflict of the Eastern and Western elements in her. The soul of the Russian people was molded by the Orthodox Church — it was shaped in a purely religious mould. And that religious mold was preserved even to our own day, to the time of the Russian nihilists and communists. But in the Russian soul there remained a strong natural element, linked with the

Nicolas Berdyaev, *The Origin of Russian Communism*, trans. R.M. French (Ann Arbor, MI: University of Michigan Press, 1969), pp.8–11, 13–14, 143–155.

The eleventh century Sveti Tskhoveli ("Life-Giving") cathedral was built in the Caucasus Mountains where Georgian Christians believe the robe of Christ is buried.

Courtesy of Paul D. Steeves.

at the beginning of the nineteenth century, the tsar ordered the Catholicos of the Georgian church to take a seat on the Holy Synod of the Orthodox Church. This move effectively destroyed the independence of the Georgian Orthodox Church. It became an exarchate of the Russian church. Only after the revolution in 1917 was the Georgian church able to regain its independence within the communion of Orthodox churches.

The revered metropolitan center of the church is Mtskheta, a small town nestled in the Caucasus Mountains above Tbilisi, where the magnificent cathedral of Sveti Tskoveli is located.

Religion and national identity are so closely linked that today, even though they are a part of the Soviet Union where atheism is promoted, the overwhelming majority of Armenians and Georgians consider themselves Christian believers.

immensity of Russia itself, with the boundless Russian plain. . . . In the typical Russian, two elements are always in opposition — the primitive natural paganism of boundless Russia and an Orthodox asceticism received from Byzantium, a reaching out towards the other world.

A natural dionysism and a Christian asceticism are equally characteristic of the Russian people. A difficult problem presents itself ceaselessly to the Russian — the problem of organizing his vast territory. The immensity of Russia, the absence of boundaries, was expressed in the structure of the Russian soul. The landscape of the Russian soul corresponds with the landscape of Russia, the same boundlessness, formlessness, reaching out into infinity, breadth.

In the West is conciseness; everything is bounded, formulated, arranged in categories, everything (both the structure of the land and the structure of the spirit) is favorable to the organization and development of civilization. It might be said that the Russian people fell victim to the immensity of its territory. Form does not come to it easily, the gift of form is not great among the Russians. Russian historians explain the despotic character of Russian government by this necessary organization of the boundless Russian plain. Kluchevsky, the most distinguished of Russian historians, said, "The state expands, the people grow sickly." In a certain sense this remains true also for the Soviet-Communist government, under which the interests of the people are sacrificed to the power and organization of the Soviet state.

The religious formation of the Russian spirit developed several stable attributes: dogmatism, asceticism, the ability to endure suffering and to make sacrifices for the sake of its faith. . . . In virtue of their religious-dogmatic quality of spirit, Russians — whether orthodox, heretics or schismatics — are always apocalyptic or nihilist. Russians were true to type, both in the seventeenth century as Dissenters and Old-ritualists [that is, what we have called Old Believers], and in the nineteenth century as revolutionaries, nihilists and communists. The structure of spirit remained the same. The Russian revolutionary intelligentsia inherited it from the Dissenters of the seventeenth century. And there always remains as the chief thing the profession of some orthodox faith; this is always the criterion by which membership of the Russian people is judged.

After the fall [in 1453] of the Byzantine Empire, the Second Rome, the greatest Orthodox state in the world, there awoke in the Russian people the consciousness that the Russian Muscovite state was left as the only Orthodox state in the world and that Russia was the only nation which professed the Orthodox Faith. . . . The doctrine of Moscow the Third Rome became the basic idea on which the Muscovite state was formed. The kingdom was consolidated and shaped under the symbol of a messianic idea. The search for true, ideal kingship was characteristic of the Russian people throughout its whole history.

The Russian communist state is . . . based upon the dictatorship of a

> **"Two elements are always in opposition in the typical Russian — the primitive natural paganism of boundless Russia and an Orthodox asceticism received from Byzantium."**
> **Russian scholar Nicolas Berdyaev**

THE NUMBER OF BELIEVERS . . . ACCORDING TO THE 1897 CENSUS

The following are the most complete statistics on religion from the tsarist period:

Religion	Total in empire (in millions)	Proportion of population	Number in European Russia (in millions)	Proportion
Orthodox	87.4	69.5%	76.5	81.8%
Old Believers	2.2	1.7%	1.7	1.8%
Roman Catholics	11.4	9.1%	4.3	4.6%
Protestants	3.7	3.0%	3.2	3.5%
Other Christians	1.2	0.97%	0.055	0.1%
Muslims	13.9	11.0%	3.5	3.8%
Jews	5.2	4.1%	3.9	4.0%
Others	0.6	0.5%	0.32	0.3%

Source: *Bolshaia entsiklopediia* (Great Encyclopedia) (St. Petersburg, 1900–05), vol. 16, p. 457.

world view, on an orthodox doctrine which is binding upon the whole people. Communism in Russia has taken the form of an extreme "tatism" which holds in an iron grip the life of a huge country, and that unfortunately is in entire accord with the ancient tradition of Russian statecraft. The old Russian autocratic monarchy was rooted in the religious beliefs of the people; it recognized itself and justified itself as a theocracy, as a consecrated Tsardom. The new Russian State is also autocratic; it also is rooted in the beliefs of the people, in the new faith of the working class and peasant masses; it also recognizes and justifies itself as a consecrated state, as an inverted theocracy. The old Russian monarchy rested upon an orthodox world outlook and insisted upon agreement with it. The new Russian State rests upon a world outlook and with a still greater degree of coercion requires agreement with it. The consecrated kingdom is always a dictatorship of a world outlook, always requires orthodoxy, always suppresses heretics. Totalitarianism, the demand for wholeness of faith as the basis of the kingdom, fits in with the deep religious and social instincts of the people. The Soviet communist realm has in its spiritual structure a great likeness to the Muscovite Orthodox Tsardom. . . .

Russia's vast expansion is often attributed, in part, to its self-proclaimed messianic mission as the guardian of true and pure Christianity.

From *The Icon and the Axe,*
Courtesy of James H. Billington.

THE EXPANSION OF
MODERN EUROPEAN RUSSIA

Areas controlled by Moscow about 1300
1462 (accession of Ivan III)
1598 (accession of Boris Godunov)
1725 (death of Peter the Great)
1815 (after final defeat of Napoleon)
1945 (after World War II)
Russian boundaries after World War II
× Important battle sites
‡ Monasteries

The Russian people have not realized their messianic idea of Moscow the Third Rome. The ecclesiastical schism of the seventeenth century revealed that the Muscovite Tsardom is not the Third Rome. . . . The messianic idea of the Russian people assumed either an apocalyptic form or a revolutionary; and then there occurred an amazing event in the destiny of the Russian people. Instead of the Third Rome in Russia, the Third International was achieved, and many features of the Third Rome pass over to the Third International. The Third International is also a consecrated realm, and it also is founded on an orthodox faith. . . . There is growing up in Russia not only a communist but a Soviet patriotism which is simply Russian patriotism. But the patriotism of a great people must be a faith in a great and worldwide mission of that people; otherwise it would be restricted to a provincial nationalism and lacking in world perspective. The mission of the Russian people is recognized to be the realization of social justice in human society, not only in Russia but in the whole world, and this fits in with Russian traditions. . . .

Russian communism, if one looks more deeply into it in the light of Russia's historical destiny, is a deformation of Russian ideas, of Russian messianism and universalism, of the Russian search for the kingdom of truth and righteousness.

"

For 925 years, from Vladimir's baptism of Rus until the end of the tsarist system in 1917, the Russian government patronized Orthodoxy. The rulers professed it as their own and promoted it as the preferred religion of their subjects. The church and the state related to each other in a tightly knit alliance in which the church accepted a place of subordination to the power of the state in exchange for the state's protection of its prerogatives as the religious master of nearly all of the population.

While the surrender of the church's independence at times displeased some of its leaders, on balance the church showed little hesitation in acquiescing in a situation where for a person to be truly Russian meant to be Orthodox. Over 70 percent of the subjects of the empire (82 percent in the European part) were officially numbered within the Orthodox Church. The Orthodox view of reality dyed the fabric of Russia's culture.

Throughout most of these nine centuries, the rulers of Russia sought to produce religious uniformity in their realm. This policy succeeded in the main until it was overtaken by the expansionism of the very government which sought to make uniformity work. The Orthodox monopoly of six centuries ended in the seventeenth century. The state responded by accelerating its use of force to bring outsiders into the Orthodox fold. Of all Russia's rulers, only Catherine the Great displayed a tendency to practice conscientious toleration of Jews, Muslims, and non-Orthodox Christians. Two Alexanders, her grandson and great grandson, showed some weak inclination to follow her example. But they were exceptions. More typical was the third Alexander under whom, in the last two decades of the nineteenth century, violent measures against Jews and Protestants followed the long-term pattern of intolerance for ideological diversity.

The policies which came from the attempt to impose religious uniformity in the Russian Empire had direct consequences in the next stage of Russia's history, to which we now turn. The revolutionaries who replaced the old system with a new one, which they claimed to base on Marxist ideology, had to confront head-on the church which had been so closely identified with that old system.

What were the most significant aspects of Orthodox belief in Russia — and how had church-state relations evolved — before the 1917 revolution?

COMPETING FAITHS

REVOLUTIONARY IDEOLOGY
AND RELIGIOUS BELIEF

Since the 1917 revolution and the establishment of the Soviet Union, Soviet political leaders have openly and consistently stated their commitment to an antireligious policy. However, the way the government has actually treated religions has varied widely, as will be seen in this chapter. As the policies and tactics of Soviet leaders have fluctuated, so have the constraints on religion. At times, religious activity has been tightly restricted; if believers resisted, the government used strong, sometimes violent, measures to gain their compliance. At other times, religions (at least some of them) have been relatively free to carry out their basic activities.

The following brief survey of the basic policies toward religion of six Soviet leaders since the revolution—Lenin to Gorbachev—shows clearly the shifts and constants in Soviet church-state relations. According to Vladimir Ilych Lenin, the leader of the victorious revolutionary Bolsheviks, "a Marxist must be a materialist, that is, an enemy of religion." Lenin's heirs have reiterated their leader's enmity against religion in numerous statements. In 1927, Josef Stalin declared to a group of American visitors: "We carry on antireligious propaganda and we will carry on propaganda against religious prejudices. . . . The party cannot be neutral with respect to religion, and it conducts antireligious propaganda against each and every religious prejudice because it stands for science and religious prejudice goes contrary to science, as all religion is somewhat contradictory to science. . . . The party cannot be neutral towards the disseminators of religious prejudices, the reactionary clergy who poison the minds of the laboring masses. Have we repressed the reactionary clergy? Yes, we have. The only unfortunate thing is that they have not yet been completely eliminated." Stalin's hostility to religion brought about a vicious administrative assault upon religion that lasted for more than ten years. Then Stalin dramatically

What has been the impact of Communist ideology on religion in the U.S.S.R. since 1917 — what has changed, what has endured, what has flourished?

From *The Soviet Political Poster,* Courtesy of USSR Embassy, Washington, DC.

reversed his policy, and for the last ten years of his life permitted religious activity to expand.

A year after Stalin died, the Communist leaders made a new commitment to combat religion. The first official document which Nikita Khrushchev signed as secretary of the Central Committee of the Communist Party began with the words: "The Communist Party, in accordance with its program, conducts scientific atheist propaganda of the materialist worldview directed to the continuous elevation of the consciousness of the laboring masses and to their gradual liberation from religious prejudices." Khrushchev's policy brought about another assault upon religion that resulted in the forced closing of more than half of the religious congregations in the Soviet Union in the early 1960s.

Khrushchev was eventually succeeded by Leonid Brezhnev. After Brezhnev consolidated his power as leader of the Communist Party, his Central Committee issued a resolution in 1971 criticizing the failure of party and governmental entities to combat religion: "The Central Committee of the C.P.S.U. [Communist Party of the Soviet Union] notes that . . . ideological institutions have decreased the attention paid to the atheist education of the population, not infrequently permitting a conciliatory attitude to the spread of religious views." The Central Committee ordered party organizations to conduct more vigorous antireligious propaganda and urged government agencies to exercise stricter control over the observance of legislation on religious cults and to "take all necessary measures to bring an end to the activities of religious fanatics, churches, and sectarians who violate Soviet laws."

In his public statements, Konstantin Chernenko spoke more explicitly and forcefully on the subject of combating religion than any secretary of the Communist Party had for at least twenty years. The following excerpt comes near the end of a long speech he delivered to the Central Committee in June 1983 when he was second secretary of the party.

Materialy plenuma tsentral'nogo komiteta KPSS, 14–15 iiunia 1983 goda (Materials of the Plenum of the Central Committee of the Communist Party of the Soviet Union, June 14–15, 1983), p. 60.

"The revolutionary transformation of society is impossible without changing man himself. And our party proceeds on the premise that the molding of the new man is not only an extremely important goal but also an indispensable condition of Communist construction. . . . Molding and lifting man's spiritual values and actively influencing the ideological, political, and moral makeup of the individual is an extremely important mission of socialist culture. . . .

We must not let our work be weakened, in particular in dealing with the religious believers in the population. A part of the population, and, let us speak frankly, a not insignificant part, still remains under the influence of religion. The numerous ideological centers of the imperialist camp are working not only to support but also to inculcate religious sentiments and to impart to them an anti-Soviet, nationalistic bias. They are particularly counting on religious extremists. . . . What can one say to this? Our constitutional guarantees of freedom of conscience are common knowledge. Communists are consistent atheists, but they do not impose their worldview on anyone. Our method is one of enlightenment, persuasion, and propaganda. But when we encounter cases in which socialist laws have been violated or cases of subversive political activity that merely use religion as a front, we act in accordance with the requirements of our constitution. **"**

In the portion of his speech that dealt with religion, Chernenko touched on several themes that recur in this chapter. He affirmed the party's unequivocal adherence to the spread of atheism but at the same time acknowledged that, despite seven decades of antireligious activity, religion was still vigorous in the Soviet Union. While he alluded to cases where religious believers had suffered physical punishment, he suggested that in such cases religion was being used "as a front" for "subversive political activity." From his perspective, the conflict between religion and atheism thus reflected the international conflict between "capitalism" and "socialism."

For twenty-two months after Mikhail Gorbachev replaced Chernenko

Pictured here with members of the Union of Struggle for the Liberation of the Working Class in 1898, Lenin (seated second from right) viewed religion as a form of oppression which "everywhere weighs down heavily upon the masses of the people who are overburdened by their perpetual work for others." SIPA Press.

CHRONOLOGY OF EVENTS

1917   The Bolshevik Decree on Land specifies that all lands owned by churches be confiscated by the state; Church Council of Moscow revives Orthodox Patriarchate; Tikhon elected thirteenth patriarch of Moscow

1918   Decree on Separation of Church and State; Metropolitan of Kiev murdered in Monastery of Caves

1918   First constitution of Soviet Russia grants "freedom of religious and antireligious propaganda"

1919   Law on Exemption from Combat Service in Army on Religious Grounds provides for alternate service for conscientious objectors

1922   Decree orders confiscation of precious stones and metals in churches to aid victims of great famine

1925   Patriarch Tikhon dies; state prevents the election of a new patriarch of Moscow

1929   Law on Religious Associations issued; outlaws all activities by religious groups except worship which "meets religious needs"

1935   Russian Baptist Union dissolved

1943   Stalin "concordat" with religion; election of Patriarch Sergius

1944   Creation of Council for the Affairs of the Russian Orthodox Church and Council for the Affairs of Religious Cults; formation of All-Union Council of Evangelical Christians-Baptists;

1945   Election of Patriarch Alexis.

in 1985, he made no public remarks about religion. When he finally broke his silence in November 1986, he spoke almost as forcefully as Chernenko, calling for a "decisive and uncompromising struggle against manifestations of religion and a strengthening of . . . atheistic propaganda." He went on to declare: "We must be strict above all with Communist and senior officials, particularly those who say they defend our morality and ideals but in fact help promote backward views and themselves take part in religious ceremonies." Only in 1988 did Gorbachev express a much different, conciliatory attitude toward religion.

Soviet leaders in the seven decades from the revolution until 1987 — whether their policies have been strict or lenient — have believed that Communism and religion are antithetical and have sought to persuade Soviet citizens to reject religion. That desire is rooted in the ideology proclaimed by Lenin, who considered religion to be "mildew," "hum-

1946	Synod of Lviv "merges" Ukrainian Catholic Church (Uniates) with Russian Orthodox Church, effectively outlawing up to five million Eastern Rite Catholics
1947	Creation of *Znanie* (Knowledge) Society with task of conducting antireligious propaganda
1948–53	"Anticosmopolitanism" campaign raises level of anti-Jewish hostility
1954	"Hundred Days antireligious campaign"
1954–57	Post-Stalin amnesties for thousands of imprisoned believers
1959–64	Khrushchev antireligious campaign
1964	"Foundations of Scientific Atheism" made compulsory course for graduates of institutions of higher education
1966	Council for Religious Affairs created by merger of two previous councils
1967	New level of Soviet anti-Semitism in aftermath of Six-Day War spurs Jewish emigration movement
1971	Election of Patriarch Pimen
1975	Amended Law on Religious Associations places responsibility for registering religious associations in central Council for Religious Affairs
1983	Danilov Monastery in Moscow returned to Russian Orthodox Church for use as patriarchal headquarters; Orthodox printing enterprise started near Novodevichy Monastery

bug," "rotgut," and "spiritual oppression."

Lenin's starting point was Marx's famous words: "Religion is the opium of the people." Lenin gave these words his own destructive twist and drew from them a practical approach for dealing with religion in the new society he dreamed of creating. In an article entitled "Socialism and Religion," one of the few explicit statements he made about religion, Lenin wrote, "religion is a sort of spiritual rotgut in which the slaves of capital drown their human image. It is one of the forms of spiritual oppression which everywhere weighs down heavily upon the masses of the people who are overburdened by their perpetual work for others and by want and isolation."

Lenin drew the conclusion that a just and humane society would be one from which religion had been removed. However, he thought religion should be attacked indirectly, not directly. "The revolutionary proletariat will succeed in making religion a really private affair, so far as the state is concerned," he wrote. "And in this political system, cleansed of medieval mildew, the proletariat will wage a broad and open struggle for the elimination of economic slavery, the true source of the religious humbugging of mankind."

There were three aspects to Lenin's stance toward religion. First, he expressed a contempt for religion that bordered on irrational hostility. His emotional aversion to religion may have developed because the tsarist government and the Orthodox Church in the Russia he grew up in were intimately connected. For religions that had been persecuted by the autocratic regime, Lenin expressed some sympathy.

The second aspect of Lenin's stance toward religion was a more reasoned conviction that church and state ought to be separated. This, he believed, was a modern way of thinking. He wrote: "Complete separation of church and state is what the socialist proletariat demands of the modern state and the modern church."

The third and most important aspect was Lenin's strategy for achieving the elimination of religion from society — a strategy which placed priority on economic questions. As mentioned above, Lenin concluded that it would be futile to attack people's religious beliefs directly. "It would be stupid to think," he said, "that in a society based on endless oppression, religious prejudices could be dispelled." Religion could be expected to disappear from any society only after full economic justice had been instituted.

When Lenin became head of the revolutionary government in 1917, he quickly took steps to implement what he had espoused in 1905. In December 1917, he appointed a committee to draft a law on the separation of church and state. Promulgated in February 1918, the law was relatively brief, but had far-reaching ramifications. It profoundly changed the legal status of religion in Russia. For the Russian Orthodox Church, it meant the end of its favored position as the state church. Orthodoxy lost the privileges that came from its prominence in public ceremony and its right to teach religion in the public schools. The church was not allowed to own property and was thereby deprived of enormous financial resources. All of its vast properties were confiscated, and the financial subsidy which it had received earlier was terminated. Congregations were permitted to continue to use their church buildings, but they no longer owned them. For other religions, the law had a less negative impact. Some even believed they could derive considerable benefit from it because it removed (or appeared to remove) disadvantages that they had suffered previously in comparison with Orthodoxy. Formally, the decree made all religions equal before the law.

This law established the fundamental legal structure for the role of religion in Soviet society, a structure that continues today, although many other legal regulations, interpretations, and directives have affected religion's sphere of activity. The following excerpt is the full text of the law as enacted in February 1918. The six sentences in brackets

"A Marxist must be a materialist, that is, an enemy of religion."

V. I. Lenin

were removed formally in the 1980s when the laws of the country were codified. Both their original inclusion and subsequent elimination reveal the changing approach the state has taken to religion.

1. The church is separated from the state.

2. Within the boundaries of the republic, it is forbidden to publish any local laws or resolutions which would hinder or restrict freedom of conscience or would establish any kind of advantage or privilege on the basis of religious adherence of citizens.

3. Each citizen may profess any religion or profess none. All kinds of denial of rights connected with the profession of any faith or with the nonprofession of faith are eliminated.

Note: All mention of religious adherence or nonadherence of citizens is removed from all official documents.

4. Activities of state and of other public social institutions are not accompanied by any religious rituals or ceremonies.

5. The free conduct of religious rituals is guaranteed insofar as they do not disrupt social order and are not accompanied by the infringement of the rights of citizens of the Soviet Republic.

Local authorities have the right to take all necessary measures to preserve social order and security in these cases.

6. No one may refuse to fulfill his civic obligations on the basis of an appeal to religious views. [Exemption from this requirement is granted in each separate case by decision of a people's court, provided that one civil obligation is substituted for the other.]

7. Religious oaths and pledges are eliminated. In cases where necessary, only a solemn promise is given.

8. Records of civil status are keep exclusively by the state: by the departments of registry of marriages and births.

9. The school is separated from the church.
[The teaching of religious subjects is not permitted in all state and public institutions as well as in private teaching institutions in which subjects of a general character are taught. Citizens may teach and be taught religion in a private manner.]

10. [All church and religious societies fall into the category of private societies and unions and do not enjoy any privileges and subsidies from either the government or its local autonomous and independent institutions.]

11. Compulsory collections and taxes for the support of church and religious organizations, as well as measures of discipline and punishment on the part of these organizations, with respect to members are forbidden.

"Decree Concerning Separation of Church from State and School from Church" in P. V. Gidulianov, ed., *Otdelenie tserkvi ot gosudarstva v SSSR* (Separation of the Church from the State in the U.S.S.R.) (Moscow: Iuridicheskoe izdatel'stvo, 1926), pp. 615f.

"For the Russian Orthodox Church the 1918 decree meant the end of its favored position as the state church."

12. [No church or religious societies have the right to own property. They do not have the right of juridical person.]

13. All property of church and religious organizations existing in Russia is declared to be the property of the people. Buildings and objects which are used specifically for divine worship are leased, by special action of local or central state authorities, for use without cost by the respective religious organizations. **"**

Early Soviet propaganda posters hailed the Russian revolution as the beginning of a world revolution and called upon the working masses everywhere to unite in building a world free from capitalist oppression — a world where the crutch of religion would no longer be needed.

From *The Soviet Political Poster,* Courtesy of USSR Embassy, Washington, DC.

With the exception of article 12, this law seems to guarantee the free exercise of religion in a way which respects the human rights and spiritual needs of all citizens. But it would be a mistake to conclude that the law accurately described the climate for religious activity in the aftermath of the revolution: reality presented a less rosy picture. As the situation evolved, the law appeared to be a hostile attack upon religion. The decree was announced at the beginning of a civil war between the "Red" Bolsheviks, then in power, and an assorted collection of "White" opponents, including reactionary monarchists, liberal democrats, and other socialists. The Bolsheviks were simultaneously encountering opposition from religious quarters, mostly from the Orthodox Church. At the time, the church was led by its patriarch, Tikhon, who had been selected by a church council in the week after the Bolsheviks seized power in November 1917. (The church had not had a patriarch since Peter had denied it the right to choose one 216 years before.) When the decree on separation of church and state was announced, Patriarch Tikhon rallied resistance against it, setting the stage for an intense and often bloody clash between the church and the new government. He pronounced an anathema upon the revolutionaries and ordered believers to prevent local officials from taking possession of church properties as the law prescribed. The confrontation that Tikhon's actions produced, in which many church leaders were killed, is described by an American church historian.

Matthew Spinka, *The Church and the Russian Revolution* (New York: Macmillan, 1927), pp. 20–22.

" Obviously, Patriarch Tikhon played what seemed a dangerous game; for if the Soviet regime should retain its hold on the helm of the state, he was certain to be crushed by its might. Many of the members of the Sobor [the council which had elected him] tried to prevent such consequences for the Patriarch by urging him to leave Moscow and to take refuge elsewhere, perhaps even abroad. But Tikhon resolutely refused: "The flight of the Patriarch," he replied, "would play into the hands of the enemies of the Church; they would exploit it for their purposes. Let them do as they see fit." And despite this known danger to his safety, Tikhon, in October 1918, when the regime was busy with preparations for the first anniversary of the Revolution, was the only person who dared to pen a

"THERE IS NO PERSECUTION FOR FAITH . . ."

The decree of February 1918 separating the church from the state aroused considerable opposition, especially from the upper echelons of the Orthodox Church, including the newly elected Patriarch Tikhon, who pronounced a decree of excommunication against the Bolshevik rulers. One device employed by the Bolsheviks to defend their actions and calm the general populace was to display wall posters such as the following.

"TO ALL BELIEVERS. Each believer considers his faith best. And the unbeliever considers that no faith is necessary. Who is right — the Orthodox, Old Believers, Catholics, Muslims, Jews, Buddhists, or the unbelievers? Each considers himself right. Each person should be free not to believe or to believe as he wishes. The law of the workers and peasants government, the decree of the Council of People's Commissars declares: Each citizen may profess any religion or not profess any.

According to the meaning of the decree on separation of church from state, icons should be taken only from government and civil institutions, from schools, hospitals, and almshouses. And this is clear to everyone. If you want to pray, go to church or mosque or synagogue. In the bath, at the post office, in the soviet, in the barracks — these are places for work and not for prayer. At your own home you may hang as many icons as your soul wishes, but people of various religions and unbelievers frequent hospitals, almshouses and dormitories, so there you may not hang icons. Also in schools.

The decree says: Citizens may teach and be taught in a private manner. This means that in the government schools, children should learn grammar, arithmetic, historical and other sciences, and drawing, but not the law of God. Why? Because in the schools the children of Orthodox, and Catholics, and Muslims, and Jewish parents are taught. There are also children of unbelieving parents. It is therefore forbidden to teach religion in the public schools at state expense. But if parents wish, they may teach their own children, at their expense, any kind of religion they want.

Here is the truth both about icons and the schools and religion. Do not listen, then, believers, to the false slanders against the Soviet government. Do not believe the foul interventions of the adherents of the old regime and know:
THERE IS NO PERSECUTION FOR FAITH IN SOVIET RUSSIA"

Quoted in R. Iu. Plaskin, *Krakh tserkovnoi kontrrevoliutsii, 1917–1923* (The Failure of the Church Counterrevolution) (Moscow, 1968), p. 77.

When the Bolsheviks seized power, the Church Council of Bishops took the opportunity to elect Patriarch Tikhon as the church's first patriarch in over 200 years.

Soviet Life.

declaration, "the strongest of anything that he has hitherto written against Bolshevism." Even his own advisers were frightened. But Tikhon sent it directly to Lenin on the eve of the celebration. It is a marvel that the latter did not take decisive measures against the Patriarch. All that the regime did was to place him under house arrest. . . .

Under such circumstances, the conflict of the Soviet government with the Church was inevitable: it at first took the form of persecution of the hierarchs and the clergy. The ancient and historic churches in the Kremlin were closed, and the relics of the great Russian saints kept in the Cathedral of the Assumption, the most famous of them, were destroyed. The same procedure was followed in Petrograd with the relics of St. Alexander Nevsky, and in Zadonsk with the remains of St. Tikhon. Some of the relics were placed in museums, and a wide publicity was given them. . . . The second method of conflict with the Church was that of depriving it of organized leadership. Twenty-eight hierarchs were murdered: Metropolitan Vladimir of Kiev was brutally killed in

January 1918; Archbishop Vasily of Chernigov, Bishop Andronik of Perm, who was bestially tortured, Bishop Germogen of Saratov, Bishop Ephraim of Irkutsk, and Bishop Pimen were also murdered. Thousands of clerics of all ranks were thrown into prisons without any trial, and twelve thousand others were reported by the emigre press as put to death.

There can be no doubt that during the first year of his administration, Tikhon used his office for political opposition to the Bolshevik regime, as under the circumstances was not difficult to understand. But he soon recognized that the policy hitherto pursued by him and his Synod [council of bishops] was wrong. His essential greatness may be seen in the fundamental change of his orientation. . . . [Later] Tikhon assumed an "apolitical," neutral relation to the state, although it also involved him in recognition of the Soviet regime as the legal government of the country to which civil obedience is due. This new policy was based on a strict interpretation of the Constitution, which separated the Church from the state, by reason of which the Church should have enjoyed freedom and autonomy in its internal administration. **"**

Patriarch Tikhon led the church for the first seven years of the Soviet government. He spent several months in prison and more under house arrest and was constantly under threat of being tried in court for treason. When he died in 1925, the question of who would lead the church was complicated by state interference. The government refused permission for a church council of bishops to meet to elect a new patriarch. Tikhon had provided for such a contingency by naming a succession of three metropolitans who were to take over responsibility for church affairs. But when he died, two were already in exile and the third, Metropolitan Peter, was arrested soon after he assumed control of church headquarters. The person who stepped into the breech was Metropolitan Sergius Stragorodsky, who had been appointed by Metropolitan Peter to serve as his deputy in the event of his arrest. Sergius served as "acting patriarch," from the beginning of 1926 until 1943, when the government finally allowed him to be formally elected patriarch.

Sergius's first eighteen months as temporary head of the church were stormy. He was arrested almost immediately and kept in jail for two months. After a few weeks of freedom, he was thrown back in jail for another month. In the fall, he was jailed again when the police discovered that he had been trying to conduct a secret election of a patriarch.

Five months after Sergius's third release from jail, the newspapers carried an important proclamation over his signature. This document articulated what was to become the "official" attitude of the Russian Orthodox Church toward the Communist state.

Two themes emerge from the proclamation, both have been prominent in the experience of religious persons and groups within the Soviet Union. One is that international events have an impact on church-state relations in the Soviet Union. That impact takes various forms; it is not always negative, as Sergius describes it below. The proclamation was issued in a time of considerable international tension—sometimes called the "war scare" of 1927. Two months earlier, Great Britain had broken diplomatic relations with the U.S.S.R., and just one month earlier, a Russian Orthodox youth had assassinated the Soviet ambassador in Warsaw. Sergius is probably referring obliquely to these events in his proclamation. Compounding the problems for the Russian church were anti-Soviet statements and actions by Russian priests and bishops who had emigrated and then created the Karlovci Synod or the Russian Orthodox Church Abroad, a monarchist church in exile.

The second theme concerns the basic conflict inherent in church-state relations in a state fundamentally opposed to religion. How could Orthodoxy or any religion endure in the inhospitable circumstances of the new Communist regime?

Recognizing that some way had to be found to adjust to political reality, Sergius apparently wrestled with that question and ultimately decided that submission to the Communist state was the solution that would enable the church to endure through bad times (and prosper in better ones). As might be expected, not all religious believers agreed with Sergius's decision — nor do they all today — but many did, and the model of submission is still followed. The proclamation thus has great significance; some analysts claim that it is the most important document of Soviet religious history.

> **How could Orthodoxy or any religion sustain itself in the profoundly inhospitable circumstances of the new Communist regime?**

Sergius Stragorodsky, "Proclamation," *Izvestiia*, August 18, 1927, in William C. Fletcher, *A Study in Survival* (New York: Macmillan, 1965), pp. 28–31.

"

By God's grace the humble Sergey, Metropolitan of Nezhegorod, Deputy of the Patriarchal Locum Tenens, and the Temporary Patriarchal Holy Synod;

To the Most Reverend Archpastors, God-Loving Pastors, Honored Monks and all faithful members of the Holy All-Russian Orthodox Church;

Rejoice in the Lord.

One of the concerns of our late Holy Father Patriarch Tikhon before his death was to place our Orthodox Russian Church in correct relations with the Soviet government and by this to give to the church the possibility of fully legal and peaceful existence. And, of course, if unexpected death had not cut short his holy labors, he would have carried the matter through to the end. Unfortunately, various circumstances, mainly the activities of foreign enemies of the Soviet State, among whom were not only ordinary believers of our church but their leaders also, arousing a natural and just distrust by the government of church activities in general, hindered the efforts of His Holiness, and it was not allotted to him in life to see his efforts crowned with success. . . .

We must show, not in words, but in deed, that not only people indifferent to Orthodoxy, or those who reject it, can be faithful citizens of the Soviet Union, loyal to the Soviet government, but also the most fervent adherents of Orthodoxy, to whom it is as dear with all its canonical and liturgical treasures as truth and life. We wish to be Orthodox and at the same time to claim the Soviet Union as our civil motherland, the joys and successes of which are our joys and successes, the misfortunes of which are our misfortunes. Every blow directed against the Union, be it war, boycott, or simply murder from behind a corner, like that in Warsaw, we acknowledge as a blow directed against us. Remaining Orthodox, we remember our duty to be citizens of the Union "not from fear, but from conscience," as the Apostle has taught us (Rom. 13:5). . . .

"Seats reserved for ladies with babes in arms."

Courtesy of *Krokodil*, a Soviet satirical magazine.

Not in vain does the Apostle tell us that we may live "quietly and peaceably" by our piety only if we submit to the lawful government (I Tim. 2:2); otherwise, we should leave society. Only impractical dreamers can think that such an immense community as our Orthodox Church, with all its organizations, may peacefully exist in this country by hiding itself from the government. **"**

Ten years after the revolution, the Communists had managed to wrest from the leader of the Orthodox Church a statement of submissive loyalty to the new regime. As already stated, not all Orthodox Christians agreed with Sergius's proclamation. Many priests, believers, and even some bishops rejected his leadership, creating various schisms and independent church groups, the most significant of which is known as the True Orthodox Church. No reliable information is available about how many True Orthodox there are, but it is known that the group has active adherents, although their congregations have no legal existence.

Sergius's proclamation was opposed in a letter purportedly written by a trusted associate of Patriarch Tikhon, Archbishop Illarion Troitsky. As seen below, the writer uses apocalyptic terms, in a way that is reminiscent of Avvakum's characterization of those who put him on trial, against "materialism, atheism, theomacy, and satanism."

Illarion Troitsky, "Letter to the Priest P. F. Tikhon" in Dimitry Pospielovsky, *The Russian Church under the Soviet Regime*, (Crestwood, NY: St. Vladimir's Seminary Press, 1984), pp. 484–487.

"

The difficulty of our time for an Orthodox is . . . that the contemporary life of the Church demands of him a high spiritual self-discipline in personal life. He cannot rely on guidance from the official pastors (bishops and presbyters). . . . Life has posed questions that can be solved in a truly churchly manner only by bypassing mores, forms, regulations and being led by senses trained to recognize virtue from evil. Otherwise it is easy to defile the sacredness of one's soul and to allow one's conscience to disintegrate through a legalistically regulated reconciliation with fraud and profanity, brought into the Church by the bishops themselves. By means of laws it is possible to reconcile oneself even with the devil.

Aren't the latest events a confirmation of the above premonitions? . . . Hasn't Sergey's declaration, which has caused varied and fully justified negative reactions, thrown the church organization, headed by him, into the loathsome, adulterous embraces of the atheistic and blasphemous power of antichrist, and hasn't it introduced a frightening profanity into the bosom of our Church? Please note that this declaration appeared from the hands of . . . a canonical, lawful, apparently Orthodox hierarch. The main assertions of the declaration are based on scriptural texts . . . and on the historical experience of the ancient Church, as if it were similar to the current one. On the other hand, the declaration hopes to quench the essential thirst of believers exhausted by persecutions, for it

Muslims, with their distinct cultural traditions and religion, inhabit six of the fifteen Soviet republics and make up close to one-fifth of the Soviet population.

Courtesy of Howard Cooperman.

> **"We wish to be Orthodox and at the same time to claim the Soviet Union as our civil motherland, the joys and successes of which are our joys and successes, the misfortunes of which are our misfortunes."**
>
> **1927 proclamation of Metropolitan Sergius**

promises them peace and quiet. And hence multitudes, especially from the clerical ranks, are sympathetically responding to the declaration of Metropolitan Sergey and his Synod.

This symphony between the power which is making war on God and the regular Orthodox hierarchy has already produced some "blessings": some bishops (although not the best ones and not the most "guilty" ones) are returning from exile (not from a very distant one, however) and are being appointed to dioceses (not to the same ones from which they had been deported, however); ... Metropolitan Sergey has a Synod (which is more like the office of the procurator general) which consists of regular hierarchs (alas, with questionable reputations owing to their longtime and solid cooperation with the godless GPU [secret police] ...). Metropolitan Sergey's name is being elevated [in the liturgy] as

ISLAM UNDER SOVIET RULE

The following outline of the history of Islam since the Bolshevik revolution was written by two Western researchers.

Alexandre Bennigsen and S. Enders Wimbush, *Muslims of the Soviet Empire* (Bloomington, IN: Indiana University Press, 1986), pp. 11–12.

" The first period is that of the Civil War and the first consolidation of Bolshevik rule, approximately 1917–19. The characteristic feature of this period was the "calvary raids" by local Bolsheviks against (with some regional exceptions) all religious institutions, including Islam.

The second period, that of Muslim National Communism, lasted from 1919 to 1928. Muslim leaders who joined the Communist Party remained partial to Islamic culture, and exercised authority in all the Muslim republics. Islam was left relatively unhindered, but various administrative measures were adopted by the Bolsheviks to weaken the economic and cultural power of the clerics. These measures included: the liquidation of the *waqfs* [religious property], which were the basis of clerical economic power; suppression of the religious (*shariat*) and customary (*adat*) courts; and the elimination of the confessional school system (*mekteps* and *medressehs*).

The third period, 1928–41, was characterized by a frontal assault on Islam within Soviet borders. This assault resulted in the closing of thousands of mosques and the liquidation or imprisonment of most Muslim clerics. This attack also involved intense anti-Islamic propaganda. In the 1930s, especially, clerics and believers were accused of being spies, saboteurs, counter-revolutionaries and parasites. A period of more relaxed relations followed, and lasted from 1941 to 1959. The main stimulus for this change was, of course, the Second World War, during which the Soviet official position towards religious institutions underwent a dramatic change in order to secure greater support for the So-

that of the captain of the Church, but, alas, this name is but a forgery, because the real master of the destiny of the Russian Church and her bishops, both those in positions as well as the persecuted ones . . . is the current "Procurator General" of the Russian Orthodox Church, Evgeny A. Tuchkov [chief of the political police department responsible for church affairs].

Everybody with ears to hear and eyes to see knows that contrary to the decree on the separation of Church and state, the Orthodox Church has entered into a close alliance with the state. And what state? . . . A state whose government aims at the destruction of any religion on the

viet war effort. An official Muslim organization was created in late 1942, first at Ufa and then in Central Asia, on the initiative of the Mufti Abdurrahman Rasulaev of Ufa. All anti-Islamic propaganda ceased during the war.

A new offensive against Islam was launched by Khrushchev in 1959, and lasted till he was ousted from power in 1964. The majority of working mosques were closed during this period, their number falling from approximately 1,500 in 1958 to less than 500 in 1968 (compare this with the 26,279 mosques that existed in the Russian empire in 1912).

Under Brezhnev (1964–82) the massive campaign against Islam was abandoned as being counterproductive, and direct attacks on the official religious leadership disappeared completely from the Soviet press. Relations between church and state became more normal. Beginning in the late 1970s, several new mosques were opened, and religious authorities, especially those attached to the Muslim Spiritual Directorate in Tashkent, have both travelled widely abroad and entertained foreign Muslim delegations at home. During this period, the Soviet use of Islam as a strategic and diplomatic instrument [to advance its influence in the Middle East] became marked.

The current period, dating approximately from the Islamic revolution in Iran in the late 1970s and the Soviet invasion of Afghanistan, can be characterized by an abrupt backtracking on the relative liberalism of the Brezhnev years. In the early 1980s, a new anti-Islamic campaign was initiated, a reversal predicated on the Soviet leadership's justifiable fears that the Iranian and Afghanistan situations were infecting Soviet Muslim territories. At the time of going to press, Gorbachev's policies toward Islam are not entirely clear, although first indications suggest that at least the beginning of his tenure will be remembered for the vehemence of the anti-Islamic line taken by regional Soviet officials. Recent keynote speeches at the Central Asian party conferences of January 1986 are remarkable for their violent hostility to Islam and the party leaders' perception of the political damage which Islam is causing their social policies. If we are to assume that these leaders are Gorbachev's men and that they articulate his policies, it is probable that Islam under the new Soviet regime will be more persecuted rather than less so.

"

face of the earth, and the Orthodox Church before all the others, because it justly sees in her a basic world foundation of religious faith and a first class fortress in the struggle against materialism, atheism, theomachy, and satanism (practiced, according to hearsay, by some members of the contemporary powers that be).

"

In practical terms, Sergius's proclamation brought a measure of freedom to the Orthodox and put the former state church on an equal footing with other religious groups, toward which the revolutionary government seemed solicitous.

For example, less than one month after the Bolsheviks seized power, Lenin issued an appeal for the support of "all the working Muslims of Russia and the East," assuring them that their rights were "protected by the full weight of the Revolution."

V. I. Lenin, "To All Working Muslims of Russia and the East," trans. Gulhamid Sobratee, in Shaukat Burkhanov and Vladilen Gusarov, *Soviet Power and Islam* (Moscow: Novosti Press Agency, 1984), p. 11.

" **M**uslims of Russia, Tatars of the Volga Region and the Crimea, Turks and Tatars of Transcaucasia, Chechens and other highlanders of the Caucasus — all whose mosques and prayer houses were destroyed, whose beliefs and customs were trampled underfoot by the tsars and oppressors of Russia! Henceforth your beliefs and customs, your national and cultural institutions are declared free and inviolable. Arrange your national life freely and without hindrance. You have a right to that. Be aware that your rights, like the rights of all the peoples of Russia, are protected by the full might of the Revolution and its bodies of power, the Soviets of Workers', Soldiers' and Peasants' Deputies. **"**

Lenin's government set up a Central Commissariat for Muslim Affairs to represent Muslim interests to the new government and to win the sympathy of Muslims. In an overt demonstration of respect for Islam, Lenin signed the following decree: "Fulfilling the aspirations of all the Muslims of Russia, the government has decided to hand over to them the Othman Koran." This ancient copy of the sacred text had been confiscated by the tsarist government from a mosque in Central Asia and kept in the Petrograd National Library.

The Bolsheviks dealt with the Jews in a similar fashion. In early 1918, over the signature of Lenin as president of the Council of People's Commissars, the following circular sought Jewish support for the new government with a promise that discrimination and violence against Jews would be condemned.

Gerard Israel, *The Jews in Russia* (New York: St. Martin's, 1975), pp. 143–144.

" **I**n the Russian Soviet Federated Socialist Republic, where the principle of self-determination of the working masses of all peoples was proclaimed, there is no room for national oppression. The Jewish bourgeois is not our enemy because he is Jewish, but only because he is bourgeois. The Jewish worker is our brother. Every incitement to hatred against any nation whatsoever is inadmissible, criminal and shameful. The Council of the People's Commissars considers the anti-Semitic movement and the Jewish pogroms as pernicious to the revolution of the workers and peasants and calls upon all the working peoples of Socialist Russia to fight with all of their might against this evil.

The Council of the People's Commissars urges all Soviets to take decisive measures to nip the anti-Semitic movement in the bud. It commands that the pogromists as well as the agitators of pogroms be considered as outlaws.   **"**

For Jews, the party had a special Jewish section known by an acronym, Yevsektsiia, which combined the Russian words for "Jew," *Yevrei,* and "section." The Yevsektsiia was intended to appeal to the Jewish desire for a measure of self-determination and autonomy. But it also had the task of undermining the Jewish religion, as the following excerpt from a book by an American scholar shows. Thus, an instrument that had the potential to secure the rights of Jews as a national group did not protect their religious rights.

"The Bolshevik revolution brought radical changes. In the first four years of Soviet rule, the fight against religion was treated as a necessary but not immediate task. Not until 1921, four years after the Bolsheviks seized power, did they feel strong enough to initiate an organized campaign to close down houses of worship.

The Jewish Communists, the Yevsektsiia, were torn between two opposing attitudes. On the one hand, they were aware of the peculiarities inherent in the position of a minority religion which had been oppressed and debased by the Tsarist regime and by the dominant church. On the other hand, the Jewish Communists felt uncomfortable in admitting the differences in the treatment of religious groups. Therefore, they continually underscored the harmful influences of all religion and all clerics. More often than not they instigated action against Jewish clergy for a particular synagogue whenever a non-Jewish clergyman was arrested or other drastic action was taken against a Christian church.

They felt that not acting against Jewish religious institutions might provoke anti-Semitism. But linking innocent Jewish clergymen and houses of prayer with their non-Jewish activist counterparts alienated the "Jewish masses." Nevertheless, Jewish Communists insisted that such joint action be taken regardless of the Jewish reaction. . . .

In the closing of synagogues, the Jewish Communists had their own set of priorities. First on the list were the so-called "choir synagogues" which were modern and spacious and to which the wealthier Jews belonged. Then would come the systematic reeducation of the existing smaller houses of prayer, by emphasizing the pressing needs of the community for the buildings. This would be coupled, in case of compliance, with the promise of leaving other synagogues in peace.

The "pressing needs" were often real. Hundreds of thousands of

Joshua Rothenberg, *The Jewish Religion in the Soviet Union* (New York: Ktav, 1971), pp. 39–40, 210–211.

"The Council of the People's Commissars considers the anti-Semitic movement and the Jewish pogroms as pernicious to the revolution of the workers and peasants and calls upon all the working peoples of Socialist Russia to fight with all of their might against this evil."
1918 circular signed by Lenin

SOVIET CONSTITUTION ON RELIGION

Three constitutions and three party programs (see box, pp. 92–93) have been issued by the Soviet government since the Bolshevik revolution. Each has contained a long list of citizens' rights, including the right of freedom of conscience. The formulation of that right has changed in significant ways.

1918 CONSTITUTION OF THE RUSSIAN SOCIALIST FEDERATION OF SOVIET REPUBLICS.

Article 13: To secure for the toilers real freedom of conscience, the church is separated from the state, and the school from the church, and freedom of religious and antireligious propaganda is recognized as the right of every citizen.

This constitution also disenfranchised clergy. The ideological justification for this move was that in the aftermath of the revolution, the government was a "dictatorship of the proletariat" and a "dictatorship" may be forced to deny political rights to some people.

Article 65: The following persons may not vote or be elected [to the soviets]:
d: monks and ministers of the church and religious cults.

A new constitution was adopted in 1936 which was intended to reflect the changes that came from a new stage of development, namely, the achievement of Socialism in the U.S.S.R. As regards religion, the constitution did not recognize the right of religion to proselytize in public (recognition of that right had been deleted from the constitution in 1929). Freedom of conscience consisted only of the right to conduct religious ceremonies. With socialism in place, it was no longer necessary for the constitution to perpetuate the requirements of the dictatorship of the proletariat and so all categories of people were enfranchised.

1936 CONSTITUTION OF THE U.S.S.R.

Article 124: In order to guarantee for citizens freedom of conscience, the church in the U.S.S.R. is separated from the state and the school from the church. Freedom of the performance of religious rites and freedom of antireligious propaganda is recognized for all citizens.

Article 135: Elections of deputies [to soviets] is universal. All citizens of the U.S.S.R. who have attained the age of eighteen have the right to participate in the elections of deputies, irrespective of race and nationality, sex, religious profession, education, place of residence, social origin, property status, and previous behavior.

The current constitution was adopted in 1977. The definition of freedom of conscience was slightly expanded to include the right to "profess" a religion. The notion of "religious profession" may provide some latitude for the limitations on permitted religious behavior to be stretched. Reflecting the development of the "scientific atheist establishment," the new constitution replaces "antireligious" with "atheist" propaganda. The prohibition on inciting hostility, if it is interpreted simply as a strong warning against offending the feelings of believers, would provide protection for believers. But it could also threaten believers, if it is interpreted as a charge against religion for promoting divisions within society.

" 1977 CONSTITUTION OF THE U.S.S.R.

Article 52: Citizens of the U.S.S.R. are guaranteed freedom of conscience, that is, the right to profess or not to profess any religion, and to conduct religious worship or atheistic propaganda. Incitement of hostility or hatred on religious grounds is prohibited. In the U.S.S.R., the church is separated from the state and the school from the church. "

orphans or abandoned children roamed the countryside and many people were homeless as a result of the destruction of thousands of buildings. . . . Periodically, the communist Jewish press reported "successes" in having the larger synagogues closed. In many cases, the Jewish population vigorously opposed these actions as illegal because the closures were not in accordance with the wishes of the worshipers, as the law required. . . .

Propaganda against the Jewish religion and Jewish clergymen was entrusted to the Jewish section of the Communist Party (Yevsektsiia) which could not be accused of anti-Semitism or of adherence to the Tsarist anti-Jewish policies. The Jewish Communists did not hesitate to indict Jewish religious functionaries for their alleged former collaboration with the Tsarist regime and for their "opposition" to the new regime. In fact, however, Jewish religious leaders had not made any attempts to actively oppose the new government. It was hardly conceivable that they would have done so by supporting the enemies of the Soviet regime who had instigated or at least tolerated the anti-Jewish pogroms of the civil war. Yet Jewish clergymen and religious organizations were often penalized, if for no other reason than because action was also being taken against other religious leaders. "

The religious movement that benefited the most from the concessions granted by Lenin's government was evangelical Protestantism. The size of this movement grew from about 100,000 participants in the first decade of Soviet rule to over three million. The movement comprised several denominational organizations, including unions of Baptists, Evangelical Christians, Pentecostals, and Adventists. These evangelicals engaged in widespread vigorous proselytizing, taking advantage of the Soviet constitution's grant of "freedom of religious propaganda." They published an array of religious works, operated Bible schools to train preachers, organized charity programs, and created successful agricultural and manufacturing cooperatives. Suddenly, in April 1929, all these activities, which had so facilitated the growth of the Protestant evangelical movement, were banned, as Stalin consolidated his power.

By the end of the 1920s, Stalin had accomplished his goal of becoming Lenin's successor as the leader of the Communist Party and, thereby, of the Soviet state. With his nearly unqualified dictatorial powers, Stalin launched the country into a frantic, breakneck transformation which he declared would introduce full socialism. Naturally, the practice of religion was affected by his Promethean quest for a thoroughly modernized and socialized country. Laws determining what religions could and could not do were made more restrictive, antireligious propaganda and demonstrations were accelerated, and the Communists launched a direct assault on religion that left the institutions in disarray and many believers in prison.

The law of April 8, 1929, entitled "Concerning Religious Associations," imposed many restrictions. Whereas Lenin's basic decree had denied religions the right to own property and run schools, it still permitted a broad range of activities. The new law took these away. The most important activities to be prohibited were specified in article 17 of the law, which is reproduced below. Beginning in 1929, all that religious groups could do legally was to meet "for the joint satisfaction of their religious needs." The state interpreted "religious needs" very narrowly. In brief, religions were restricted to the performance of ceremony. They were even denied the right to attempt publicly to persuade people to adopt religious faith and were prohibited from functioning until they registered and were formally recognized by the state.

N. Orleanskii, *Zakon o religioznykh ob"edineniiakh R.S.F.S.R.* (Law Concerning Religious Associations of the Russian Soviet Federated Socialist Republic) (Moscow: Bezbozhnik, 1930), pp. 6–24.

" 2. Religious associations of believing citizens of all religions are registered either as religious societies or groups of believers. Each citizen may be a member of only one religio-cultic association (society or group).

3. A religious society is a local association of believing citizens, who have attained the age of 18 years, of one and the same religion, confession, movement, or sect, comprising no fewer than 20 persons who have joined together for the joint satisfaction of their religious needs.

Believing citizens who, because of insufficient numbers, are not able to form a religious society, are granted the right to form a group of believers.

4. A religious society and group of believers may begin its activity only after registration of the society or group with the designated administrative department of the local executive committee or city soviet. . . .

17. Religious societies are prohibited from the following activities: a) creation of funds for mutual aid, cooperatives, industrial associations; and, in general, the use of property placed at their disposal for any other goals than the satisfaction of religious needs; b) providing material support to members; c) organizing either special children's, youth, women's prayer and other meetings, or general Bible, literature, handicraft, labor, or religious study meetings, groups, circles, departments, as well as organizing excursions and children's playgrounds, opening libraries and reading rooms, and operating sanatoria and medical clinics. . . .

22. Religious congresses and the executive organs by them do not have the right of juridical person, and besides this, they may not: 1) establish any kind of central treasury for collection of voluntary contributions of believers; 2) establish any kind of compulsory collections; 3) acquire cultic property or use it by contract or acquire premises for prayer meetings by purchase or rental; 4) conclude any kind of agreements and transactions. . . .

57. In the buildings of the religious cult or in specially appointed premises, conforming to the construction and health regulations, prayer meetings of believers united in groups or societies may proceed without notification or permission of the authorities.

In premises not especially appointed, prayer meetings of believers proceed upon notification [of appropriate authorities]. . . .

59. Religious processions, as well as the conduct of religious rituals and ceremonies under the open sky are permitted with special permission for each instance.

"The Kingdom of the Church is the Kingdom of Chains"
Antireligious poster, 1932.

From *Mastera Sovetskoi Karikatury:*
M. Cheremnykh,
Courtesy of USSR Embassy, Washington, DC.

"

In addition to the provisions cited above, the new law also contained lengthy provisions for closing religious buildings, a procedure ultimately invoked against thousands of synagogues, mosques, and churches. Although the ownership of religious buildings had been transferred to the state in 1918, until the 1929 law, congregations still were able to enjoy relatively unhindered use of their buildings. But the new "church closing" procedures drastically changed the situation for religion because congregations rapidly lost opportunities to conduct their services.

The essential provisions of the 1929 law remain in effect in 1988, although recently there have been public promises that they may be changed. (Article 22 was rescinded after World War II in order to permit the officially recognized national organizations of various denomina-

In what ways did the treatment of different faiths vary in the early years of the Soviet state?

tions to conduct their activities.)

The acceleration of antireligious activities and the direct assault on religious institutions and believers are described in the next three excerpts. The first is by a British journalist.

Trevor Beeson, *Discretion and Valour* (Glasgow: Collins, 1982), pp. 65–66.

> **"The intensified persecution, part of the general terror inflicted upon Soviet society by Stalin's Promethean quest for a thoroughly modernized country, struck all religions with devastating force."**

"The persecution of the Church was accompanied by a highly organized campaign to promote atheism and to destroy Russia's religious culture. The League of Militant Atheists was formed in 1926 and by 1930 had recruited three million members. Five years later there were 50,000 local groups affiliated to the League and the nominal membership had risen to five million. Children from 8–14 years of age were enrolled in Groups of Godless Youth, and the League of Communist Youth (Komsomol) took a vigorous antireligious line. Several antireligious museums were opened in former churches and a number of Chairs of Atheism were established in Soviet universities. Prizes were offered for the best 'Godless hymns' and for alternative versions of the Bible from which the concept of God had been removed. Antireligious caravans were sent on missionary tours of the villages, films and radio programmes were produced to demonstrate the foolishness of religion and the wickedness of the Church, and there was an extensive publications programme of books and pamphlets. Much of this antireligious propaganda was extremely crude—embarrassingly so for some party intellectuals — and probably did not greatly harm the Church, though the long-term programme of indoctrinating children and young people in atheism has clearly helped to produce two generations of adults who are largely alienated from the Church and from Russia's traditional culture and piety.

One effect of the savage persecutions of the 1920s and early 1930s which was not foreseen by the Communists, but came as no surprise to Christian historians, was the beginning and rapid growth of an underground Church. The hermits and wandering monks who had been a feature of the Russian religious scene for three centuries or more became highly significant figures. They were joined by a large number of bishops and priests who had either been expelled from their posts or forced to flee for their lives. . . . Speaking at a conference of trade unions held in Moscow in April 1939, the leader of the League of Militant Atheists, Yemelian Yaroslavsky, said: "When a priest is deprived of his congregation, that does not mean that he stops being a priest. He changes into an itinerant priest. He travels around with his primitive tools in the villages, performs religious rites, reads prayers, baptizes children. Such wandering priests are at times more dangerous than those who carry on their work at a designated place of residence."

The intensified persecution, which was a part of the general terror inflicted upon Soviet society by Stalin's policy, struck all religions with devastating force. Whereas in the 1920s the state's attack on religion concentrated principally on the leaders of the Orthodox Church—there were 150 bishops in prison by 1930 — the havoc Stalin wreaked in the 1930s reached into the parishes throughout the countryside and extended to non-Orthodox religions as well. The brief period of apparently favorable treatment for Muslims and Protestants came to an abrupt end.

The following excerpt shows how some Baptists, writing in 1967 to commemorate the centennial of the Baptist religion in Russia, recalled the period of persecution of their church in the 1930s.

"
n 1929, even though there was a law on the freedom of religion, the resolution "Concerning Religious Associations" was published, reducing religious freedom to zero. Already in the summer of that year the publication of the journals *Khristianin* [by Evangelical Christians] and *Baptist* [by Baptists] was forbidden and it has never been resumed. All over the place congregations were being closed. The atheists tried to bring down the church through action against the leaders of the unions of our brotherhood. Many fraternal workers of the [Evangelical Christian and Baptist] unions exerted all of their energies in order to keep the brotherhood faithful to the Lord and they resisted all suggestions that they cease preaching the Gospel and cooperate with the authorities with the answer: "We submit unconditionally to all the laws of the state so long as they do not violate our convictions. If you should publish a law that we believers must not preach the Gospel to anyone, then such a law cannot be binding upon us since the law of God is above the law of the state. If you should publish a law that people must not believe in God, then that law, too, would not obligate us."

For such faithfulness to the Lord they all, with few exceptions, received imprisonment and several, like Odintsov, Bukreev, Kostiukov, Vins, and many others gave their lives. In these severe years, the congregations were subjected to conditions which sapped their spiritual life. Membership in a church was determined not by faith but by registration forms. . . . In 1935 the Union of Baptists was closed and the Union of Evangelical Christians ceased its religious activity. Everywhere the congregations of Evangelical Christians and Baptists were closed and the prayer buildings were confiscated.

But the year 1937 was especially severe for our brotherhood. It is difficult to state the number of believers who were taken off to prison in these years and who died through torture in the severe Siberian conditions and on Solovki Island. The terms of imprisonment were so long that for many they seemed to be for life. Thrown into the wild taiga forests, deprived of the right of correspondence, tormented by hunger and weakened by labor, the true children of God died by the thousands. Only a few of those who went through these nightmares returned home,

Vestnik spaseniia (Herald of Salvation), no. 3 (1967), pp. 24–25.

and they had become invalid old men. . . . And how many orphans and widows, despised as families of state criminals, suffered in those years without the basics of subsistence since they were denied the right to work. . . .

In those years the church of Christ passed through the valley of the shadow of death. By 1940 there remained in the whole country only a few open congregations. To the enemies of the work of God it seemed that religion was finished. In reality, the church continued to live even in these incredible conditions. Here is what the picture was like in the congregations: the presbyter was arrested; the church elected another for leading meetings; he was seized; a third was elected. And so on until all were awarded chains. The modest, wretched apartments of believers, the forests and ravines were the places of worship services. Many expected deliverance from the Lord which they imagined would come with the imminent advent of Christ for the church. **"**

> **Do the various approaches to religion adopted by the Soviet state under Lenin and Stalin reveal the existence of fundamentally different attitudes toward religion, or are they simply different political tactics?**

As Trevor Beeson explained in an earlier excerpt, ordinary believers responded to the closure of churches with various expedients. Some of these are described in the following excerpt from a study of underground Orthodox activity.

William C. Fletcher, *The Russian Orthodox Church Underground, 1917–1970* (London: Oxford, 1971), pp. 84f, 93f.

"The formation of "house churches" became a widespread practice. Where other means of worship were not available, dispossessed parishioners would organize religious services in their homes or apartments. Such "churches in the home" conducted complete liturgies (when clergy were available), truncated liturgies led by members of the minor clergy, lay services, or even prayer meetings of individuals or small groups of laymen. . . . Fully operational secret churches were also established during this period. If the local clergy survived the closure of their church it was not unlikely that the church would continue to function, but at locations which were not known to the state authorities. . . .

A common phenomenon during this period was the wandering priests, roaming the Russian countryside at will without any stable parish. . . . Generally these priests were paid in kind by the population for performing religious ceremonies, and thus managed to make their living. The need for their services was immense. In one case a wandering priest baptized eighteen children at once, ranging in age from one to fifteen years. . . . Concurrently with the phenomenon of the wandering priests who could bring the consolations of the Church to the people, the practice grew up of having ceremonies conducted by correspondence. Rites could be conducted *in absentia* or by proxy. Weddings could be conducted by sending the wedding ring to a priest for his blessing, and, similarly, funerals could be performed by the priest blessing a bit of earth sent to him from the grave. In addition to priests, the desperate need for religious literature induced some to become wanderers serving as colporteurs, distributing what little was available to meet this need. Similarly, religious minstrels occasionally appeared, making their living by singing religious songs in the villages. **"**

Stalin's attack upon religion directly contradicted the counsel that Lenin had given in 1918: "It is necessary to fight against religious prejudices extremely cautiously; those who offend religious feelings bring much harm. It is necessary to fight by means of propaganda and education. If we inject ridicule into the struggle, we can embitter the masses; such a struggle divides the masses on the basis of religion, and our strength lies in unity." In 1921, Lenin had guided the Central Committee of the party to issue a directive reprimanding party members who were violating his counsel of 1918: "Emphatically avoid everything that would give a basis for any individual nationality to think, and our enemies to say, that we persecute people for their religious faith." The Stalinist program of the 1930s clearly offended "religious feelings" and gave abundant evidence that people were persecuted for their religion.

By 1939, religious institutions in the Soviet Union were devastated. No denomination had a central organization. Only four Orthodox bishops in the whole country remained out of prison (there had been 163 before the revolution). Despite the terror, Metropolitan Sergius remained committed to his 1927 proclamation, pledging his and the church's obedience, although all outward signs seemed to indicate that his submission had failed to protect the church from Stalin's efforts to eradicate it.

But the church was rescued in the aftermath of the German invasion of the U.S.S.R. in June 1941. Under Sergius's leadership the church rallied the nation to rise up against the aggressors and, in appreciation, Stalin abandoned his quest for the church's destruction. Within twenty-four hours of the Nazi invasion, before even Stalin had made any public statement, Sergius issued a bold and stirring patriotic summons to Orthodox believers.

In the 1930s, cheering workers burned precious icons as authorities closed thousands of churches, converting some, such as this one in Bogorodsk, into workers' clubs.
AP/Wide World Photos.

" I n the last few years we residents of Russia have consoled ourselves with the hope that the flames of war which had ravished most of the world would not touch our country. But fascism, which knows only the law of naked force and scoffs at the lofty demands of honor and morality, has behaved true to itself. The fascist criminals have attacked our motherland. . . . The times of [the Mongol leader] Batu, the German knights, the Swedish King, and Napoleon are being repeated. The wretched heirs of the enemies of Orthodox Christianity again want to try to bring our people to their knees before falsehood and to compel them by naked force to sacrifice the welfare and integrity of our

Sergius Stragorodsky, "Summons to Orthodox Believers" in Metropolitan Nikolai Yarushevich, ed., *Pravda o religii v Rossii* (The Truth about Religion in Russia) (Moscow: Moskovskaia patriarkhiia, 1942), pp. 15–17.

motherland and the vital principles of love for our fatherland.

But this is not the first time that the Russian people have had to endure such trials. With God's help they will again pulverize the hostile fascist might. Our ancestors did not lose heart even in worse conditions because they heeded neither personal dangers nor advantages but their sacred obligation before the motherland and the faith. . . .

We recall blessed leaders of the Russian people like Alexander Nevsky and Dmitry Donskoy who laid down their lives for the nation and the motherland. . . .

Our Orthodox Church always has shared the fate of the people. The church has gone through trials with them and has rejoiced in their triumphs. It will not abandon the people now. . . . In such a time as this when the fatherland calls everyone to the task, it will be unworthy of us, the pastors of the church, to look on in silence at what is going on all around and not to encourage the timid, nor console the grief-stricken,

THE COMMUNIST PARTY ON RELIGION

Each of the three political programs written by the Communist Party since the revolution — in 1919, 1961, and 1986 — contains a statement of the party's position on religion.

" PROGRAM OF THE RUSSIAN COMMUNIST PARTY
(Bolshevik) 1919

Point 13: With respect to religion, the RCP (Russian Communist Party) is not satisfied with the already decreed separation of church from state and school from church, that is, measures which bourgeois democracy declares in its programs but never carries out in the final analysis because of the effective links of capitalism with religious propaganda.

The RCP is guided by the conviction that the complete disappearance of religious prejudices will come about only with the achievement of planning and consciousness in all of the social and economic activity of the masses. The party strives for a complete severance of the links between the exploiting classes and the conduct of religious propaganda, facilitating the practical liberation of the laboring masses from religious prejudices and conducting scientific, educational, and antireligious propaganda on the widest scale. At the same time it is necessary to avoid assiduously any offense against the feelings of believers, which only leads to a strengthening of religious fanaticism.

PROGRAM OF THE COMMUNIST PARTY OF THE SOVIET UNION (1961)

The party views the struggle with manifestations of bourgeois ideology and morality and with

nor remind the waverer about duty and God's will. And if, moreover, the silence of a pastor and his indifference to what his flock is passing through are to be explained by calculation based on what might be gained by siding with the enemy, this simply would be treason against the motherland and a failure in pastoral duty. The church needs pastors whose service is rendered "for the sake of Jesus and not for the sake of a morsel of bread. . . ." We shall lay down our lives alongside those of our flock. Untold thousands of our Orthodox warriors affirmed their worth by laying down their lives for our motherland and the faith in every time of enemy invasion. They died not thinking of glory; they thought only about how their motherland needed their sacrifice, and they meekly surrendered their all.

The church of Christ blesses every Orthodox believer who defends the sacred borders of our motherland.

May the Lord grant us victory.   **"**

vestiges of private property psychology, superstitions, and prejudices as an essential part of the work of communist education. . . .

The party uses ideological persuasion for the education of people in the spirit of the scientific and materialistic worldview and for overcoming religious prejudices, without permitting any offenses against the feelings of believers. It is necessary to conduct systematically a wide range of scientific atheist propaganda, patiently explaining the baselessness of religious faith, which arose in the past on the basis of the oppression of people by the elemental forces of nature and social oppression as a result of ignorance of the true causes of natural and social phenomena. In doing this it is necessary to take advantage of the achievements of contemporary science.

PROGRAM OF THE COMMUNIST PARTY OF THE SOVIET UNION (1986)

In the Field of Ideological and Educational Work

The affirmation of communist morality. In the gradual advance towards communism the creative potential of communist morality, the most humane, just, and noble morality, based on devotion to the goals of the revolutionary struggle and the ideals of communism, manifests itself ever more fully. Our morality has assimilated both universal moral values and the norms of conduct and norms governing relations between people which have been established by the popular masses.

Atheistic education. The Party uses ideological means for the broad dissemination of a scientific materialist world outlook and for overcoming religious

prejudices, while at the same time respecting the feelings of believers. While calling for the strict observance of the constitutional guarantees of freedom of conscience, the Party condemns attempts to use religion to the detriment of society and the individual. A highly important aspect of atheistic education consists in heightening the people's labor and public activity, raising their educational level, and the broad dissemination of new Soviet traditions and customs.

The struggle against manifestations of alien ideology and morality and all negative phenomena, connected with the vestiges of the past in the minds and behavior of people . . . is an integral part of communist education.   **"**

During World War II, Stalin consolidated and rallied the support of numerous Orthodox believers and monks, such as these decorated war veterans, by relaxing restrictions he had previously placed on the church.

Soviet Life.

Sergius's statement is all the more remarkable when the circumstances are taken into account. He rejected the course that he might have taken — and which some religious people did take — of standing by passively in hopes that the Stalinist government would be overthrown. While Stalin himself was strangely silent in the face of the German attack, the acting patriarch called his flock to defend the native Russian soil. True to the long Russian tradition, Sergius placed the resources of the Orthodox Church at the service of the state.

Sergius's outspoken patriotism was eventually rewarded, but he waited more than two years for clear evidence that his loyalty had been recognized. Within hours of his patriotic summons, he was evacuated from Moscow as the Germans approached. For months German armies occupied most of the U.S.S.R. west of Moscow, and the country's future hung in the balance. Finally, the tide of battle turned with the Soviet Army's destruction of the German Sixth Army at Stalingrad in February 1943. The Soviet Army seized the offensive and in repeated successful battles drove out the invader. With ultimate victory more and more certain, Stalin delivered his reward to Sergius.

On September 2, 1943, word reached Sergius unexpectedly that he must return to Moscow on the next day. He was being called to a fateful meeting with Stalin, who must have concluded that the church did not pose the threat to his program for Soviet society that he once thought it did. The following dramatic account of that meeting comes through reliable channels from one of the participants in it, Metropolitan Nikolai.

" Events unfolded with cinematographic rapidity. On the next day, early in the morning, the train arrived in Moscow. At the station the metropolitan was met by Metropolitan Alexis, the future patriarch, who had just arrived from Leningrad, and by Metropolitan Nikolai of Kiev.

Surprise followed upon surprise: Metropolitan Sergius was taken not to his quarters on Bauman Lane, where he had lived for fifteen years during the time when he headed the church, but to Chisty Lane, to a luxurious home, which before the war had been the private residence of the German ambassador. . . . Sergey was informed that a visit to the Kremlin was scheduled for the evening.

At 9 P.M. a state car arrived at Chisty Lane. Metropolitans Sergius, Alexis, and Nikolai got in. None of the metropolitans had any idea where they were being taken. They could only guess.

In ten minutes the car entered the Kremlin and after another ten minutes they entered a large, wood-paneled office where behind the table sat two men who they knew well from their portraits: Stalin and Molotov.

Handshakes were exchanged and they took their seats. Molotov began the conversation with the declaration that the government of the U.S.S.R. and Stalin personally wanted to know the needs of the church.

Two metropolitans, Alexis and Nikolai, maintained a confused silence. Unexpectedly, Sergius began to speak. Before the trip to the Kremlin, he had put on a hearing aid which had been sent to him from abroad and which he had never used. The metropolitan began calmly, occasionally stuttering, with the business-like tone of a man who is accustomed to speaking about serious matters with the most highly-placed people. (When Stalin was a seminarian, Metropolitan Sergey was already a bishop and held the post of rector of the Petersburg Ecclesiastical Academy.)

The metropolitan mentioned the need for widespread opening of churches, whose number was completely insufficient for the religious needs of the people. He also stated that a church council and election of a patriarch were needed. Finally he said that there was a need for a widespread opening of church educational institutions since the ranks of the church's clergy were depleted.

Here Stalin unexpectedly broke his silence. "And why do you lack clergy? What has happened to them?" he asked, removing his pipe from

A. E. Levitin-Krasnov, *Ruk tvoikh zhar* (The Warmth of Your Hands) (Tel Aviv: Krug, 1979), pp. 105–108.

UKRAINIAN CATHOLICS

The Ukrainian Eastern Rite Catholic Church is the largest proscribed denomination in the Soviet Union. This church began in 1596 when Orthodox Russians and Ukrainians then living within the kingdom of Poland united with the Roman Catholic Church in what was known as the Union of Brest. While accepting the religious authority of the pope, these Orthodox believers retained their Slavic church regulations, and therefore they are called Eastern Rite Catholics or Greek Catholics. (They are also referred to as "Uniates" but they do not like this name.) The most distinctive characteristics of the Eastern Rite Catholics were that they used the Slavonic language in worship and their priests were allowed to marry.

In the era between the two world wars, more than four million Eastern Rite Catholics lived in the western regions of Poland and Czechoslovakia. These regions became part of the Soviet Union after World War II, and the Russian Orthodox Church and the Soviet government collaborated in liquidating the Eastern Rite church organization. The Orthodox Church always considered Eastern Rite Catholics to be "wandering sheep" who should be returned to the true flock under the Moscow patriarchate. The state viewed them as Ukrainian nationalists, a separatist force which resisted becoming a part of the Soviet Union.

In March 1946, 233 priests and laymen from Eastern Rite churches (fewer than half were represented) attended a Council of the Greek Catholic Church in the city of Lviv and voted to abolish the Union of Brest. No bishops

his mouth and staring at his audience.

Alexis and Nikolai were shaken by the fixed gaze of the green eyes: everyone knew that the clergy had been slaughtered in the camps. But Metropolitan Sergius was not shaken. Having weathered the gaze of the green eyes, the old man answered, "We lack clergy for several reasons. One of them is that we train a priest and he becomes the Marshall of the Soviet Union."

A satisfied smile crossed the lips of the dictator. He said: "Yes, yes, indeed. I am a seminarian. That's when I heard about you." Then he began to recall his seminary years and the inspector who had an uncanny ability to discover cigarettes which the seminarians had hidden.

Metropolitan Sergius, it seems, knew this inspector and knew many of the teachers of the Tiflis seminary, since he had been the head of the academic committee of the Holy Synod for a long time.

Then Stalin said that his mother had regretted to her dying day his never becoming a priest. The dictator's conversation with the metro-

participated in this council and therefore its actions were not sanctioned by church law. Nevertheless, the government declared the Ukrainian Eastern Rite Catholic Church "dissolved" and it closed all of the church's parishes and cloisters.

Today, forty years after the Council of Lviv, Eastern Rite Catholics remain active. Reliable statistics about them are difficult to obtain, but they probably number between three and four million. They make up what is often called the "Catacomb Church." In addition to the main concentration of Eastern Rite Catholics in Ukraine, others are dispersed throughout the country, especially in Western Siberia, Kazakhstan, and Central Asia. Soviet researchers have shown that the proportion of believers in Western Ukraine is more than double that in other Ukrainian and Russian areas — well over 50 percent.

Eastern Rite Catholics fall into three groups, each choosing progressively more covert forms of existence and religious practice. The largest group attends Orthodox churches, pretending to be Orthodox, but maintaining links with underground clergy. The next group, comprising these underground clergy, including several secret bishops, conceal their identity by working at secular jobs and provide services to many believers at the risk of being arrested, fined, and imprisoned. Finally, those Eastern Rite Catholics known as *Pokutnyky* (penitents), are radically alienated from Soviet society, refusing to work, to send their children to school, to vote, and to serve in the army. They must lead a thoroughly underground existence.

politan took on an easy character. Then, after tea had been served, the conversation got down to business.

The conversation lasted until 3 A.M. Besides Stalin, Molotov and the metropolitans, technical experts participated. This conversation can be called historic, in the fullest sense of the word. At the time of this conversation were worked out the constitution of the Russian Church and the conditions under which it has existed to the present.

As is known, this situation is subjected at present to much justified criticism, since it means the absolute subordination of the church to the antireligious state. But at the time, after over two decades of terror directed against the church, the new order undoubtedly seemed to be a progressive step, since it gave to the Orthodox Church the possibility of a legal existence.

At the end of the conversation, the aged, sick metropolitan was completely exhausted. . . . Stalin, having taken the metropolitan's arm, carefully, like a genuine acolyte, led him down the stairway and said to him upon parting: "Your Grace! This is all that I can do for you at the

Ukrainian Catholic women imprisoned for their religious beliefs created the Tapestry of the Church in Flames, a marker for Holy Books which symbolizes the destruction of the Ukrainian Catholic Church.

Courtesy of the Ukrainian Catholic Dioceses of Stamford and St. Josaphat.

present time." And with these words he bade the bishops farewell.

After several days, a council of bishops gathered in the house on Chisty Lane (it was not difficult to gather it because in the Russian Church at the time there were only seventeen bishops) and on Sunday, September 12, on St. Alexander Nevsky Day, in the Cathedral of the Epiphany, the newly elected patriarch, Metropolitan Sergey, was enthroned. The Russian Church after an eighteen year hiatus was again crowned with a patriarch.

"

The conversation with Stalin marked such a significant change in the fortunes of religion in the U.S.S.R. that it is sometimes called Stalin's "concordat" with religion. Stalin acknowledged the church's participation in the effort to defeat the Germans. In addition to the millions of Orthodox men and women who fought in the army or partisan bands and worked in the war factories, the faithful donated about 150 million rubles to the church's Fund for the Defense of the Country. The Orthodox were not alone among religious groups in supporting the war effort. The much less numerous Evangelical Christians and Baptists, for example, donated 80,000 rubles to purchase a medical airplane. The Muslim Board of Central Asia and Kazakhstan followed suit, and their chairman received the following note of thanks from Stalin: "Please convey to the Muslim clergy and the believers of Central Asia and Kazakhstan, who collected 1,280,000 rubles in cash and 117,000 rubles in loan bonds, as well as grain and cattle for the Defense Fund of the U.S.S.R., my greetings and the gratitude of the Red Army."

Stalin's "concordat" permitted open religious activity under state control. As the civil instrument of that control (reminiscent of the tsarist Holy Synod) Stalin created two state councils: the Council for the Affairs of the Russian Orthodox Church and the Council for the Affairs of Religious Cults. Little information about these councils was made public, and no law defining their work was ever published. The TASS news agency's announcement of their formation stated simply, but mysteriously, that they were to deal with the "problems" of religious organizations "which require the permission of the government." The most authoritative description of these councils appears in the *Great Soviet Encyclopedia.*

Bolshaia sovetskaia entsiklopediia (Great Soviet Encyclopedia), 2nd. ed. (Moscow, 1956), vol. 39., p. 523.

"

The basic tasks of these institutions are as follows: supervision of the correct and timely implementation throughout the U.S.S.R. of the laws and resolutions directed to the strict observance of the principle of the separation of the church from the state and the school from the church; adoption of necessary measures for securing freedom of conscience for citizens of the U.S.S.R.; cooperation with religious associations in resolving questions which they direct to various state agencies. The activity of the Council for the Affairs of the Russian Orthodox Church is linked with appropriate organizations of the Russian Orthodox Church, and the Council for the Affairs of Religious Cults [and] with all other religious associations (Catholics, Protestants, Muslims, Baptists, etc.). The councils have their commissioners in the governments of [the fifteen Union republics and the] autonomous republics. **"**

In the next few years, believers throughout the country reopened their churches. By 1949, the Council for the Affairs of the Russian Orthodox Church reported that about 22,000 Orthodox Churches were operating. This figure includes 17,000 churches that had been closed during the Stalinist repression of the 1930s. Other religions experienced vicissitudes in their fortunes similar to those of the Orthodox. The following three paragraphs continue the Baptist account from which we heard of the terrors of the 1930s.

" But by the will of God, that very ruler under whom believers were suppressed so unimaginably permitted the opening of the prayer meetings at the end of the last war.

The following period in the life of our brotherhood was a period of new revival. Those who had been terrorized and weakened in their faith in the days of the harsh persecutions returned to the church in repentance. Even though there was a severe shortage of preachers, the Word of God had a mighty effect upon those who heard and everywhere there were mass conversions.

In October 1944 the All-Union Council of Evangelical Christians and Baptists was formed. In the main it was composed of officers of the former unions who had been released from prison after they had agreed to form the union on specified conditions. Senior presbyters were appointed to oversee the life of the churches of the union. In 1947, work on the registration of congregations was begun and a few churches received official permission for conducting services. Societies and groups of believers which had not managed to organize themselves in this brief period were subsequently denied registration by local authorities. **"**

Vestnik spaseniia (Herald of Salvation), no. 3 (1967), pp. 25f.

"With the onset of the Cold War, Catholics, Jews, Muslims, and Protestant Evangelicals became the victims of renewed propaganda attacks and restrictions."

As mentioned in the excerpt, the "brief period" of liberality came to an end with the onset of the Cold War, which brought with it a new set of conditions for the practice of religion. While the Orthodox Church generally continued to enjoy the new liberties that came from the "concordat" with Stalin, Catholics, Jews, Muslims, and Protestant Evangelicals abruptly found their opportunities curtailed. They became the victims of renewed propaganda attacks and restrictions which continued until Stalin's death. The renewal of anti-religious activities was part of a Stalin-inspired campaign of russification and anti-cosmopolitanism. What all of the restricted religions had in common was that they were perceived as suspect because of their links with large communities of coreligionists outside of Russia. The Stalin regime viewed them as untrustworthy and lacking a Russian spirit. The Catholics obeyed the pope in Italy; the Jews had just then received a restored homeland in Israel; the Muslims felt a kinship with the world of Islam and wished to make the pilgrimage to Mecca; and the Protestants had been members of the World Baptist Alliance since its founding at the beginning of the century.

The persisting problems faced by Jewish citizens of the U.S.S.R. who want to practice their religion or to move to Israel date from this era. Official anti-Semitism became virulent. Jewish intellectuals were attacked as "homeless cosmopolitans." The Yiddish magazine *Ainikeit* was closed, and Yiddish books were banned from publication. In August 1952, twenty-four leaders of Yiddish culture were executed. Joshua Rothenberg describes the long-term significance of this substantial change in the Jews' circumstances.

Joshua Rothenberg, "The Fate of Judaism in the Communist World" in Bohdan R. Bociurkiw and John W. Strong, ed., *Religion and Atheism in the U.S.S.R. and Eastern Europe* (Toronto: University of Toronto Press, 1975), pp. 228–229.

Although anti-Jewish sentiments were encouraged by Stalin, at the time of his conflict with Trotsky [in the mid-1920s], and although restrictions against Yiddish culture were ordained in the middle 1930s, a differential treatment of Jews in the area of their civil rights and status became apparent rather suddenly and dramatically in the "anti-cosmopolitan" campaign and during the "Doctors' Plot" [when nine Kremlin physicians, six of them Jews, were arrested on trumped-up charges of conspiring to kill Communist leaders] in the years 1948–53. The Jews called this period the "Black Years. . . ."

The period of the Black Years was a turning point in the history of the Jews in the Soviet Union and in the relationship between the Soviet regime and Soviet Jews. Nothing that happened later or is happening now in Soviet-Jewish relations can be properly understood without a deep comprehension of the effects of the experience on Soviet Jews and non-Jews alike. It demonstrated for the first time the never anticipated possibility of the existence of an anti-Semitism condoned and fostered by socialist authorities. It ushered in a deep-seated and long-lasting emotional conflict and antagonism between the Jews of the Soviet Union and the Soviet leadership, an antagonism which by its inner logic almost inescapably led to the present-day violent confrontation and open revolt of many young Jews and Jewish intellectuals who want to leave for Israel. It brought out attitudes which were a breeding ground for later Soviet policies, . . . and the character — not the fact but the peculiar quality — of the anti-Israel barrages. The gnawing suspicion grew among Jews, and was steadily reinforced, that the anti-Jewish attitudes were not just a temporary aberration of a Stalin, a Beria [the head of the secret police] or another clique, but had become an integral part of the Jewish condition in the Soviet Union.

"

Stalin's death in 1953 and the subsequent de-Stalinization movement in which parts of the Stalinist system were dismantled, marked a major turning point in Soviet history and affected many aspects of Soviet life, including religion. In a speech to the Twentieth Congress of the Communist Party in 1956, Nikita Khrushchev began the attack upon the "cult of personality" that had held Soviet society in a hysterical and terror-stricken thrall.

Thousands of Soviets imprisoned for their religious beliefs were released from labor camps. Many of these survivors returned with increased zeal for their faith and injected new vigor into their congregations. The lessening of international tensions and Khrushchev's policy of peaceful coexistence, allowed Orthodox, Baptists, and Muslims to accelerate contacts with Christians and Muslims abroad. The Orthodox Church and All-Union Council of Evangelical Christians–Baptists joined the World Council of Churches of Christ.

But one important consequence of de-Stalinization boded ill for believers. An atheist writer named Zybkovets pointed to it: "In the postwar years, in connection with the cult of Stalin and through his personal fault, scientific atheist propaganda in our country was weakened. Only after the Twentieth Party Congress decisively condemned the cult of Stalin was it possible to develop the ideological struggle against religion" (*Voprosy istorii religii i ateizma* [Questions of the History of Religion and Atheism], vol. 11 (1963), p. 39). These words are deceptive. The struggle that actually developed was much more potent than an ideological dispute, as the following letter written by two Orthodox priests in 1965 shows.

In what ways have international relations restricted or enlarged the ability of Soviet citizens to practice their religious beliefs?

" T o His Holiness, the Most Holy Patriarch of Moscow and All Russia, Alexis;

From the priests, Nikolai Eshliman and Gleb Yakunin, Moscow.

This letter is the fruit of earnest prayers, of spiritual struggle and severe doubts. But, forced by Christian conscience and pastoral duty, we considered it necessary to turn to you and in your person to the mother of us all — the Russian Orthodox Church. . . .

The basic legislative documents of the Soviet state concerning the church . . . establish definite juridical bases for the principle [of a free relationship between church and state]. Besides this, in order to ensure observance of the laws which define the relationship of the state to the

Nikolai Eshliman and Gleb Yakunin, "An Open Letter to the Patriarch," *Religion in Communist Dominated Areas,* vol. 5, no. 11–12 (1966), pp. 90–95.

church, and in order to arbitrate between the church and the state in civil affairs, a special department was established in the Soviet government: the Council on the Affairs of the Russian Orthodox Church.

Under an atheist government in which the church is concerned with the strictest observance of the principle of separation of the church from the state, the existence of a special department which guarantees this principle is perfectly justifiable from the point of view of the church. It is important, however, that this department does not misuse its functions and does not overstep its powers.

However, during the 1957–1964 period, under personal pressure from Khrushchev, who allowed "subjectivism and administrationism," and was later condemned by the Communist Party and the Soviet government, the Council on the Affairs of the Russian Orthodox Church radically changed its function, becoming instead of a department of arbitration an organ of unofficial and illegal control over the Moscow Patriarchate.

At present in the Russian church a situation has arisen in which not one aspect of church life is free from active administrative intervention from the council, its representatives and local governmental departments. This intervention is aimed at the destruction of the church! . . . The fact is that during recent years in the vast majority of parishes a "system" has been introduced under which the sacrament of baptism is performed only after prior and obligatory registration. Everyone who wishes to be baptized himself or to secure it for his children is bound first of all to submit his passport to a representative of the church council, who registers it on a special form. Moreover, for the baptism of children the presence of both parents is required. Similarly, illegal registration is necessary for other ceremonies: matrimony, unction, communion at home and funerals. . . .

During the last forty years the Russian Church has undergone two periods of mass closure of churches. The first time was during the period of Stalin's personality cult, the second was during the rule of Khrushchev. Over the short period 1961–1964 thousands of Orthodox churches were closed. They were closed contrary to the wishes of the believers, in violation of the stated law and not in accordance with the procedure envisaged by the law. . . .

Ten thousand closed churches, and tens of closed monasteries are the undeniable evidence of the fact that the Moscow Patriarchate did not fulfill its duty before Christ and the Russian Church, for only with the assurance that the highest church administration would remain silent could the atheists close the churches of God. **"**

When Orthodox priest Gleb Yakunin spoke out in 1965 against what he considered to be the patriarchate's supine complicity in Communist suppression of the church, the patriarch banned him from performing his priestly functions; his duties were restored in 1987.

Courtesy of Religion in Communist Dominated Areas.

Fathers Eshliman and Yakunin listed specific examples of places where "disaster struck the Russian Church." Orthodox seminaries in Kiev,

Stavropol, Saratov, Volynia, and Zhirovitsy were closed, as were monasteries in the Carpathians, Moldavia, and Ukraine, including the Pochaev (the most ancient Russian monastery), the Kievan Monastery of the Caves, and the Glynskaia Pustyn. These forced closings were part of a flood of restrictions on religious activity between 1960 and 1964 commonly referred to as the Khrushchev antireligious campaign. During this campaign, more than half of all buildings used for religious purposes were appropriated by the government. Over 11,000 Orthodox churches were closed. The official number of functioning Baptist churches dropped from 5,400 at the beginning of the Khrushchev era to about 2,000 in 1965. In the same period, the number of mosques fell from over 1,300 to about 450. Official government figures for synagogues showed 450 in 1959 and 97 in 1965.

The official rationale for closing religious buildings is revealed in the following report from a newspaper from the southern part of the Russian Republic, on the edge of the Caucasus Mountains. The Tat people, a small group of mountain dwellers, are Jewish by long-established religious tradition.

"The Tats have representatives among the Dagestan scientists, instructors in higher educational institutions, engineers, physicians, and teachers. Though small in number, the Tat people have their own literature, writers and poets. In other words, the Tat people gives its modest contribution to the building of communism and is full of gratitude to its own Communist party and its elder brothers in the family of Soviet nations.

At the same time, we still find in the small family of the Tat people, backward elements, carriers of harmful survivals of the past, who hamper our progress. One of these factors is the existence of a synagogue in Buinaksk. Though it is frequented by a few dozens of aged people only, the mere fact of its existence brings great harm.

All harmful survivals and rites such as circumcision, old marriage customs, ceremonies, and many other things are inspired and supported by the synagogue, which contributes to their preservation and revival, similarly to the mosque and the Moslem Spiritual Board in Buinaksk.

It may consequently be said with certainty and without exaggeration that the synagogue brings harm to the subsequent Communist education of the Tat youth, the building of communism and the subsequent evolution of the Tats.

Time has therefore come for Tat public opinion to raise the question of the synagogue closure. This does not mean, of course, that we ignore the religious feelings of the believers. They can perform their necessary religious rituals without hindrance in their homes, without a synagogue, just like believers in the Lower Dzhengutal and in other auls do."

"We Will Sweep Away the Vestiges of the Past, Is a Synagogue needed in Buinaksk?" *Kommunist,* July 7, 1960, trans. in *Jews and the Jewish People,* vol. 1, no. 2 (1960), p. 1.

The synagogue in Buinaksk, a regional capital in the Dagestan Autonomous Republic, was subsequently closed. If it was closed for the reasons mentioned by this writer, then it is surprising that more places of worship were not closed in the early sixties than actually were. The same reasons could apply to all religious buildings, for they all perpetuate religion and stand as visible proof that religion still has not been excised from socialist society.

Khrushchev's antireligious campaign was second in ferocity only to the worst days of the Stalin regime of the 1930s; nevertheless, the leaders of officially recognized religious organizations adopted the public stance of ignoring the attacks or at times even denying their existence. This policy can be seen in the following excerpts from an interview of Orthodox Metropolitan Nikodim, who was the director of the Foreign Relations Department of the Russian Orthodox Church in the 1960s and 1970s. Nikodim, the second most influential leader of the Russian Church after the patriarch, clearly was endeavoring to provide a positive image for the Soviet government before world opinion. The text of this interview appeared in 1964 in *L'Humanite*, a communist newspaper published in Paris.

> **"Khrushchev's antireligious campaign was second in ferocity only to the worst days of the Stalin regime of the 1930s."**

"Is It True that Christ Is Agonizing in Moscow?" *L'Humanite*, March 14, 1964, in *Religion in Communist Dominated Areas*, vol. 3, no. 8 (1964), pp. 59–60.

Question: Is it fair to speak of repression and antireligious persecution in the U.S.S.R.?

Answer: There is no repression of religion in the U.S.S.R. That is not true.... As regards the persecution of religion, one must take into account that people often mix two different ideas. When they talk in the West of the intensification of antireligious propaganda in our country, many see persecution of religion, but it is something else: the struggle of ideas. Persecution means administrative measures against believers. However, among us the equality of rights of all citizens is not only proclaimed by the Constitution, it is implemented in fact. Religious discrimination is prohibited by law, as is national or racial discrimination, etc., and believers make active use of their rights. The nonbelievers have neither the right, nor the possibility, of interfering with these rights.

I must add this in conclusion, that it seems to me that any unprejudiced person who became acquainted with the life of our country could not but be convinced that there is absolutely no antagonism of any form between the believers and the nonbelievers among us. The believer in the U.S.S.R. is a fully qualified citizen.

Khrushchev was removed from office in late 1964, and the storm of his antireligious campaign passed. His successors abandoned his coordinated, countrywide administrative assault upon religious activities and institutions and introduced new ways of dealing with religion. But the new policies contained contradictory elements. Two formal administrative changes were made. The Criminal Code, which established penalties for violating the laws on religion, was amended so that punishable actions by religious persons were more carefully defined. Such actions included the following: refusing to register religious societies with the state; organizing special children's and youth meetings or other groups or clubs that have nothing to do with the conduct of worship; distributing documents advocating violation of the

When this picture was taken in 1986, trucks were stored in Leningrad's Holy Trinity Church.

Courtesy of David Snelbecker.

legislation on religious cults; and conducting religious ceremonies in ways that disturb public order. The penalties set were a fine of fifty rubles for the first conviction and three years of imprisonment for a repeated offense.

The second administrative change was the creation of a Council for Religious Affairs within the government to replace the two councils Stalin had formed in 1944. While creation of the new council did not represent a major alteration in the treatment of religion, it did signify an increasing centralization and regularization of that treatment.

The chairman of the new council was more publicly outspoken than the chairmen of the predecessor councils had been. In his statements, Vladimir Kuroedov tried to project the impression that government policies toward religion were not as restrictive as critics of the government portrayed them. In the following excerpt, from an interview in *Izvestiia*, the government newspaper, Kuroedov asserts that Soviet laws "strictly uphold the right of believers."

"Some Questions about Religion and the Church," *Izvestiia*, August 29, 1966, trans. in *Religion in Communist Dominated Areas*, vol. 5, no. 22 (1966), pp. 174–177.

"Question:* Are there many believers in the U.S.S.R.? How do Soviet laws define the position of religious organizations and the order of their activity?

Answer: It is impossible to say how many believers there are in the Soviet Union since in the country there is no government registration of people according to religion. No official documents anywhere indicate what religion a man professes or whether he is an atheist. It is necessary to emphasize this since this is one of the conditions ensuring freedom of conscience in the U.S.S.R. In order to ensure freedom of conscience in the U.S.S.R., says the Soviet constitution, the church is separated from the state and the school from the church. . . .

Knowing that a portion of the population is made up of believers, the Soviet government permits freely functioning church associations where they can satisfy their religious requirements. These associations have been given church buildings to use free of charge and the right to train clergymen, publish religious literature, manufacture articles used in religious services, and so on.

Soviet law strictly upholds the rights of believers. To offend the feelings of believers or to discriminate against them in any way is punishable by law.

Under the conditions that have been created in the Soviet country, each citizen is really ensured the right to believe in God or not to believe in God, the right to perform religious rites and the right to conduct antireligious propaganda. . . .

From time to time, however, periodicals in the west make slanderous and insinuating statements about the status of religion in the U.S.S.R. The *Parisien Libere*, for example, reported as sensational news on April

4 that new laws affecting the church had been passed in the Russian Federation and drew the categorical conclusion that "a new offensive against Christian cults" was being organized in the Soviet Union.

What actually happened was that early this year the presidium of the Supreme Soviet adopted two decrees and passed a decision concerning legislation dealing with religious cults. . . . After reading these documents any unprejudiced person will see they do not in any way represent an "offensive" against the church or the rights of believers, or infringement of those rights.

The decrees and decision were adopted in order to regulate the existing legislation concerning cults. . . . The new legislation defines more definitely what violations of the law constitute crimes. Up to now, the criminal code did not make this concrete. It should be especially emphasized that the sphere of criminal punishment has been significantly narrowed. . . . The new laws are in no way a persecution of religion or a violation of the principle of freedom of conscience.

Freedom of conscience, however, does not mean that the activities of religious organizations are not restricted in any way, as certain churchmen abroad would like, so that these organizations can do as they wish and ignore the laws and order of things in the Soviet Union. . . .

Q: Some people think that the best way to overcome religious delusions is severely to restrict the activities of all religious organizations in our country or to prohibit their activities altogether. Are they right or wrong?

A: They are undoubtedly wrong, because it has long been known that imposing bans or using administrative pressure will not change religious ideology. Atheistic convictions, like any other convictions, cannot be imposed on anyone by force, or through decrees or other administrative measures. . . .

The Soviet government's policy on religion and its legislation on freedom of conscience are based on the Marxist-Leninist understanding of the essence of religious ideology. Consequently, if there are people in our country who believe in God, the state must ensure them the freedom to worship.

> "From time to time, periodicals in the West make slanderous and insinuating statements about the status of religion in the U.S.S.R."
>
> **Chairman of the Council for Religious Affairs Vladimir Kuroedov**

Kuroedov's answers repeat the official line on religion in the Soviet Union. This line—standard since the revolution — claims that the state is neutral on religious matters (therefore it does not know anything about the religion of its citizens), that religious organizations function freely, and that the laws prohibiting some religiously sponsored activities do not violate freedom of conscience. The implication regularly drawn from this line of reasoning is that when people are arrested for religious activity, they are not being punished because they are believers but because they are criminals.

In the post-Khrushchev years, most Jewish and Christian congregations were able to perform their acts of worship inside of their buildings without very much hindrance by secular authorities, provided that they maintained a low profile. Some groups, notably scattered congregations of Baptists and Pentecostals, openly rejected such arrangements. They held religious meetings in their homes or outdoors, they conducted regular classes for children, and they refused to conform to the authorities' requirements that they obtain legal registration of their groups and supply the state with information about their activities. For such actions they were punished under the new provisions of the Criminal Code.

The Khrushchev-inspired attempt to curtail religious practice produced one surprising difference from the Stalinist attack of the 1930s. Whereas in the Stalinist years believers had gone underground in response to oppression, the Khrushchev years brought dissent into the open. The letter to the patriarch from fathers Eshliman and Yakunin is a widely publicized example of this open dissent. Much of the dissent was loosely organized, consisting of letters signed by a local congregation like the one from Kirov mentioned by Igor Shaferevich. However, some dissent was well structured. Dissident Baptists, in particular, created a widespread network of congregations led by a committee known as the Council of Churches of Evangelical Christians–Baptists. A similar development among the Seventh Day Adventists produced the True and Free Adventist Church. These "new" denominations rejected the accommodation to the state of their parent groups. Other new organizations included the Committee for the Defense of Believers' Rights and the Council of Prisoners' Relatives. These two groups (the former crossed denominational lines while the latter was a Baptist group) publicized violations of the civil rights of believers.

Such civil rights activities were provoked by legal reprisals against believers. Several thousand were required to pay fines of from fifteen to fifty rubles because they refused to desist from religious activities which local officials considered illegal but which to them seemed essential to the exercise of their religious convictions. A few hundred especially aggressive protesters were put in prison, most for three-year terms.

The open resistance to Khrushchev's campaign, in contrast to the response to Stalin's, reflected the difference in the tactics used by the authorities. The arbitrary violence and terror of Stalin's times were absent—or at least much less common—in the early 1960s. Khrushchev had announced his administration's adherence to "socialist legality," and consequently authorities made some semblance of following orderly procedures. But the use of orderly procedures in closing churches and bringing violators of the law to trial encouraged the protestors likewise to use legal avenues of appeal.

While the number of persons who were punished for their religious behavior was, at the most, two thousand, the number of persons who continued their religious practices without punishment reached the tens of millions. In the next excerpt, a Ukrainian writer sums up the situation in the aftermath of the Khrushchev antireligious campaigns.

Today we are deceiving ourselves again: "many believers in our country have left the church and religion." This is freely self-delusion. It is true that there are no churches and no ministers in a large part of the Soviet Union. But there are believers. If they are not Orthodox, then they are members of one or another of the multitude of finely differentiated sects. Where do they come from? From the ranks of those who leave the church. . . . For, as has been said in official statements, closing a parish does not make atheists of believers. On the contrary it strengthens the attraction of religion for people and it embitters their hearts besides.

G. Kelt, "Educated Atheism," *Komsomolskaia pravda*, August 15, 1965, trans. in *Religion in Communist Dominated Areas*, vol. 4, no. 22 (1965), p. 170.

In the post-Khrushchev years antireligious sentiment focused most noticeably upon Jews. Open hostility to Jews intensified when anti-Zionist propaganda in the media became commonplace, often echoing the conspiracy theme of the notorious "Protocols of the Elders of Zion." The reasons for this new outbreak of hostility are explored in the following excerpt.

There is ample evidence that the so-called anti-Zionist attacks in the Soviet Union are actually an antisemitic, anti-Jewish campaign and, to the best of my knowledge, it is the longest such campaign in the history of the Soviet Union. . . . In the early 1960s, and more particularly later after the Six Day War, it became an open anti-Zionist, anti-Jewish campaign which continues till today.

The question which arises is: why should Zionism have become such a crucial element in Soviet propaganda? . . . I think the explanation is the same as it was in pre-revolutionary times. It was one of the surest ways of gaining popularity and being assured of public support. It would seem that because of their political and social difficulties, the Russian and Soviet authorities searched for topics which could bring them popularity in public opinion, and to this end the existing antisemitic feelings were very useful, as can already be seen in the pogroms of the 1880s. . . .

The attempts to connect all Jews with (vilified) Zionism, to present every person of Jewish origin and every Jewish organization as agents of the Zionist "elders," were further expressions of the antisemitic character of the anti-Zionist campaign. Furthermore, the demand of the Soviet authorities that all Jews (and sometimes non-Jews also) who

Shmuel Ettinger, "The 'Jewish Question' in the U.S.S.R.," *Soviet Jewish Affairs*, vol. 15, no. 1 (1985), pp. 11–15.

Сионистский тенетник

Клевета
СИОНИЗМ
провокации
антисоветчина
еврейский вопрос
антикоммунизм

За любимой «работой».

Рис. А. Зенина.

"The Zionist Spider" weaves a webb of "slander, lies, provocation, anti-Sovietism, and anti-Communism." Printed in *Sovetskaia Moldavia*, August 27, 1971.

YIVO Institute for Jewish Research.

wanted to emigrate from the U.S.S.R. should apply for Israeli visas and not for visas to any other country, was not only because they wished to avoid claims from members of other minorities to their right to emigrate, but also to be able to designate all potential emigrants as being under the influence of "Zionist enemies." If you evince a desire to emigrate, you are in the camps of the "sons of darkness," you are a Zionist, a traitor. . . .

Another aim of the anti-Zionist campaign is to demoralize the Jews inside the Soviet Union, and to prevent the emergence and consolidation of a Jewish representative body, of a Jewish leading group which could speak for the Jews as a national entity. Today the Jews of the U.S.S.R., whether as an ethnic, or a national, or even as a religious group, have no central representation at all, and the Soviet authorities are afraid of what such a leading body, if it were to be established, would do. . . . The Soviet Jews as a group are disorganized and distrusted by the majority of the public as potential emigrants and traitors. The situation is, of course, tragic for the very large numbers of Soviet Jews who do not consider emigration at all and would, on the contrary, like to be integrated into Soviet society. But all their attempts at integration and acceptance are rejected by great parts of the general public whose distrust of the Jews as a group is growing. As a result, such Jews are very demoralized.

"

Aside from its official harassment of Jews, the official Communist Party took a more intellectual and systematic approach to combating religion than was characteristic of the Khrushchev and Stalin eras. Two of these new approaches will be examined: the study of scientific atheism and the introduction of nonreligious ceremonies to mark important events in people's lives.

Beginning in the early 1960s, every student at an institution of higher learning was required to take a one-semester course called "Foundations of Scientific Atheism." The explicit purpose of this requirement was to ensure that the intelligentsia was well-grounded in the conceptions of materialistic philosophy. When these people became the leaders in all spheres of society — especially the school system — they would thus be able to promote atheism. The university textbook on scientific atheism described the purpose of the course in the following way.

" The subject of scientific atheism consists of the following parts: criticism of religion as a false representation of reality; scientific explanation of the causes of religion's origins, evolution, and disappearance; study of the objective and subjective conditions for overcoming religion and for the formation of a scientific and atheistic understanding of the world. From the definition of scientific atheism it is obvious that it includes two basic aspects.

The first aspect consists in disclosing the insubstantiality and illusoriness of religious notions. The criticism of religion prepares the ground for replacing false views and notions in the consciousness of believers by true and scientific ones.

The second aspect of scientific atheism consists in the formation of atheistic awareness and conviction. These must be built upon a system of scientific knowledge about the world and its laws. In criticizing religion, scientific atheism at the same time becomes an important means by which people can be correctly oriented to their environment on the basis of a scientific worldview. It does this because it provides a dialectical materialist understanding of nature, society, and humanity. . . .

The Twenty-Fourth Congress of the C.P.S.U. [Communist Party of the Soviet Union] assigned to Marxist science the great tasks of . . . developing a dialectical materialist worldview and overcoming the

Nauchnyi ateism (Scientific Atheism) (Moscow: Izdatel'stvo politicheskoi literatury, 1976), pp. 8, 9, 13, 14.

"The subject of scientific atheism consists of . . . disclosing the insubstantiality and illusoriness of religious notions and replacing false views and notions in the consciousness of believers with true and scientific ones."
University textbook, *Scientific Atheism*

vestiges of the past in the consciousness and conduct of the people. Marxist atheism has a great role in the performance of these tasks.

Scientific atheism is the theoretical basis for overcoming religion in practice. In capitalist societies where, as Lenin said, one can see "how the class interests and class organization of the contemporary bourgeoisie are linked with religious organizations, institutions and propaganda," only the class struggle of the proletariat, whose goal is the revolutionary transformation of society, can liberate the working masses from the oppression of religion.

SECULAR RITUALS: A WEDDING CEREMONY

N. Zhubasova and A. Beisekov, comp., *Grazhdanskie obriady i prazdniki* (Civil Rites and Holidays) (Alma Ata: "Kazakhstan," 1984) pp. 21-24.

"On the day of the ceremonial registration of marriage the bride and groom, with parents and guests, arrive at the ZAGS [the acronym for *zapis aktov grazhdanskogo sostoianiia*, which may be freely rendered as the Bureau of Vital Statistics] office, the House of Culture, etc., ten to fifteen minutes before the start of the ceremony. The bride and groom proceed to their room.

At the appointed time, the bride and groom, along with parents and guests, are invited into the hall of the ceremonial registration of marriage.

The master of ceremonies says: "This is the ceremonial registration of marriage of citizens of the Union of Soviet Socialist Republics, (names of the bride and groom). The ritual of marriage is being conducted by the deputy of the regional soviet of people's deputies, (name), and the director of the department of ZAGS, (name)."

The music begins and the young people, their witnesses, relatives, and friends approach the table and stop several paces from it. Behind the table is the ZAGS official and the deputy of the soviet.

The MC says: "Respected bride and groom! The day of the ceremonial registration of your marriage is a significant event, which you will remember all of your life. You are making an honorable and noble union, which will establish your family, your happiness and also the happiness of your future generation. In creating a new Soviet family, you take on a great responsibility not only before each other but also before Soviet society. You take on the great and honorable responsibility to live in love and concord as well as to raise healthy and happy children for the benefit of our motherland.

Before you there is a long and splendid path of love, labor and happiness. You are entering into the stage of family life. Therefore, allow me to ask you these questions before we proceed to

In developed socialist societies, where the social roots of religion have been destroyed, the system of atheistic education has great significance. . . . Getting believers actively involved in the resolution of economic, political and cultural tasks of Communist construction . . . will play an important role in overcoming their religion . . . and will make possible useful and active atheistic education. A solid understanding of the social nature and function of religion and of the peculiar characteristics of religious consciousness and religious modernism will determine the basic means for exerting atheistic influence upon people. "

the solemn registration of your marriage:

— Do you freely, mutually, and sincerely desire to enter into marriage? You, the bride? (Yes) You, the groom? (Yes).

— Do you promise before the law of our Soviet motherland, your parents, friends, and comrades to join harmoniously the interests of your family with the interests of society for the good of our state? You, the bride? You, the groom?

— Are you ready to live together in joy and sorrow, in celebration and routine?

— What surname have you decided to use after the registration of the marriage?

— I ask the bride and groom to approach the table and ratify their family union with their signatures. (Chimes are sounded and first the bride and then the groom sign.) I ask the witnesses for bride and groom to approach the table and witness the registration of marriage.

— In accordance with the Law on Marriage and the Family of the Kazakh Soviet Socialist Republic, in the presence of the deputy of the city soviet of people's deputies, this day (day, month, year) your marriage is registered. We declare you to be husband and wife. We ask the couple to exchange rings as a symbol of your faithfulness, love, and consent. As the song says: "A wedding ring is not a simple decoration; From two hearts one resolution is made — a wedding ring." (The hand of the bride must be gloveless.)

— The groom puts a ring on the fourth finger of his wife's right hand, and she does the same for him. The newlyweds kiss.

[Then a speech of congratulations and encouragement is made by a deputy of the city soviet. At the end of the ceremony the wedding march from "Aida" accompanies everyone's exit from the hall.]

After the ceremony, the newlyweds lay flowers at some memorial. "

The second new approach, the state-sponsored, nonreligious rituals, originated in 1964 when the Council of Ministers of the Russian Soviet Federated Socialist Republic adopted the resolution "on the introduction of new civil rituals into the life of Soviet people." A deputy minister of justice of the R.S.F.S.R., V. T. Gubarev, who participated in the early implementation of this resolution, reflected on its purpose and effects in the following interview which was published in *Science and Religion*.

"Linking the Person and Society," *Nauka i Religiia* (Science and Religion), April 1985, pp. 20–22.

" *Question:* Vladimir Timofeevich (Gubarev), the very first question: What was the cause of the resolution?

Answer: The most important events of human life — birth, maturity, marriage — have always been accompanied by ritual celebrations. Their role is enormous: they interrupt the ordinary routine, demonstrate the importance of the events which have special meaning both for the individual person as well as for the society as a whole, and they strengthen the link between the individual and society. Here is accumulated the social experience, a healthy sense of the nation, everything which is necessary to pass on to the new generations. At the same time the special form of ritual, its extraordinariness, clarity, and celebration work an effect upon not only the mind but also upon the emotions of a person, awakening the feeling of unity with the society in which the person lives, as well as feelings of obligation and personal responsibility before it.

Over many centuries ritual celebrations in our country were basically religious in character. The church invariably gave to them very great meaning and by means of the impressive, carefully worked out rituals it strengthened its authority — both spiritual and material — over the person. . . .

As our country moved steadily along the road of constructing a socialist society, there developed an active process of supplanting the old church rituals with new religionless ones. By the sixties we had instituted a system of new rituals — as an essential part of the spiritual culture and the Soviet way of life. In many places there were well established rituals of the solemn registration of marriages and births, bestowal of passports upon citizens of the U.S.S.R., induction into the Soviet Army, entrance of a young person into the labor force, etc. In Moscow and Leningrad wedding palaces were opened.

At the same time there were difficulties associated with the new rituals. In many places registration of marriage and of the birth of a child were conducted in a trite fashion . . . so they produced dissatisfaction and justified complaints of the workers. A more responsible approach was needed. In 1964 the Council of Ministers of the R.S.F.S.R. adopted its special resolution which recommended that local governments . . . introduce new civil rituals and rites, viewing them as an important factor in communist education and in overcoming vestiges of the past in the consciousness of the people. . . . "

One might question where these new approaches are leading. Are they contributing to the gradual demise of religion, or are they creating a surrogate religion? In the following excerpt, an American Unitarian minister argues that Orthodoxy has been displaced by a new "official state religion."

" In spite of the disestablishment of the Russian Orthodox Church in 1918, there is in fact an official state religion in the Soviet Union. Originally, it was called "The Science of Marxism" or "Dialectical Materialism," the philosophy of Marxism. But since 1954 the year after the death of Stalin, by decree of the Central Committee of the C.P.S.U. [Communist Party of the Soviet Union], it has officially been dubbed "Scientific Atheism." This religion — or counter-religion — is spearheaded by a think-tank of some forty scholars comprising the Institute for Scientific Atheism, headquartered in Moscow, a division of the Academy of Sciences, founded in 1963. The institute is the major center for religious studies in the Soviet Union, apart from the few remaining Russian Orthodox . . . seminaries (which are not noted for their scholarship, in any case). It carries on research, publishes a learned journal and a popular magazine, and coordinates the activities of some fifty-one local Houses of Scientific Atheism. . . .

One of the most important tasks of the parent institute is to design the curricula for the required university one-semester course on scientific atheism, which was introduced in 1964. It also supervises both the doctoral programs for scholars in the field of religious studies and instructors for the compulsory university courses. And it has close ties with the nation's largest Museum of the History of Religion and Atheism in the magnificent old Kazan Cathedral in Leningrad. . . .

Scientific atheism, on its theoretical side, is a peculiarly Russian concept. The official university curriculum, for example, does not attempt to disprove the existence of God by refuting any of the classical "proofs" enumerated by St. Thomas Aquinas and others. Atheism is simply taken for granted by the modern provenance of the physical sciences or simply because Lenin said so. The approach to religion is almost entirely sociological and historical: from primitive times, religion in all its forms has been a tool of the ruling classes. . . .

The institute is the most visible symbol of the official Soviet state religion, but it is not yet a church in the full sense. It maintains no shrines. It conducts no services. It has no priesthood. These functions are as yet decentralized, yet a kind of "church" is emerging. . . . Marriages are performed with great dignity in stately wedding palaces by specially trained officials. Comparable rites of passage are regularly performed at baby palaces, for newborns, and at crematoria, where trained funeral directors conduct funeral services. The school system takes care of other rites of passage for young people.

It seems to have dawned on those in charge of the state antireligion

Robert M. Hemstreet, "Religious Humanism Meets Scientific Atheism," *The Humanist*, January/February 1987, pp. 6, 7, 34.

that religious faith is not only a matter of the head but of the heart and that people are religious not simply out of their personal deficiencies or because of their socio-economic oppression but because they need to celebrate the great events of life and to express hope in their personal, familial, and social future. The Soviet atheists are becoming more sophisticated in providing vehicles for the expression of such aspirations.
"

The people responsible for the "scientific atheist establishment" obviously do not wish to view their own activities as religious. They insist that their mission is to liberate people from religion, which they view as an impediment to healthy human development, and to create a new kind of person. In the following description of the Soviet rituals, the writer — a Ukrainian — emphasizes the atheistic orientation of the ceremonies.

N. M. Zakovich, *Sovetskaia obriadnost i dukhovnaia kultura* (Soviet Rituals and the Spiritual Culture) (Kiev: Naukova dumka, 1980), pp. 168–185.

"

In conditions of developed socialism the necessary material, socio-political, moral, and psychological prerequisites for forming the new man have been created. Soviet ceremonies fulfill various functions. They have emotional and intellectual effects, and they produce devotion to the cause of Communism along with love for the socialist motherland and for labor.

There is an important atheistic function in socialist rituals. . . . [They are] an effective form of atheistic education as well as a device for eliminating religious ritual. . . . The clergy views religious ritual as a means for propaganda, through which it will be possible to attract even nonbelievers to religion. . . . Such life-changing events as the birth of a child, getting married, the death of loved ones, fear of death, personal loss, etc., occasionally encourage people to have recourse to the services of the church. . . . It is no secret that many believers came to religion through the emotional effect of its ceremonies. . . .

In recent years, the custom of the ceremonial registration of infants has achieved relatively widespread acceptance. The ritual of the ceremony has been developed. Already there are examples of interesting and impressive performances of this ceremony. For example, in the Karelian A.S.S.R. certain days of the month have been assigned for the ceremonial registration of newborn babies. In rural regions of Estonia it is performed once each quarter. . . . The new ritual contains many beautiful elements which impart to it a special character and emotion. At present almost every family marks the birth of a child with a festive ceremony. However, the registration sometimes is conducted formally. Frequently it happens that registrations of several infants are done simultaneously. Naturally, this detracts from the educational impact of the new rite for in this instance an individual approach is very important.

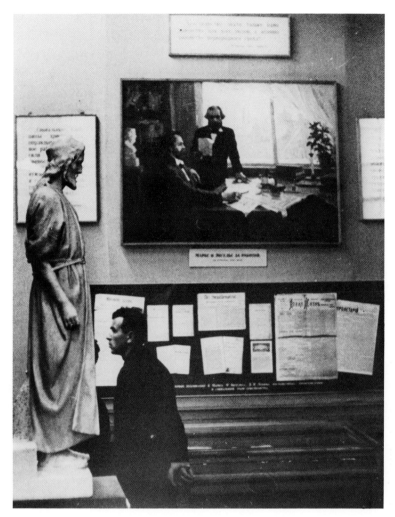

Closed as a place of worship in 1932, Leningrad's Old Kazan Cathedral is now the Museum of the History of Religion and Atheism, a museum which highlights the ugliest features of religion and portrays scientific atheism, based on the writings of Marx and Engels (who are depicted in the background), as the way to salvation.

AP/Wide World Photos.

Leningrad has acquired valuable experience in the ceremonial registration of infants. The country's first "Maliutka" ["Baby"] palace was opened here in 1965. In the palace the new ceremony is performed separately for each parent couple. The ritual consists of two parts: official and celebrational. The official part begins with the entry of the parents into the room. The presider delivers a short speech about the significance of this event and about the family. Then the registration is completed and the name of the infant is announced. At the end of the official part the Soviet State hymn is played in honor of the new citizen of the Country of Soviets. Then a deputy of the city soviet warmly congratulates the parents and all present and hands the parents the birth certificate, a medal, and a congratulatory letter from the soviet. The medal is presented as a souvenir to the new citizen in honor of the home city. Again festive music is heard and the relatives and friends congratulate the parents and give them flowers. 🎵

Zakovich goes on to describe other surrogate rituals which the state offers as substitutes for traditional religious ceremonies: acknowledgement of citizenship in place of confirmation, wedding palaces to replace marriage in church, and "religionless funerals," which "function on the social and psychological levels." With the commitment of considerable resources to such secular ceremonies, the Communist leadership of the Soviet Union moved beyond mere repression to a strategy of providing a creative substitute for meeting the basic human needs which religion serves.

While available evidence suggests that this strategy has enjoyed little success, it is certainly more in keeping with Lenin's counsel that confronting religious institutions head on would impel believers to cling even more tenaciously to their religions. Until comparatively recently, the Soviet state that was created in the revolution generally ignored Lenin's advice, trying in various overt ways — some of them brutal — to restrict the practice of religion in the Soviet Union. In the early months after the revolution, the government tried to destroy the principal bases

Although religious and folk customs have been largely eliminated from state wedding ceremonies, this bride (pictured at the Alma Ata Wedding Palace) is wearing a traditional Kazakh wedding gown.

J.P. Laffont/Sygma.

of the Orthodox Church's influence (and to a lesser degree the bases of other institutional religions) by confiscating the property of the church and prohibiting it from educating children. The Orthodox Church resisted this attempt and suffered the consequences. Most other religions found that the conditions created by the revolution provided them with an opportunity to expand their activities.

After a dozen years, at the end of the 1920s, a veritable "war on God" accompanied Stalin's aggressive policy of rapid industrialization and forced collectivization of agriculture. The first goal of Stalin's anti-religious policy was to undermine religion's influence on society; the second was the complete elimination of religion itself. By the end of the 1930s, organized religious life had almost ceased to exist in the Soviet Union.

World War II changed the situation dramatically. Many religious leaders called for a defense of the country against the Nazi invaders. Stalin reversed his policy on the church, and the situation for religion improved steadily until the end of the 1950s when Nikita Khrushchev unleashed another antireligious war, somewhat less vicious than Stalin's of the 1930s, but still very effective in abolishing about half of the operating religious congregations.

Khrushchev's campaign against religion ended when he was removed from office in 1964. Under Leonid Brezhnev's leadership, administrative assaults on religion declined considerably — though they did not disappear — while the program for educating and conditioning people in the spirit of scientific atheism became more systematic.

As the 1970s progressed, restrictions were gradually eased. However, life was still difficult for Jews, especially those whose requests to leave the country were rejected and for dissenting religious congregations that refused to conform to the laws on religious activity or to cooperate with officially recognized organizations.

At best, the attempts of almost seven decades to curtail religion achieved marginal success. Religious practice in the Soviet Union remains vigorous in the 1980s and that evident vigor is the subject of the next chapter.

In addition to their legally required state wedding, some couples choose to have a church wedding like this Orthodox "crowning," a ceremony which symbolizes the dignity and purity of marriage by capping the bride and groom with crowns picturing the Virgin Mary and the Savior, respectively.

Furnished by the Moscow Patriarchate, Courtesy of J. Martin Bailey.

RELIGIOUS LIFE

CONTEMPORARY PRACTICES AND PROBLEMS

Outside observers, familiar with the history of repression in the Soviet Union, are often surprised to find that religion is actually practiced with great fervor there. Signs of vitality exist in the churches, synagogues, and mosques where believers gather to worship in great numbers. Benefiting from more hospitable circumstances than existed in the past, religious institutions have recently been striving to publish enough books, train enough seminarians, and otherwise provide the resources to meet the religious needs of believers. Some observers even claim that the Soviet Union is experiencing a religious renaissance. This chapter examines these signs of vitality and ends with a discussion of how the "official" Soviet estimate of the number of religious believers in the Soviet Union compares with the estimates of Western observers. The numbers may surprise many Americans.

The tenacity with which Soviet citizens have clung to their religions since the revolution is explained below by a perceptive British journalist writing about religious conditions in the early 1980s. Trevor Beeson offers several theories about why "religious communities are still very much a part of the Soviet scene" despite the state's efforts to ensure "that religious bodies shall wither away and die."

How do people of faith in the Soviet Union practice their beliefs?

" **A**lthough in theory Lenin's position left open the possibility of mutual respect and co-existence between Church and State, the policy of successive regimes in the U.S.S.R. has included the destruction of religious institutions and the elimination of religious belief. It has been, and is, the intention of the Soviet government that religious bodies shall wither away and die. This is a fact which cannot be ignored in any examination of the religious

Trevor Beeson, *Discretion and Valour* (Glascow: Collins, 1982), pp. 150–153.

■ 121

situation in the U.S.S.R.

The policy on religion has achieved only limited success. . . . There can be no doubt that since 1917 all the Christian churches and Jewish synagogues of European Russia have been very seriously reduced in number and seriously disabled. Moreover, the combination of atheistic teaching and creeping secularism has had a significant effect upon the incidence of religious faith and practice. There are fewer church-goers than there were 50 years ago, for oppression and propaganda do have their results.

Yet, in spite of all the Communist efforts, the religious communities are still very much a part of the Soviet scene. Not only are they still there; if we look at the situation as a whole, they are there in considerable strength. The number of Russian Orthodox believers is generally estimated to be in the area of fifty million [out of 190 million Ukrainians, Belorussians, and Russians] — hardly a figure to be overlooked or dismissed as unimportant. The various religious sects are of course smaller, but there are signs here and there that they are very much alive, with some even growing and attracting significant numbers of young people. The persistence of personal belief obviously cannot be quantified, but it is at least interesting that icons are still to be found in a surprising number of Soviet homes and that surveys carried out over the last two decades show that many people still have their children baptized and still have religious burials. . . .

The persistence of religious belief and the survival of the churches in the Soviet Union is a plain fact. But serious difficulties are encountered as soon as any attempt is made to offer an explanation for this phenomenon. . . . Nonetheless, study of the continuing life of religious communities in the Soviet Union leaves certain impressions.

Chief among these is the fact that the culture and the traditions of a people cannot be destroyed and replaced overnight. The Marxist-Leninist revolutionaries of 1917 were firmly convinced that religion would disappear as soon as man ceased to be alienated from the fruits of his labours, and they did not foresee any undue delay in the completion of this process. But they made a serious miscalculation. . . . Russian Orthodox culture, for example, with its intricate intertwining of the sacred and the secular, the mystical and the ethical, the personal and the institutional, had been evolving for almost a thousand years and was not ready to collapse at the wave of a red flag. . . .

A second element in the persistence of religious belief and the survival of the churches is to be found, perhaps paradoxically, in the nature of Soviet society itself. For more than a half a century the main organs of corporate life and expression have been held in the suffocating grips of a government even more authoritarian than its predecessor. Rigorous control, censorship, elaborate systems of espionage, propaganda and much else have been developed to maintain the power of the Communist Party over almost every part of life. It is not surprising that

"The persistence of religious belief is a plain fact. The culture and the traditions of a people cannot be destroyed and replaced overnight."
British journalist Trevor Beeson

since Stalin's death a growing number of Soviet citizens have become more and more unhappy about this arrangement, and have begun to look for areas in which they can breathe a different air. The churches and the synagogues provide one of the few places — perhaps the only place — where such air exists. . . .

Institutional durability is yet another factor which has worked to promote the survival of religion. The historic churches have developed a quite remarkable facility for adjusting their life to meet new challenges. Like those parts of the natural order which are obliged to change in order to survive, the churches seem to have been able to move through every disaster, if not actually unscathed at least with their essential life intact. The adjustments, though, have been far from easy, and the demand for courage and self-sacrifice has been enormous — perhaps especially so for the responsible leadership. More than anything else, it seems, the creative tension which has arisen between courageous leaders and their courageous critics, between the forces of conscientious

Overcrowded churches show simultaneously the vitality of religious faith and the shortage of open churches.

Clayton Jones/*The Christian Science Monitor.*

accommodation and conscientious resistance, has nurtured the durability of religious institutions. . . . There can be no disputing that many millions of religious believers in the Soviet Union today are sustained by their belief in the ultimate indestructibility of the community of faith and, by their deep devotion and heroic courage, they are turning this belief into reality.

"

Since the mid-1970s, the Soviet government's greater tolerance for religion has resulted in what might even be called "normalization" of conditions for believers. Congregations of Pentecostals, Adventists, Mennonites, and independent Baptists, which previously had been declared illegal, are now officially registered, although other denominations (Ukrainian Catholics and Orthodox, Jehovah's Witnesses) remain proscribed. While certainly not providing for broad freedom of religion as Americans understand it, conditions today allow many believers to express their religious aspirations, as a number of firsthand accounts demonstrate.

In the following excerpt, an American describes the Easter vigil service, the most significant evening service of the Orthodox Church year, as it was celebrated in the chief cathedral of the Orthodox Church in Moscow.

Suzanne Massie, "You Can Pray for Us," *Guideposts*, February 1985.

"

Because Easter is the most cherished Orthodox holiday — one of fervor, fasting, exuberance, and feasting — I had always wanted to celebrate it in Russia. You can imagine my excitement when I knew that I would at last be visiting Russia during Easter week last spring.

In Moscow, I attended an Orthodox Easter service, a liturgical re-enactment of the first Easter. Outside, police in uniforms watched. So did the plainclothed KGB and the red-armbanded *druzhiniki* vigilantes. Being watched is routine for Russian worshipers.

At 10 P.M., an hour before the service, more people had gathered than the 18th century church could hold. Everyone, upon entering, had bought red beeswax candles. I managed to squeeze to a place in front, and there I waited, pressed into the crowd. They were all ages. Old women, bearded men, students, workers, young couples holding hands. Men waited with sleepy children in their arms and women close beside them. Icons of the apostles, of Christ and Mary, looked on us as we stood beneath the blue, star-painted ceiling, called the "dome of heaven," where prayers of the faithful are caught and sent on their way.

As 11 P.M. approached, a mass of people remained outside, unable to press in. Then the priests, in long flowing vestments, began intoning the lamentation, echoed by the choir. (All Orthodox services are sung *a cappella*.)

In the darkened church, we stood in sadness. Men and women, old and young alike, their faces marked by personal sorrow, wept openly. Heads bowed under the stress of everyday life.

These people have known a history of hardship. Theirs is a spirituality that has endured 250 years of Mongol domination, Napoleon's invasion, World War I, the Revolution, civil war, World War II, and the terror of Stalin. Not a family hasn't been touched by tragedy, and yet here they were, having endured everything, holding fast to their belief in God.

As midnight approached, the priest lit a candle held by someone in the front row. Swiftly the flame was passed from candle to candle. A young woman offered her flame to me; I passed mine to the man beside me; he to the next one.

In this way, from hand to hand, the church burst into light. We were all part of that light. Each of our candles added to its intensity and it seemed that the brightness around me was a symbol of the Orthodox believer, who sees man as a link between heaven and earth, as one who may not see the end result, but without whose faith the end result would not be possible.

Continuing an age-old tradition, these Moscovites have brought Easter breads and eggs to be blessed at an Easter church service.
UPI/Bettmann Newsphoto.

HOW MANY PEOPLE OF FAITH LIVE IN THE SOVIET UNION?

While it is impossible to obtain precise and complete statistics about religious groups, generally reliable estimates for the early 1980s are available from researchers. Although these figures are generally higher than those from official sources before Gorbachev's era of glasnost, they are based on a variety of sources within the Soviet Union which appear to be reliable. The question marks indicate that no figure can be determined.

Religion	Believers	Congregations	Clergy
Orthodox	50 to 70 million	7,000	6,500
Muslims	35 to 43 million	450	2,000
Eastern Rite Catholics	>3 million	700	?
Georgian Orthodox	3 million	200	100
Roman Catholics	>2 million	625	>800
Armenian Apostolic	2 million	500	?
Baptists	½ to 2 million	5,000 to 8,000	?
Old Believers	>1 million	?	?
Lutherans	600,000	350	200
Buddhists	500,000	?	>300
Jews	500,000	60	few
Pentecostals	100,000	?	?
Adventists	40,000	?	?
Mennonites	40,000	?	?
Methodists	3,000	12	?
Jehovah's Witnesses	?	400	?

Source: compiled by author from Soviet data

A deacon's voice from the rear of the church boomed, "Why do you seek the living among the dead? He is not here. *Khristos Voskrese!*" (Christ is risen!).

That was our signal to follow the priests, holding brilliant banners, in the traditional *Krestny Khod* (Search for Christ). Our long candlelight procession wound around the outside of the church three times, as together we sang and searched, accompanied by the tolling of bells outside.

On the doorstep, the priest thrice joyously proclaimed *"Khristos Voskrese!"* And three times the vast crowd responded, *"Voistinu Voskrese!"* ("Indeed, He is risen!").

The doors were thrust open. The church interior was ablaze with light. The crowd surged back inside, and the choir burst into hymns of rejoicing, punctuated by the repeated cry "Christ is risen!" The crowd gave response in a rousing chorus of joy and excitement.

We had been standing for three hours — there are no pews in Russian churches because worshipers feel it is sacrilegious to sit in the presence of God — but we felt elated.

At 3:30 A.M., after the communion service, we lined up to kiss the cross held aloft by the priest. Many gave him a colored Easter Egg. Then smiling, exchanging the Easter greeting, *"Khristos Voskrese!"* we kissed one another heartily on alternating cheeks and surged out.

People separated into groups on their way home, where they would break their seven-week *Veliki Post* (Great Fast) with a feast of *Kulich*, a tall, cylindrical Easter bread, decorated with frosting and the letters *XB* ("Christ is risen"), and thick, creamy white spread, *paskha*, a cheese-cake–like Easter treat made in a triangular mold. And, of course, eggs — hard-boiled and dyed.

"

In another firsthand account, a Jewish traveler from Czechoslovakia describes Jewish religious life in Moscow. The writer, a graduate of the rabbinical seminary in Budapest, has since become the rabbi of the Jewish synagogue in Prague. (Because his account appeared originally in the monthly magazine of the Jewish Religious Communities in Czechoslovakia, its contents had to be approved by Czech authorities.)

"About 300,000 members of the Jewish nationality now live in the Soviet capital. There function in Moscow two synagogues in which believing Jews are able to lead a religious life and thus preserve the thousand-year-old traditions of their ancestors.

The principal Moscow synagogue is the Choral Synagogue in Archipov Street, not far from Red Square. The synagogue is also the seat of the religious community. The Moscow community is one of the few in which younger people are in charge. The chairman of the Jewish religious community is Boris Mikhaylovich Gram, 36, who has been performing his taxing functions for four years now, to the complete satisfaction of the members. The Chief Rabbi is Adolf Shaevich, 46, from Birobidzhan, the main town of the Jewish Autonomous oblast. Shaevich completed his studies in Budapest in spring 1980. . . .

Daily services — *shahrit, minha, ma'ariv* — are held in the Choral Synagogue. For example, four "minyanim," three of Ashkenazi and one of Sephardi Jews, meet for the morning service. On Saturday, two or

Daniel Meyer, "Moscow's Choral Synagogue," *Soviet Jewish Affairs*, vol. 14, no. 2 (1984), pp. 63–65.

three hundred believers participate in the prayers. Services take place from 10 a.m. to 1 p.m. and are accompanied by a cantor and choir. After reading the week's portion of the Torah, the Chief Rabbi recites a prayer for peace and tranquility on earth. One characteristic of the Sabbath services is that not only one Scroll of the Law is taken from the *Aron Ha-kodesh* [Ark], but five or six; later the respective number of *minyanim* is formed in the synagogue, and each reads its own Scroll independently.

The service and attendance at the Moscow synagogue during the High Holidays are a veritable experience for any of our Central European co-religionists. For instance, this year there were inside and in front of the synagogue over eight thousand believers, of whom about forty per cent were young people.

There is therefore considerable variety among the community's members. One can meet people who visit the synagogue through tradition and to honour their ancestors, *hasidim* of several tendencies, and highly observant young believers, who wear *peot* [side curls] and *tsitsit* [a small fringed shawl].

Although the precise number of synagogues operating in the Soviet Union is a source of ongoing dispute, it is clear that Jewish services, such as this one in Moscow's Choral Synagogue, are severely restricted.

Courtesy of Lew Freedman/*Anchorage Daily News*.

Lukasz Hirszowicz, who translated the previous excerpt into English, provided the following notes which illuminate and clarify some of Meyer's statements. Hirszowicz's comments were free from the censorship to which Meyer's were subjected.

The two synagogues referred to are the Choral Synagogue in Arkhipov Street and the small wooden synagogue in the suburb of Maryina Roshcha. A third synagogue functioned in the suburb of Cherkizovo until the 1960s.

No religious community in the generally accepted sense exists in Moscow or elsewhere in the U.S.S.R. Soviet religious law demands the existence of a group of twenty people in order to form a religious association and acquire the use of a place of worship. Such a religious association is also the legal framework in which the Moscow Choral Synagogue operates.

The prayer for peace introduced by Rabbi Schliefer appeared in the prayerbook he published in 1957. It begins: "Our Father in Heaven! Bless the Government of the U.S.S.R., the defender of peace in the whole world. Let us say Amen."

Many people who do not feel Jewish in a religious sense assemble in front of the Choral Synagogue on Jewish religious holidays, especially *Simhat Tora*. These gatherings have acquired special significance with the development of the national and emigration movement among Soviet Jewry.

Lukasz Hirszowicz, "Moscow's Choral Synagogue," *Soviet Jewish Affairs*, vol. 14, no. 2 (May 1984), pp. 65–66.

As Hirszowicz indicated, the religious activity of Soviet Jews has undergone a change in the years since the resurgence of public anti-Semitism promoted a new desire for emigration. In the 1968–1982 period, 271,165 Jews requested permission to leave the Soviet Union permanently; of these 8,838 (or about one in twenty-five applicants) were refused permission. These "refuseniks" have returned to religious observance in great numbers. The impact of their presence on Soviet Jewish religious experience is assessed in the following observations of a Canadian traveler.

"Soviet authorities have unquestionably, if unintentionally, helped spark the return to religion among the refuseniks ... social isolation leads naturally to association with other like-minded Jews."

Although most informed readers in the West have heard about the plight and the heroism of the refuseniks—those Soviet Jews who, after being refused an exit visa, find themselves in limbo, deprived of their professional base and relegated to a life of poverty, discrimination, and intimidation—relatively little has been written about the recent phenomenon of return to religious observance among hundreds of refusenik families. . . . To those familiar with the history of Russian Jewry since the 1917 Revolution, and the Soviets' early persecution of religious Jews by such state organs as the infamous Yevsektsia, the new religious awakening among young Russian Jews must rank as one of the most poignant sagas of our time. . . .

Some refuseniks who had been studying Hebrew in preparation for aliyah [return to the land of Israel] came to the realization that in order

Henry H. Weinberg, "Soviet Jewry: Faith and Defiance," *Midstream*, August–September 1987, pp. 11–13.

RELIGIOUS
LIFE

129

not to lose their Jewish consciousness, they would have to acquire a deeper knowledge of Jewish culture and traditions. . . . Progressively, those who attended circles for the study of Hebrew gravitated to Seminars on Torah and the Talmud. There appeared a new breed of Soviet Jews who came to the conclusion that a commitment to Judaism made sense only when it is based on knowledge of traditional texts and on religious practice. . . .

Reliable estimates indicate that in Moscow alone there are more than 300 families (about 1,000 individuals) who observe the mitzvot, and by

THE JACKSON-VANIK AMENDMENT AND JEWISH EMIGRATION

In 1974, the United States Congress added a provision to the foreign trade law which was intended to give official support to Jews and persons of other nationalities who wished to leave the U.S.S.R. This provision drew a direct link between a country's emigration policy and access to trade with the United States. If a country did not allow its people to move from their home country without hindrance, that country could not reap the benefits of trading with the United States. Popularly known as "Jackson-Vanik," this amendment did not name specifically either Jews or the Soviet Union as the targets of its concerns, but people of all countries understood its intent. Soviet spokesmen objected to this action as an example of American lawmakers improperly meddling in their internal affairs. American supporters of the measure took pride in its expression of humanitarian concern.

An excerpt from the text of the amendment follows.

Public Law 93-618, January 3, 1975.

"Section 402: Freedom of Emigration in East-West Trade

(a) To assure the continued dedication of the United States to fundamental human rights, . . . products from any nonmarket economy country shall not be eligible to receive nondiscriminatory treatment (most-favored-nation treatment). . . .during the period beginning with the date on which the President determines that such country —

(1) denies its citizens the right or opportunity to emigrate (2) imposes more than a nominal tax on emigration or on the visas or other documents required for emigration, for any purpose or cause whatsoever, or

(3) imposes more than a nominal tax, levy, fine, fee, or other charge on any citizen as a consequence of the desire of such citizen to emigrate to the country of his choice, and ending on the date on which the President determines that such country is no longer in violation."

all reports their numbers are growing. Significantly, only five years ago the figures were close to zero. . . .

In Leningrad, after the Sabbath morning services in the city's only functioning synagogue, we were approached by a group of young men who invited us for Kiddush. . . . In the apartment of "Sasha" we learned that every one of the five young men in the group was in the process of "returning" and had reached a different level of competency in Hebrew. . . . "Sasha" had only a rudimentary reading of Hebrew but he had been attending Sabbath services for over a year and had surrounded

The chart below shows, among other significant things, one of the Soviet reactions to the Jackson-Vanik Amendment; the rate of emigration of Jews dropped markedly during the period it was being debated (1974) and after its adoption. The rate of emigration eventually recovered, peaking the year the second Strategic Arms Limitations Treaty (SALT II) was signed by Presidents Jimmy Carter and Leonid Brezhnev. After the Soviet invasion of Afghanistan at the end of 1979, emigration dropped dramatically. After Brezhnev's death in 1982, a time when U.S. — Soviet relations were severely strained, it was reduced to the merest trickle. After the Iceland summit, in conditions of expanding perestroika in the U.S.S.R., there was a substantial recovery in the rate.

Source: National Conference on Soviet Jewry

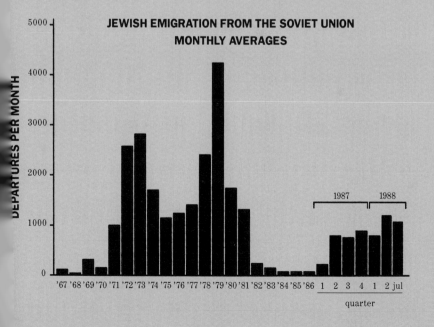

JEWISH EMIGRATION FROM THE SOVIET UNION
MONTHLY AVERAGES

Compiled by the author.

himself with a variety of Jewish and Israeli objects in his apartment. . . .

The Soviet authorities have unquestionably helped to spark the return to religion among the refuseniks. . . . The social isolation leads naturally to an association with other like-minded Jews, and to a quest for a way of life and a culture they can adhere to and transmit to their children. . . . The renewal of interest in the Jewish religion in Soviet Russia represents a reversal of a trend that originated in the days of the *maskilim* [promoters of humanistic enlightenment]. It is a vivid demonstration that modern Zionism can lead to religious commitment — not just away from it. **"**

As the preceding excerpts show, individual congregations are manifesting a new vitality. But what about seminaries, religious publishers, and denominational headquarters, for example? Have their activities also accelerated? In the following excerpt, the president of the Council for Religious Affairs at the end of the Brezhnev era argues that the freedom of religious institutions to carry out supporting activities, such as training and publishing, proves that the Soviet Union does not violate the right to freedom of conscience.

V. A. Kuroedov, *Religiia i tserkov v sovetskom obshchestve* (Religion and the Church in Soviet Society) (Moscow: Politizdat, 1984), pp. 111–119.

" At the present time in the U.S.S.R. there is a total of about 20,000 religious societies and groups of various denominations: Orthodox, Catholic, Muslim, Jewish, Lutheran, Old Believer, Buddhist, Evangelical Christian–Baptist, Seventh Day Adventist, and others. . . .

An important concrete guarantee of the enjoyment of freedom of conscience is the granting to religious associations (to their centers) the possibility of regularly publishing the literature that is necessary for satisfying their religious needs. The Russian Orthodox Church, for example, puts out the monthly *Journal of the Moscow Patriarchate* in Russian and English. *Theological Works*, the organ of the higher academic institutions (the ecclesiastical academies of the Russian Orthodox Church) is published annually. An Orthodox church calendar is published in a massive edition in two variants: an illustrated table calendar with explanatory articles about Orthodox theology and a wall calendar in the form of a table with the dates of church holidays. Besides this, every month the *Orthodox Herald* comes out in Ukrainian. . . .

In the last fifteen years there have been four editions of the Bible published in large editions (in 1983 the publishing run was 75,000 copies). The New Testament and the Psalms have been frequently published. Liturgical books have also been published: a Typicon, Missal, Service Book, and many others. The works of the late Patriarch Alexis were published in four volumes and recently a volume of the works of Moscow Patriarch Pimen was published. . . .

Do Soviet authorities see their own statements about freedom of conscience as hypocritical in light of repeated official antireligious statements?

Substantial publishing activity is also carried out by other religious associations. For example, the Spiritual Directorate of Muslims has frequently published the Koran in recent years (in 1983 it published an edition of 40,000 copies); the Muslim lunar calendar is regularly published, as is the journal *Muslims of the Soviet East* in four languages. . . .

In the last five years the Catholic dioceses of Lithuania and Latvia have reprinted the New Testament, Psalter, Prayer Books, Missals, and materials of the Second Vatican Council in Latin and the national languages. Periodically there are produced calendars and journals of Evangelical Christians–Baptists, the Echmiadzin Catholicate, the Moscow Old Believer Archbishopric, Patriarchate of the Georgian Orthodox Church, Consistory of the Evangelical Lutheran Churches of Estonia, Latvia, and Lithuania, the presbyteriate of the Council of Seventh Day Adventists, and others. The All-Union Council of Evangelical Christians–Baptists has produced three editions of the Bible, a hymnbook, the collected sermons of the famous church leader A.V. Karev, and albums about the life of Evangelical Christians–Baptists in

This Baptist congregation is one of five such congregations in Kiev, the capital of the Ukraine, where most Baptists are concentrated.

Courtesy of Gene Williams.

the U.S.S.R. Old Believers have published a church service book in three volumes and decisions of the Old Believer council. The Armenian Apostolic Church has published a New Testament twice, the book of Vazgen, Patriarch of the Armenians, describing the patriarch's trip abroad, and the albums *Echmiadzin* and *Armenian Churches*.

Religious associations in the U.S.S.R. have available to them shops for the production of objects needed for religious purposes and church utensils, candles, matzo, etc. Churches have forty such specialized institutions to satisfy fully the needs of believers for cultic objects. . . . In Moscow, as well as in other dioceses, there are candle factories which provide Orthodox parishes with candles. In 1979, in the suburbs of Moscow, a large factory was built for producing a wide variety of liturgical objects. . . .

At the present time there are eighteen institutions of theological education operating, including six Orthodox academies and seminaries, two Catholic seminaries, an Islamic institute and *medressah*, and a Jewish *yeshivah*. The Armenian Apostolic Church has an ecclesiastical academy, the Georgian Orthodox Church prepares clergy in a seminary, and the Evangelical Christians–Baptists conduct a correspondence course. . . . Many clergy of the Russian Orthodox Church have been educated abroad. And at the present time there are groups of Orthodox students studying in Athens and Rome. At present students from our country are studying in various countries: Baptists in the Baptist seminar in Bukov (G.D.R.); Catholics in the Paris Catholic Institute and the Advanced Catholic School in Warsaw; Muslims in the State University of Jordan, the Islamic University in Libya, and Damascus University; and Buddhists in Nepal at the Higher Buddhist School of Ulan Bator.

"

While recognized religious organizations are certainly permitted to function, they carry out their activities under the tight control of the Communist government. Some observers, like the German scholar whose analysis of this issue is excerpted below, claim that Communist government control exerts a "destructive influence on the church."

Otto Luchterhandt, "State Authorities for Religious Affairs in Soviet Bloc Countries," *Religion in Communist Lands,* vol. 13, no. 1 (Spring 1985), pp. 57, 61f.

" The Council for Religious Affairs . . . has the last (and very often the first) word in all important questions of church organization, appointments, finance, economics, training institutions, and publishing. . . . In practice the CRA, improperly using its position of overwhelming power, . . . successfully exerts a destructive influence on the church. . . .

The concentration of state power over church affairs in a single authority represents a considerable danger for religious communities. . . . At best a mere fig-leaf veils the fundamentally self-contradictory situation in which the state authorities for religious affairs find themselves. On the one hand, even a communist state sets itself the task of maintaining peace under the law, that is to say of protecting all non-criminal citizens and their organizations, including the churches. . . . On the other hand, this protective function is in direct opposition to its policy of discrimination against religious citizens in numerous ways and of restricting, oppressing and indeed even destroying religious communities. In view of this unresolvable contradiction, the communist authorities for religious affairs find themselves in a schizophrenic state of tension.

"

Kuroedov's long litany of the number of books published and seminarians graduated raises a serious question: Are these quantities sufficient to meet the need? Moreover, Kuroedov exaggerates. Although his statistics are accurate — so far as can be ascertained — his generalizations are not. For example, he describes the publication of the Koran and Bible as "frequent," yet these books have not been published on an average of even once every three years over the past fifteen. His claim that 75,000 Bibles is a "large" edition sounds hollow, for millions of Jewish and Christian believers have never owned a copy of their scriptures.

Still, the opportunities presented to religious organizations have expanded year by year. Perhaps the more lenient government stance is intended to reward the church for enduring without open defiance the blasts of various storms unleashed by the officials against religion. But for some the subservience of the church to rulers hostile to religion has never been acceptable. In a famous open letter to the Orthodox patriarch in 1972, the Nobel laureate Alexander Solzhenitsyn condemned the subservience of the church's leadership. Solzhenitsyn speaks with the zeal of a recent convert to the church and as a Russian nationalist.

"

The study of the last few centuries of Russian history leaves one with the conviction that it would have advanced in an incomparably more humane and harmonious manner if the Church had not renounced her independence. . . . We have been losing and forfeiting the shining moral Christian atmosphere in which for a millennium our mores, our style of life, outlook, folklore, even the very name of the people — *krestiany* ["peasants," derived from *krest*, which means "cross" and identifies the peasants with the Christian symbol] — have stood firm. We are losing the last characteristics and traits of a Christian nation. . . .

For every church in use there are twenty razed and irreparably damaged and twenty more in desolation and profanation — is there a more heartrending sight than these ruins, left to the birds and

Aleksandr I. Solzhenitsyn, "A Lenten Letter," *Religion in Communist Dominated Areas*, vol. 11, no. 1–3 (1972), pp. 5–6.

storehouse keepers? How many population centers are there in the country without any church within 100 or even 200 kilometers? And our north is left without any churches whatsoever — that north which from ancient times has been the repository of the Russian spirit and, one can expect, will most faithfully show it forth again in the future. Workers, almsgivers, and donors meet with obstacles at every attempt to restore even the smallest church because of the one-sided laws of the so-called

"MORAL CODE OF THE BUILDER OF COMMUNISM"

The ethical values that the Communist Party seeks to promote appear in the Constitution of the Party. The rules of the party require that members adopt these standards. In 1968, a law was passed which stated that parents have the legal obligation to bring up their children according to the "moral code of the builder of communism." Some have concluded that this requirement poses a threat and a dilemma for religious parents.

Pravda, November 3, 1961, p. 3.

" The party organization must see to it that every communist observes in his own life and cultivates among working people the moral principles set forth in the Program of the Communist Party of the Soviet Union — the moral code of a builder of Communism:

— loyalty to the Communist cause, love of his own socialist country, and of other socialist countries;

— conscientious labor for the benefit of society: he who does not work, neither shall he eat;

— concern on everyone's part for the protection and increase of social wealth;

— a lofty sense of public duty, intolerance of violations of the public interest;

— collectivism and comradely mutual assistance: one for all, and all for one;

— humane relations and mutual respect among people: man is to man a friend, comrade, and brother;

— honesty and truthfulness, moral purity, unpretentiousness and modesty in public and personal life;

— mutual respect in the family circle and concern for the upbringing of children;

— intolerance of injustice, parasitism, dishonesty, careerism, and profiteering;

— friendship and fraternity among all peoples of the U.S.S.R., intolerance of national and racial hostility;

— intolerance of the enemies of Communism, the enemies of peace and those who oppose the freedom of the peoples;

— fraternal solidarity with the working people of all countries, with all peoples. "

separation of church and state. We do not even dare to ask about the ringing of church bells — but why is Russia deprived of her ancient adornment, her finest voice? And why speak of the churches? — we cannot even get the Gospels anywhere, even the Gospels must be brought in from abroad. . . .

Does the Church make a stand for anything whatsoever? All ecclesiastical administration, the appointment of pastors and bishops — everything is carried out secretly according to the directives of the Council on Religious Affairs.

A church directed dictatorially by atheists is a sight unseen for two millennia. All administration of church business, as well as the use of church monies — those coppers dropped in by pious fingers — are given over to their control. . . . Priests are without rights in their parishes, only the conducting of divine worship is still entrusted to them, and that only within the churches, while before stepping outside to visit the sick or to go to the cemetery it is first necessary to ask permission of the city council.

On what evidence can one convince himself that the systematic demolition of the Church, body and soul, at the hands of the atheists is her best way of preservation? Preservation — for whom? Certainly not for Christ. Preservation — by what means? By *lying*? But after lying what shall be the kind of hands offering the Eucharist?

"Millions of Jewish and Christian believers have never owned a copy of their scriptures."

People who know a great deal about religion in the Soviet Union do not agree on how to evaluate its current status. The tone and approach of the next two excerpts — both by well-informed Americans — are greatly at odds with each other. The first is by an assistant secretary of state in the American government. He shares Solzhenitsyn's view that state control of religion is morally reprehensible, although he also observes the continued vigor of religious practice.

I n recent years, to be sure, we have heard eye-witness reports from highly respected American religious personalities as to the tolerance of religious observance in the Soviet Union. These visitors to the Soviet Union reported accurately and fairly what they saw. They were, of course, unable to report what was hidden from their view.

What these recent visitors to the Soviet Union may have thought they might encounter was an active crusade against all forms of religion, a continuing deep, publicly-manifested commitment to atheism. They were pleasantly surprised not to encounter evidence of an overt atheistic campaign. What they failed to understand fully is that a newer approach to the repression of religion had taken the place of the earlier campaign for atheistic doctrine.

Statement of Hon. Richard Schifter, *Congressional Record*, July 31, 1986, pp. H5229–H5230.

Although Easter is the most important and elaborately celebrated of all Russian Orthodox holidays, the grandiose Easter services that Westerners often observe in big city churches are generally more lavish than typical rural Easter services.

Kevin R. Locke, Closer Image Studios, © 1988.

Atheism was undoubtedly an important element of the ideological foundation on which the Bolsheviks erected their state. But, like other facets of that ideology, the commitment to atheism has been significantly attenuated. In this, the 69th year of its existence, the Soviet state is committed largely to maintaining in power its ruling class. . . . It is in this context that the Soviet attitude toward religion can be readily understood. To the extent to which religion can serve the ruling class it will be used. To the extent to which it interferes with the objectives of the ruling class it will be suppressed. . . .

The Soviet government allows the performance of traditional rituals, traditional prayers, and traditional religious practices which do not involve significant interaction among religious believers. To illustrate the point I just made: believers may pray together, may sing together, but they may not engage in discussions on religious topics.

What is true of the individual believer, is also true of the clergy. The clergy may perform rituals, may lead congregations in prayer, but may not otherwise interact with believers. Moreover, what is expected of the clergy is support of the state when called upon, including support of the state's foreign policy objectives at international gatherings or on visits abroad. There are some clergymen who may perform the tasks assigned to them by the state out of conviction. There are others who view these tasks as the price they must pay in order to be able to carry on their religious traditions. . . .

What the visitors don't see is what goes on with regard to religious observance in the Soviet Union outside the officially sanctioned ceremonial occasions. What they don't see are the unlicensed activities which are carried on illegally and at serious risk to the participants. What the totalitarian system of the Soviet Union does not tolerate is any form of association of individuals outside the duly licensed pattern. . . .

To the chagrin of the authorities, interest in religion on the part of the Soviet people has been on the increase in recent years. This has included not only participation in governmentally-authorized religious obser-vance but also in what in the Soviet Union are deemed illegal religious activities. Violations of the law have become too numerous to permit them to be enforced rigidly and consistently. . . .

The practices which I have here described are all in contravention of the provisions of such international instruments as the Universal Declaration of Human Rights and the Declaration Against Religious Intolerance, documents approved by the General Assembly of the United Nations without objection from the Soviet Union. They are also in violation of the Helsinki Final Act, a document subscribed to in 1975 by General Secretary Brezhnev. . . .

What we who believe in freedom of religion need to do is make it clear that such conduct is not acceptable, that it will be noted, will be publicized, and the Soviet Union will be criticized for its failure to observe the internationally-recognized standards of freedom of reli-gion. **"**

An opinion quite different from Schifter's is expressed in the following excerpts from a recent book by Howard Parsons, a professor of philosophy at an American university. This writer takes a different stance on the history of religion in the Soviet Union since the revolution. He points the finger at Orthodoxy for its abuses before the separation of church and state and suggests that, in the context of Russian history, the present is an improvement over the past.

" In accordance with the constitution, the laws, and social practice in the U.S.S.R., Christians today are free to believe and to worship in keeping with their convictions. They are likewise free to organize congregations, to rent, construct, and use buildings for the purpose of worship, to hold services, to conduct rituals and celebrate religious holidays, and in these ways and others to transmit their faith to the younger generation. Some denominations — the

Howard L. Parsons, *Christianity Today in the U.S.S.R.* (New York: International Publishers, 1987), pp. 153–160.

Russian Orthodox, Roman Catholic, Armenian Apostolic, Lutheran, Georgian Orthodox — have their own seminaries in the U.S.S.R. Church leaders have free access to the leaders of other denominations in the Christian faith and other faiths in the U.S.S.R. as well as to their counterparts abroad.

Many people in the West perceive the Revolution of 1917 as the initiation of the repression of Christianity. But in several senses the reverse was the case. By the Revolution scores of millions of Christians were liberated from the long drawn-out sufferings and terror of "theocratic caesaropapism." . . . The faithful of Orthodoxy were liberated from the arbitrary and cruel rule of the hierarchy, some of whom were shaken out of their autocratic assumptions by the popular thrust of the Revolution. The small sects and the denominations like the Baptists, who had been suppressed minorities under the iron heel of Orthodoxy, enjoyed a new freedom. Comparing their prerevolutionary state, both mundane and spiritual, with their postrevolutionary state, the vast majority of the faithful today would not care to turn the clock of history back.

But this liberation was not an unmixed blessing. The wholesale and merciless oppression of tsarism and the Orthodox Church, once toppled, produced a bitter reaction against Christianity among its victims. Once the centuries-old burden had been lifted from peasants and workers, once the huge difference that liberation made dawned on them, their resentment often knew no bounds and could not be contained. And it deepened, and their zeal was still more energized, when they listened to the acute critique that the trained Communists brought to the ideological struggle against religion. The result was an excessive crusade in both theory and practice — a result that Soviet scholars today are ready to admit.

Like believers in other faiths, all Christians with few exceptions accept the conditions, limits, opportunities, and moral values of Soviet society and contribute to it. They are ready and willing to live in it, obey its laws, work in and for it, and labor alongside others to solve their common problems. They subscribe to its basic moral values, norms, and aims. They try to carry out these in their personal and social lives. . . .

Under the constitution Christians enjoy the same freedoms and rights as everyone else — the right to work and to choose one's type of job in accordance with one's "inclination, abilities, training and education, with due account of the needs of society"; the right to rest and leisure; the right to health protection; [etc.]. . . . Such rights are guaranteed to everyone quite apart from personal belief and ideology; for Article 52 of the constitution guarantees to all "freedom of conscience, that is, the right to profess or not to profess any religion, and to conduct religious worship or atheistic propaganda." Thus it is forbidden by law to require one to state one's belief on any official form or document. Refusal of a job or of admission to a school or college to any citizen, or expulsion from a

To what extent are disagreements among Westerners about the state of religious freedom in the Soviet Union disputes about facts or disputes about values?

job or school, on the basis of belief is contrary to law and punishable by law. Likewise interference with the performance of a religious ritual and with the distribution of atheistic propaganda is illegal.

I have heard from Soviet people occasional stories of the denial of educational rights to religious persons, and critical literature is quick to make such allegations but thin in their substantiation. But we should not be surprised at the existence of more than a few such cases, considering circumstances of Soviet life and history. . . .

For many years a loud hue and cry has been raised in the West by those who have supposed that "religious dissenters" [in the Soviet Union] have been tried, convicted, sentenced, fined, and jailed for their religious beliefs. But this supposition is not supported by the evidence. People are punished for specific acts of law-breaking. If a specific illegal act, such

Living mainly in regions bordering Mongolia, Buddhists remain on the fringe of Soviet society and are generally left alone or ignored by the government.
Tass from Sovfoto.

REGISTRATION REQUIREMENTS FOR RELIGIOUS ASSOCIATIONS

At the heart of much of the tension in church-state relations in the Soviet Union is the registration requirement. According to a law passed in 1929, all religious groups must obtain permission from the government to exist and function. If a group meets regularly for religious purposes without registering, its members are liable to criminal prosecution for "violating the laws on separation of church and state." The penalty for this crime ranges from a fine of fifteen rubles to as much as three years of imprisonment and can be supplemented by additional penalties.

There are many congregations which are not registered. Some denominations have been declared ineligible for registration because the government deems their practices to be socially harmful. Such groups include the Eastern Rite Catholics, Jehovah's Witnesses, True Orthodox Christians, and some Pentecostal and Adventist sects. Some unregistered congregations belong to denominations which are eligible for registration, but local officials arbitrarily refuse to register them

Приложение № 2

В _____

_____
(указать наименование районного или
городского исполкома Совета депутатов
трудящихся)

Заявление

Для совместного удовлетворения религиозных потребностей, мы, граждане, в числе _____ человек, принадлежащие к_____

_____

_____

_____ , желаем образо-
(вероисповедание, культ, направление или толк)

вать религиозное общество. Район деятельности религиозного общества будет распространяться_____
(село, город, район)

Просим зарегистрировать наше _____
(указать название и адрес общества)

_____
(село, город, район)

Подписи всех учредителей:

Приложение: список учредителей по установленной форме

< ____ > _____ 19 ___ г.

(see box, pp. 148–149). Still other congregations refuse to accept registration, even when officials offer it, because they believe that they would violate the principles of their religion if they did so. (See next box for example.)

There are many illegal congregations, for when a congregation is not registered, it breaks the law simply by meeting. These congregations are not, however, all treated in the same way. For example, in some areas, local officials know about the illegal congregations but leave them alone. In other places, officials take action against a congregation sporadically in the form of fines and short prison terms, but the believers go on meeting pretty much openly. In some cases, officials make a concerted effort to prevent the group from meeting and the believers are forced to meet clandestinely. What the officials do seems to depend partly on what religion the congregation is practicing and partly on the attitude of the officials themselves.

REGISTRATION PROCEDURES

1. Application for registration: The group desiring to register fills out a simple form, indicating its wish to register. That form says: "To _____ (name of local executive committee of the soviet of workers' deputies). DECLARATION. For joint satisfaction of religious needs, we, citizens, numbering _____ persons, belonging to _____ (name of religion) wish to form a religious society. The region of activity of the religious society will incorporate _____ (village, city, or district). We request registration of our _____ (name and address of society) _____ (village, city, or district)."

2. Signatures of charter members: The list asks for the following information for each founding member, of which there must be at least twenty: full name; year and place of birth; occupation, position and place of employment; address of residence; signature.

3. Certificate of registration: The registration is confirmed on a form which says: "Hereby registration is confirmed, on the basis of the decision of the Council on Religious Affairs of the Council of Ministers of the U.S.S.R. of (date) of 19 (year), protocol no. _____ for religious society (group) of believers of _____ (religion) _____ (besides place of meeting show also the region of activity of the society). Commissioner of the Council on Religious Affairs of the Council of Ministers of the U.S.S.R. _____ (region, territory, republic). _____ (date)."

as organizing a congregation without registering it with the government or printing and distributing an unlicensed religious tract is carried out, what is punishable is not the religious content of such an act but the status of the act under the law. Critics may object that the law is too restrictive. [It] may or may not be so; in any case, that is an issue for the Soviet people to decide. Furthermore, secular laws generally do not protect religious people *ad libitum*. From time to time in the United States one reads of a person who murders another "because God told me to do so." But to try and imprison such a murderer is not regarded here as an infringement on the person's religion. That Americans may print and distribute unlicensed religious tracts shows that the legal bounds we draw around religion are different from those in the Soviet Union.

TO REGISTER OR NOT TO REGISTER

The forms used for registration seem to be very simple and straightforward (see box, pp. 142–143). Why, then, are there problems? The religious believers who have been most outspoken in their refusal to register are the dissident Baptists of the Council of Churches of Evangelical Christians-Baptists (C.C.E.C.B.). The C.C.E.C.B. is an unofficial body which opposes the officially recognized leadership of the large Protestant denomination, the All-Union Council of Evangelical Christians-Baptists (A.U.C.E.C.B.). The following C.C.E.C.B. declaration explains why this group conscientiously refuses to submit to registration. The declaration is in the form of a letter to Protestant congregations.

Bratsky listok (Fraternal Leaflet), no. 1–3 (1975), quoted in *Religion in Communist Dominated Areas*, vol. 14, no. 7–9 (1975), pp. 114–117.

" **U**nder the guise of the law they [i.e., the registering authorities] present to us something that is contrary to it and, in undertaking the obligation to fulfill the legislation on cults, congregations violate the law and depart from the commands of Christ.

The point here is that relations between Church and State are entirely regulated, not by the law, but by a whole series of secret instructions and resolutions, directed to the struggle against the church. These instructions are not law, but should only explain the law, without exceeding its limits. However, they grossly contradict the law and even contain points categorically prohibited by the Decree of 1918.

Contrary to law, these instructions require the church and its members to submit to state agencies systematic and detailed information about the internal affairs of the congregation and about all the changes within. . . . These instructions literally turn officers of the congregation and ministers into state

And the definition of those bounds did not drop out of the sky; it came out of seventeenth century England and the struggle of political and religious radicals against the Crown and our own distinctive economic, political, and religious history — as the Soviet definition of the legal position of religion came out of their history. "

The positive tone of Parson's description of religion in the Soviet Union contrasts sharply with what Schifter and Solzhenitsyn and others say. The difference is not so much a matter of factual accuracy as it is personal predilection. People who see things differently than Parsons cannot put their finger on one of his statements and say, "this is a clear

informers. . . .

We always fully recognize and respect the government as such. In our Christian work there are no signs of a disloyal attitude toward the state, as the authorities themselves know well. . . .

The sin of cooperation by the All-Union Council of Evangelical Christians-Baptists with the authorities is the cause of the division and sufferings of the people of God. When representatives of the Council of Churches of Evangelical Christians-Baptists pointed out that cooperation with the authorities is wrong, representatives of the A.U.C.E.C.B. declared: "Since authority is from God, it means that the KGB is also of God. We should give the information which the authorities demand of us." To the present, the A.U.C.E.C.B. has insisted that we submit to the same legal authority. . . .

If the registering agencies could resolve the question of reg-istration without establishing any illegal conditions, and in accordance with the Decree of 1918 and the Constitution of our country, then these acute problems would not arise . . . We must recognize that, contrary to law, the registration of congregations has become a matter of forbidding or permitting: a congregation agrees to accept the conditions that are ruinous for the church — it is registered and consequently its activity is permitted; it does not accept such conditions — it is not registered, its meetings are dispersed, buildings are confiscated, believers are fined, ministers are sent to prison and into exile.

Essentially, this protracted battle is an argument concerning the church, involving the question: who will rule the church, Christ or those who call themselves His enemies? "

error of fact." But they can — and do — challenge the implications of his writings. For example, in the first paragraph Parsons uses the word "free" three times in listing a broad range of religious activities. That word hardly fits the Soviet situation. It is true that the law permits the activities on Parson's list in the sense that they are not legally forbidden. But believers are not "free" to carry out their religious activities whenever or wherever they reasonably desire. Laws narrowly circumscribe religious activities, and local officials frequently add their own restrictions, often in violation of the law. Thus, believers have often found themselves not "free." Moreover, Parsons does not even mention activities prohibited by Soviet law that believers elsewhere consider a natural and vital part of their religion: holding classes, preaching in public, providing charity, broadcasting worship services, and running parochial schools.

Parson's description illustrates how an observer's frame of reference changes the way a situation is perceived. According to his interpretation, the Soviet situation is understandable, defensible, and therefore tolerable, while others find it abhorrent. How sympathetic or hostile people feel toward the principles which the Soviet government espouses inescapably colors their assessment of the facts, and their own political, religious ethical, and even artistic values affect their judgement.

To whatever extent knowledgeable observers may disagree about the degree of religious freedom in the Soviet Union, they usually agree that religion is not only surviving but also growing vigorously in a profusion of forms, both traditional and nontraditional, highly organized and very informal.

Since the mid-1970s, a wide range of witnesses, including new emigrants from the country, Soviet church leaders, and writers of antireligous literature, have been talking about a "religious renaissance" in the Soviet Union. They have pointed to the obvious increase in the numbers of persons performing religious ceremonies and attending religious services — many of them young adults who had been educated in schools with atheist teachers and raised by nonreligious parents. Atheist writers sometimes raise the subject of the "religious renaissance" with the purpose of denying its existence; but it often seems that their eagerness to declare that there is no such renaissance provides evidence of its reality.

While more and more people, including the young, have rediscovered traditional religion within the synagogues and churches, non-traditional religions, such as Hare Krishna, also have drawn many adherents. It is pertinent to note that this renewal of interest in religion began in the Soviet Union at about the same time that people were talking about the "Jesus movement," the "resurgence of the religious right" (traditional fundamentalism), and the "journey to the east" (interest in Asian religions) in the United States.

Some Soviet citizens have explored traditional religions in unofficial study groups like the "Christian Seminar on Problems of the Religious Renaissance," which is described in the following excerpt from an article by a British scholar.

"

The Christian Seminar was formed to meet a need among young, newly-converted Orthodox Christians in the U.S.S.R. Many of these young people with intellectual tastes needed a forum where they could discuss their faith. Alexander Ogorodnikov, a student who had recently become a member of the Russian Orthodox Church [i.e., baptized as an Orthodox believer] and who felt the need for a religious education and Christian fellowship, founded the Christian Seminar in Moscow in 1974. Dissatisfied with the mere "performance of a religious cult" [note: this refers to the law of 1929 which said that this was all a religious association could do legally], having no opportunity to receive a religious education, and in need of brotherly Christian relations, we began in October 1974 to hold a religio-philosophical seminar. . . . We were . . . convinced that our problems were being raised neither in church sermons, which are the only means for the religious education of believers, nor in the pages of the church journal, the *Journal of the Moscow Patriarchate*, which, moreover, is inaccessible [i.e., unavailable] to the ordinary Christian. Most important of all, in the Russian Church the parish is not like a brotherly community where Christian love of one's neighbor becomes a reality. The State persecutes every manifestation of church life, except for the performance of a "religious cult". Our thirst for spiritual communion, religious education and missionary service runs up against all the might of the State's repressive machinery.

So far as is known, the Christian Seminar has confined its activities to discussing religious questions, usually verbally, but also in writing. Subjects discussed have included the Church and the modern industrial world, *The Two Sources of Morality and Religion* by Bergson, Vladimir Solovyov's concept of the God-Man, and the sermons of Billy Graham. . . . In addition to its discussion, the Christian Seminar began to produce a journal, *Obshchina* (Community), but, unfortunately, this attempt has been thwarted by the authorities. Only one issue of the journal has reached the West. . . . Despite the harmlessness of its activity, the KGB have persecuted the Seminar's members in a manner more appropriate to an armed subversive cell which aims to overthrow the Soviet State. The members of the Seminar have met in private homes for their discussions. On many occasions they have faced police harassment. . . .

As of 1980, five members of the Christian Seminar have been forcibly interned in psychiatric hospitals . . . [and] five members are in prison. . . .

The Christian Seminar has made contact with other young people's religious (mainly Orthodox) groups in the U.S.S.R. . . . The Seminar sees

Jane Ellis "U.S.S.R.: The Christian Seminar," *Religion in Communist Lands*, vol. 8, no. 2 (Summer 1980), pp. 92–97. (Text of the letter, "Young Russia to Young America," is from *Sparks*, October–December 1981, pp. 4–5.)

"Our thirst for spiritual communion, religious education and missionary service runs up against all the might of the state's repressive machinery."
Founder of "Christian Seminar" Alexander Ogorodnikov

itself as a movement for Russian young people, operating within Russia — no members appear to live in non-Russian republics of the U.S.S.R. — and it made no attempt to export its ideas to the West or to develop contacts abroad until its members began to be persecuted and support from the West was needed. . . . Later the desire for contact with western Christians grew, or at any rate was more openly expressed. Several letters signed by Seminar members have been addressed to young Christians in different countries. . . . One of the most expressive is a letter to American young people which states:

"The time has come for us, living as we do on different continents and raised in different historical traditions, to open our hearts to each other and unite our efforts in creative searching. We feel your influence around us at every step. You have now really become the cultural leaders of man. Because of your example, thousands of young people in our country have broken out of stifling totalitarian ideological constraint. They have become apostates and outsiders. . . . They sing your songs, wear your

THE "APPEARANCE" OF THE VIRGIN MARY

The sighting of the Virgin Mary in three areas of the Ukraine was reported in the *Moscow News*, an official newspaper published in many languages for circulation inside and outside of the Soviet Union.

This incident and others like it, as well as the existence of unofficial religious study groups such as the "Christian Seminar," provide insight into the spiritual longing felt by many Soviet citizens. The article excerpted below sympathetically acknowledges that the Virgin Mary was seen in the Ukraine "because people very much wanted to see her."

"The Inertia of Simplification," *Moscow News*, September 20–27, 1987, p. 13.

"One morning, a girl, a fourth-form pupil in Gurshevo Village (Dragobych District, Lvov Region) came out of her home, looked at the church (which was not in use) and thought she saw a woman's figure on a small balcony. She told her playmates and they ran to look. Adults started to go to the church. A day later crowds went to Grushevo from Dragobych, Truskavets and Lvov. People crowded around the church fence and peered intensively. A woman would cry out suddenly:

"I see! I see!" People rushed to her: "Where?" "Why, there she is, dressed in white, holding a baby in her arms."A couple of days later, Our Lady was "seen" in Ternopol, Ozernaya, Berezhany, and Kamenka-Bugskaya — in a window of a cathedral, on a church roof, on the wall of a hospital, shop or school. There were no mystifications involved, nor any of nature's tricks when sunlight is refracted. The slightest event sparked off people's imagination. The leaves of an aspen tree moved by the wind

clothes, and accept your fundamental values, especially those of freedom, sincerity, humanity, and love of the earth. Renouncing an existence grounded in conformity, fear, egoism, and calculation, they embrace a life which is socially less significant but morally more pure. . . . We are grateful to you for that spirit of freedom which has spread to us through the crevices of the customhouses and the infernal wailing of radio jammers.

"But we also want to tell you that from this call arises another call. . . . At the brink of human despair, having caught a glimpse of the abyss, we heard the saving call — this was the voice of our predecessors, our fathers. We found Russia. Like archaeologists, we saw the signs of Russian religious history and culture even through the curtain of misinformation and prohibition. The mystery of the presence of the Church in Russia and Christ in the world was partially revealed to us. We understood that only Christ can free and unite us as persons. So we have come to the Church in order to find there freedom in Christ. . . . In the

are reflected on windowpane, or there is a curious spot of rust on a roof — and someone inevitably starts yelling with elation — "I see!"

Virgin Mary was seen because people very much wanted to see her . . . The events we're speaking about are clearly defined in space — Our Lady "appeared" in three regions of the Ukraine — Lvov, Ivanofrankovsk and Ternopol (in the past this area was called Galicia) . . . Not ill-wishers, but conventional, earthly misfortunes brought together those who wished to see the Virgin Mary.

Offences are especially painful for those with religious feelings. "Where didn't we write to, so that our community would be registered."

Moscow News has already written about this, but the prob-

lem remains. It is especially grave here — in the western regions of the Ukraine. Believers ask, with full legal right, for a church to be opened, but they inevitably meet with refusals. Last year, 120 of such complaints were sent to superior organizations in the Ternopol Region alone.

The local leaders and the Council on Religious Affairs attached to the Council of Ministers of the Ukraine apparently think they can "defend" atheism only by violating the law and trampling on the believers' rights. The result was the explosion of religious fervour this summer — mass pilgrimages to the places where the Virgin Mary "appeared. . . ."

Only major social transformations can change the composition of the soil which begets the need for supernatural help. Only such

transformations will rid man of all and sundry fears, improve his conditions of life, protect his rights and guard him against the arbitrariness of bureaucrats, against caddishness and heartlessness.

And it is even more important that the present-day movement toward democracy and glasnost gives people back their dignity, and the possibility for each individual to feel that he or she is a personality and not just a grain of sand, carried at will by the wind.

"

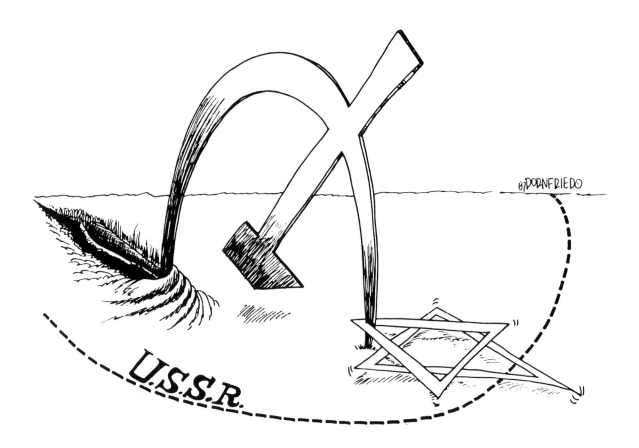

depths of our beings our souls hear the words of Sergei of Radonezh, the spiritual mentor of the Russian people, 'Looking at the unity of the Holy Trinity is to conquer the hateful divisions of this world. . . .' We sense that we are the living material from which Christ will create everything new — a new society, a new culture, a new family, a new type of man and a new type of woman. In essence, he will create a new people out of us. But at the same time this is a returning to the original roots of the Russian soul, flung open toward God's world and all peoples in it.

"Rejecting the ideologies which greedily grasp for our souls, we long to build an independent and inwardly free world, a world full of love and meaning."

How do Soviet officials explain the persistence of religion in the Soviet Union?

A similar renewal of interest in religion was observed among Jews, although it is apparently quite limited. The next excerpt, by an American political scientist, is taken from an article tracing the history of Jewish culture in the Soviet period. Zvi Gitelman makes a distinction between official and unofficial Jewish culture, the former being "an artificial creation of the 1920s, . . . limited to one language, Yiddish," while the latter is a genuine product of Jewish creativity, expressed in Hebrew and Russian. Gitelman's analysis of the causes of this religious renewal to some extent also applies to non-Jewish persons whose attraction to religion seems to be growing.

" In a word, then, I think official Jewish culture is a closed chapter in Soviet Jewish history. Remarkably, however, simultaneously with this closure, there has begun a new chapter, and that is unofficial Jewish culture. This takes the basic form of a study of Hebrew and Jewish history and a kind of quest for religion.

The study of Hebrew has now gone on unofficially and at best semi-legally since the rise of the emigration (or "aliya") movement. While it is limited to the large cities, and to the intelligentsia in those cities, it has made quite a significant impact even on those who do not participate in it. Those who are engaged in it, whether as students or teachers, seem to have developed a remarkably efficient teaching method. I have been greatly impressed by the amount of Hebrew people have been able to learn in these conditions, and perhaps the way they have done so may be a model for others.

Along with this has come a very limited religious revival which has occurred also in other contexts. . . . Perhaps revival is too strong a word to use, and it would be more correct to say that this religious interest is the effect of three causes. One is simply the search for an alternative both to Marxism-Leninism as well as the growing Soviet materialism. I think there is considerable disenchantment with both of these dominant value systems.

Secondly, there is a recognition by those who began in the Zionist movement or who came to it after leaving the Democratic movement, that the further one looks into the history of the Jewish people and their culture, the greater looms the role of their religion. For those who are able to make a personal commitment to religion, this is a logical next step. Clearly, not everyone can or wants to do that. But there is a logical connection between national consciousness and religious observance if one has theological conviction.

Thirdly, and the most recent phenomenon, perhaps only of the last few years, is, in the absence of external emigration, an increase in internal emigration. It is obvious to Soviet citizens today that the immediate possibilities for leaving the country are very small. . . . What then should one do if interested in Jewish commitment? Without being cynical, I suggest that one alternative is to turn to religion. We have seen that many individuals who began as secular Zionists have become increasingly personally religious. This is a phenomenon which may be growing and cannot be dismissed out of hand. . . .

Finally, as regards religion, the synagogue remains the only physical central address of the Jewish people in the Soviet Union and it has therefore acquired a kind of symbolic and social importance, no less than its religious importance. There are no other places in the country

Zvi Gitelman, "The Abridgement of the Rights of Soviet Jews in the Fields of Nationality, Culture, and Religion," *Soviet Jewish Affairs*, vol. 15, no. 1 (February 1985), pp. 79–87.

"The synagogue remains the only physical central address of the Jewish people in the Soviet Union and it has therefore acquired a kind of symbolic and social importance, no less than its religious importance."

where large numbers of Jews can meet together. It is the last remaining symbol of Jewish historical and religious culture on a communal basis. It therefore serves as a magnet for many who are not particularly religious but who do wish to identify themselves as Jews and to meet other like-minded people. **"**

Religious activity among Muslims has increased also. This excerpt from a relatively long article in *Pravda*, the central newspaper of the Communist Party, carried the dateline, Dushanbe, the capital of the Tadzhik Republic, which borders Afghanistan.

A. Tursunov, "Atheism and Culture," *Pravda*, January 16, 1987, in *Current Digest of Soviet Press*, vol. 39, no. 3, p. 8.

" t is no secret that religious feeling is on the rise here and there in our country, and not just among people who are not permanently employed, but among young people as well. It is now apparent that the earlier notion of a direct connection between the degree of religious feeling and the level of a person's education was an oversimplification. There are, after all, known cases of members of the intelligentsia (including teachers) joining a religion, to say nothing of the fascination with all sorts of occult "sciences" on the part of people with a higher education (and even advanced degrees!). At the same time, in declaring that religion is a thing of the past, we cannot simply brush aside the obvious fact that the overwhelming majority of believers were born in the Soviet period and were brought up in an atheist environment. . . .

The number of followers of Islam, for example, is increasing not only as a result of natural population growth, but also via a huge number of converts (Islam is ceasing to be a purely Eastern phenomenon). How does it manage to do this? Many interrelated causes and conditions could be pointed out here. We will point out only one, perhaps a rather important one. That is Islam's capacity for spiritual mimicry, its ability to adapt itself to local spiritual needs and aspirations and then adapt those needs and aspirations to its own ends. . . .

Let's take the problem of religion among women, for example. At first glance, the root cause of the relatively large influence of Islam on Central Asian women is the fact that fewer of them are employed outside the home. But behind that is a whole chain of other factors. Thus, a large percentage of those not employed in production are mothers with many children. . . . If we add that, from the beginning, religion has focused special attention on the so-called ultimate conditions of human existence (birth, death, life's tragedies), then the substantial role of the above mentioned factor in the growth of religion among women will become obvious. For as Lenin noticed, "Gemuth, (feeling — Ed.), the practical side, the search for something better, for protection, for help, etc., is extremely important in religion." Obviously, it is our under-

With the Muslim population growing at two to three times the rate of the country's Slavic and European population, and with fundamentalism gaining momentum in many Muslim communities, nationality conflicts in Soviet Muslim regions are rapidly becoming a major source of instability within the U.S.S.R.

Soviet Life.

estimation of this that also explains the return of some pensioners (former atheists!) to the bosom of religion. This "conversion effect" may have both inward causes (such as a spiritual crisis brought about by personal, family or other traumas and upheavals) and outward ones (such as a new appreciation of social values that the person had held previously).

"

The interest of Soviet officialdom in the growth of Islam in the Soviet Union is explained in the following excerpt by Alexander Bennigsen, professor of Turkic history at the Ecole des Hautes Etudes en Sciences Sociales in Paris and a leading Western expert on Islam in the U.S.S.R. In the article from which the following excerpt is taken, he shows why the revival of Islam is viewed with alarm in the Soviet Union.

Alexandre Bennigsen, "Winning the War for Afghanistan," *National Review*, May 8, 1987, pp. 36–38.

"**F**or sixty years, Moscow has been trying, unsuccessfully, to eradicate Islam. In 1917, in Czarist Russia's Muslim areas, there were thirty thousand mosques, each with its attached Koranic school. Today fewer than 450 mosques remain. . . . For more than half a century, Moscow kept the Soviet Muslim population, heirs to an ancient and brilliant Irano-Turkic culture, isolated from the rest of the Muslim world.

But by invading Afghanistan, the Red Army itself lifted the Iron Curtain that has artificially isolated Soviet Tadzhiks, Uzbeks, and Turkomans from their brethren in Afghanistan and Iran. . . . In part because of this mingling of Soviet and Afghan Muslims, the new spirit of the Afghan Jihad [holy war] is slowly but steadily spreading into Soviet

While these Hare Krishna followers practicing their faith in a Leningrad park do not typify most Soviet youth, they do represent a group that, far from accepting atheism, has turned to new, nontraditional religions.

Courtesy of Michele Kelemen.

Muslim territories. The war in Afghanistan is followed with an intense and passionate interest by nearly all Muslims in Central Asia. In the last two years, strong evidence, unreported in the world press, has emerged of a number of acts of solidarity between Central Asian Muslims and the Afghan resistance. . . . A number of Soviet Muslims—Uzbeks, Tadzhiks, and Turkomans — fled to Afghanistan; some have joined Afghan resistance guerilla units. . . . Because of the success of the Afghan resistance, Islam — which Soviet propaganda has portrayed as an outdated medieval relic—now appears to be younger and more dynamic than aging, dusty, and bureaucratic Marxism-Leninism. For the first time since the October Revolution, Central Asian Muslims have rediscovered the Muslim "ummah," the "community of believers." They have discovered a new sense of kinship with the Afghans and, through them, with the entire Muslim world. . . .

Soviet officialdom is clearly worried about the adverse political effects of the Afghan war. The Soviet mass media themselves have begun linking it with the Islamic religious revival in Central Asia. This revival is not a growth in the domesticated "official Islam" the Soviets permit, but an outbreak of radical, strongly anti-Communist and anti-Russian Islam such as the Sufi brotherhoods. . . . (Sufi brotherhoods are secret Islamic societies. Though forbidden by Soviet legislation, they are of growing importance within the U.S.S.R. Each Sufi brotherhood is bound by a complicated set of rules governing every aspect of an adept's life. They are united as well by a common raison d'etre: the defense of Islam against the rule of the unbelievers and the turncoat Muslims who serve them.) . . . Several Soviet rulers have publicly worried that the Islamic revival is exacerbating anti-Russian sentiment among the Muslims of Central Asia.

"Several Soviet rulers have publicly worried that the Islamic revival is exacerbating anti-Russian sentiment among the Muslims of Central Asia."

The *Pravda* article about Islam in the Tadzhik Republic mentioned that some well-educated people had turned to "occult sciences." The growth of interest in nontraditional religion among the intelligentsia is an important development in the Soviet Union. In 1988, the American Helsinki Commission reported that 10,000 Soviet citizens participate in the religion of Krishna Consciousness. This number is significant given that the movement began only about fifteen years ago. The spread of this religion to cities throughout the Soviet Union has evoked considerable attention in the Soviet media, including television programs in 1987 in the capitals of Armenia and Ukraine, as well as in Moscow.

The Hare Krishna movement is just one of several nontraditional religions that have profoundly disturbed the leaders of the antireligious establishment and those whose task it is to neutralize the attraction of religion, especially for the younger people and people who are well educated. In early 1988, the director of the Institute of Scientific

Atheism wrote in the Soviet journal *Science and Religion,* "In recent years in a number of large cities there have appeared adherents of the so-called nontraditional cults, especially among students and intellectuals" (January 1988, p. 11). Interest in nontraditional religions suggests that lectures on scientific atheism and secular ceremonies substituting for baptisms, weddings, confirmations, and funerals have not satisfied the human thirst for religion.

Details about Hare Krishna activity come from an extraordinary number of official, and consequently hostile, newspaper accounts as well as from the followers of Krishna Consciousness who send information out of the country through unofficial channels. These accounts show that Krishna adherents have been treated in the same manner as the Orthodox young people of the Christian Seminars. Although official and unofficial sources present divergent opinions and interpretations, they agree on two points: the Krishna movement is meeting some deeply felt needs on the part of Soviet intellectuals, and officials have treated its followers as both criminal and insane. The following excerpt is from an official source.

B. Timofeyev, "Under the Protection of Magnetism," *Trud* (Labor), August 28, 1983, in *Current Digest of Soviet Press,* vol. 36, no. 9, p. 25.

"After work they gathered at the apartment of their leader, or sometimes at the home of one of the group members. They lighted sticks of incense and sat before a portrait of the Hindu god Krishna. Those present were given beets, green peas and dried bread crusts, which they ate with great reverence. This was not simply food, but a "prasad" — a time-honored ritual meal. Candles were lit and to the monotonous accompaniment of a tambourine, the group chanted mantras.

These were not aborigines of some forgotten tribe, but people who thought of themselves as intellectuals; many, such as V. Kozelsky, a senior engineer in the Urals power system, had higher degrees.

This all started a few years ago when a so-called "health group" was formed in Sverdlovsk by a certain Valeria Aleksandrovna Sukhova. . . .

So fragrant incense and candles burned, while doleful mantras were chanted by an editor in the Russian Republic Office of Trade Advertising, a senior instructor in the Russian language department of the state university, senior researchers in the Urals Research Institute of Chemistry, and others. And V. Bochkova, an astronomer, who has come to believe in the existence of the god Krishna, has herself become not only a servant but a zealous propagandist of this mystical dogma."

The literature of the antireligious establishment, while repeatedly proclaiming that religion is steadily dying out and that there is no such thing as a "religious renaissance," also supplies sufficient information about religion in the Soviet Union to corroborate evidence from other sources that many young people are turning to religion.

The following excerpt, from an article in the popular antireligious magazine, *Science and Religion,* provides advice for people who give public lectures as a regular part of atheist educational programs. The author suggests that to make the point that false information about the status of religion is being circulated, lecturers should discuss freedom of conscience, alleged violations of human rights, and the so-called "myth of the religious renaissance."

"Despite the sharp crisis which it is experiencing, religion continues . . . in the Soviet Union as the only legally existing ideology that is alien to Marxism-Leninism. In these conditions, our enemies, on the one hand, persistently try to establish bridges between foreign anti-Soviet religious centers and believers in the U.S.S.R. and, on the other, calculate that in the world of capitalism, many religiously minded people are not immune to repeated assertions that in the Soviet Union the adherents of religion are objects of cruel persecution. . . . [The author goes on to give an outline for the lecture.]

In the third part of the lecture it is necessary to deny the myth of the imaginary "religious renaissance" in the U.S.S.R., about which today the anti-Soviet falsifiers speak so avidly. It will be helpful to explain to the listeners, right off, that this fantasy is closely connected with notions of the persecution of believers which have been discussed already. According to the "logic" of our opponents, the supposed attempts to eradicate religion by administrative measures have led only to its strengthening and to a "religious renaissance."

Here the slanderers contradict themselves. For if one starts from the idea that the church in our country is oppressed and doomed to silence, then how can one understand the triumphant reports of bourgeois propaganda about "always overflowing churches"? It must be concluded that at least one, perhaps both, of these ideas are baseless myths.

What supports the fantasy of a "religious renaissance"? Practically nothing at all if one does not consider the earnest wish of the falsifiers of the Soviet way of life to discover what does not exist. Overcrowded churches? Well, sometimes that can be observed, but by no means everywhere, and only on days of the most important religious festivals.

And what else is there? Crosses on the Kremlin cathedrals, witnessing that the "godless regime" has been forced to reckon with the wave of religious "renaissance" that is rolling over the popular masses? Or concern for the preservation of the monuments of antiquity, which include churches? For the clerical "restorers of holy Rus" all of these are indubitable signs of a "spiritual rebirth." But for us they simply constitute the Leninist approach to the cultural achievements of the nations of the U.S.S.R., for "by no means has Marxism discarded the

M. Goldenberg, "Against Falsification of the Situation of Religion in the U.S.S.R.," *Nauka i religiia* (Science and Religion), October 1984, pp. 26–30.

THE SPIRITUAL PILGRIMAGE OF VLADIMIR PORESH

Vladimir Poresh was about 25 years old when he was baptized into the Orthodox Church. His evolution from materialism to religious faith is described here by Tatyana Shchipkova, a teacher at the Smolensk Pedagogical Institute, who refers to him as Volodya.

Tatyana Shchipkova, "The Spiritual Pilgrimage of Vladimir Poresh," *Religion in Communist Lands*, vol. 8, no. 2 (1980), pp. 101–103.

" I n the autumn of 1966 my first-year French class was joined by Volodya Poresh, who was then 17 years old — a tall adolescent with large hands and honest, kind eyes, a simple person without the faintest suspicion of the existence of the camps [detaining religious prisoners] and convinced that religion developed as the result of fear of the forces of nature. He soon began to work in my group. After each lecture he would ask me questions, delighting me with the lack of banality of his vision and the accuracy of his argument. It was a pity to lose such a pupil, but I was glad when he was able to go on to Leningrad University.

He was very much alone in Leningrad. Thrown back on his own reflections, he at last came face to face with questions of universal significance. His anxiety found expression in his letters of that period. First of all he realized the senselessness of life without spirituality.

All too often recently I have been faced with questions that have no answer, like a machine in perpetual motion. It is as if I have gone into a room where I have seen a mechanism — no one knows how it works or the reason it is there, or even why it was made. First of all, I saw that the world is senseless, like a cat running across the street. Everything is senseless from begin-

most valuable achievements of the bourgeois era, but, on the contrary, has adopted and adapted everything that was of value in the more than two thousand years of development of human thought and culture. Only by further work on this basis and in the same direction can a truly proletarian culture be realized."

With special persistence our ideological opponents seek out "proofs" of this "renaissance" among the youth, which is easily explained: because whichever ideology wins the minds of the youth today will determine the spiritual climate of Soviet society tomorrow.

The West German magazine *Osteuropa* comes to the conclusion that while "the old generation of Bolsheviks hated the Orthodox Church with conviction and fanaticism," now among a large part of the youth there is to be observed an attraction toward it going hand in hand with "disillusionment with Communist ideals." This fabrication can be debunked by the lecturer if he will turn to the believers themselves, if there are any in the auditorium, who will undoubtedly confirm that in

When used to describe the status of religion in the Soviet Union, what is meant by "renaissance"?

ning to end. . . . It is senseless to keep searching, but I shall go on searching for this very reason.

At last, after these meanderings, the crisis came in 1970: the total recognition of his own spiritual enslavement and that of everyone around him. He came to Smolensk for the winter holidays. He seemed so completely changed that I thought there had been some sort of catastrophe and fearfully asked him what had happened. He sat down without taking off his coat and said: "I understand everything!" "What do you mean, everything?" "Everything!" I understood of course because I, too, could not think of anything else at that time and had reached the same dead end. We were both heading towards the same conclusion in different ways, with an age difference of 19 years. . . . "I came to the conclusion that God exists. He cannot not exist, otherwise there would be no sense in anything." But faith was still along way from this deduction. To become involved in life, discover its meaning and become its embodiment — that was what he was striving for.

I forget which month it was in 1973 when he arrived in a joyful and enthusiastic mood, and told me: "I have begun a new phase of my life: I've got to know someone called Sasha Ogorodnikov. We have decided to create a culture within a culture." His search for a spiritual foundation for this culture led him to Russian religious philosophy: "Besides this, I am reading Russian philosophy now . . . I am discovering a number of very interesting things. I have read Nicholas Berdyayev's essay on Khomiakov, a few things by Vladimir Solovyov and some Dostoyevsky. . . ."

Volodya was baptized on 20 October 1974. The slow, difficult process of involvement in the Church began. . . .

After graduation from Leningrad University, Poresh worked as a specialist in Romance philology in the Academy of Sciences Library. He became a leader of the Leningrad group associated with the Christian Seminar on Problems of the Religious Renaissance. He was arrested 1 August 1979 on the charge of "anti-Soviet agitation and propaganda" because of his part in editing an underground religious journal, *Obshchina*. [Poresh was sentenced in 1980 and released in February 1986.]

"

Orthodox churches (and not in them only) the overwhelming majority of worshippers are old folk. There has been no change of proportion in the direction of youth. Besides, the presence in religious buildings of some young men and women most often is to be explained not by religious motives but by the desire to observe church "exotica" which are passing away. . . .

It is necessary to turn attention also to the way religious articles attract some young men and women. One should suggest that, for example, the conservative French *L'Aurore* would not be able to entitle one of its anti-Soviet diatribes: "Why do so many members of Komsomol wear crosses?" if some of our young dandies were not sporting these decorations.

It is especially necessary to emphasize that the myth about the "religious renaissance" is tied up with the fantasies about another "renaissance," which is supposedly being experienced by our country, the rebirth of nationalistic prejudices.

> **"The religious renaissance reflects a certain profound improvement in the consciousness of the whole of contemporary Soviet society."**

Despite intellectual debates and official interference, religion remains an integral part of everyday life for many Soviet citizens.

AP/Wide World Photos.

At this point one should deal briefly with the preparation by the anti-Soviet emigration for the celebration of the millennium of the "baptism of Rus," as if it were marking the return of the Russian people to the bosom of "its own" religion and a recovery of its "lost national distinctiveness." . . .

These same "renaissance processes," according to these clerical observers, also have reached an impressive extent in regions where there has been wide diffusion of Islam. When, for example, the Swiss Islamic scholar M. Buazar (and not he alone) determines that the number of Muslims in the U.S.S.R. is 50 million, he is including all residents of those republics which can be labelled as "Muslim." In such an approach, even Communists, Komsomol members, and propagandists of scientific atheism are accounted as faithful followers of Allah.

Such "luminaries" of anti-Sovietism as A. Bennigsen and H. Carrere d'Encausse, for example, compose odes of praise in honor of the vestiges of feudalism associated with Islam and attempt to reckon the peoples of a number of our republics as members of some mythical "world Muslim nation." It does not take much insight to figure out that the imagined "renaissance" of Islam has been invented for the provocative and hopeless goals of creating nationalistic and confessional isolation and raising hatred for the Russian and other "Christian" peoples. . . .

Along with the myth about a "religious boom" in our country, there also is much ballyhoo about a corresponding imaginary decline of atheism and of the scientific-materialist worldview as a whole. Supposedly, despite all their efforts, Communists have not been able to achieve their declared aim — to destroy the church and to eradicate religion. For example, the chief ideological mouthpiece of the Catholic Church, the Jesuit journal "Civilta catolika," made such a triumphant declaration. But, it may be asked, where and when have Marxist-Leninists ever declared such an absurd goal?

Attempts to establish the triumph of religion and the bankruptcy of atheism with such inconvenient devices can be opposed by the lecturer with widely known facts and figures. According to Yaroslavsky, by the second half of the thirties, over one third of the population in the village and no less than two thirds in the city had made the break with religion. And by the end of the 1970s, according to sociological research, the number of active believers was no greater than 10 per cent of the adult population of the country.

The real purpose of this article is a puzzle. Supposedly this line of reasoning is for use by lecturers speaking to average Soviet citizens. Why would average citizens need to be told that there is no religious renaissance? How would they have drawn the conclusion that there was one, unless, of course, they had seen some evidence of it? Some Western observers might suggest, perhaps cynically, that the atheist workers need to make claims such as these to show that they are doing their job of combatting religion. Reading this article brings to mind Shakespeare's line that "The lady doth protest too much, methinks."

Perhaps the label "religious renaissance" is a bit grandiose to describe what has been happening in the Soviet Union. That, at least, was the conclusion reached by four Orthodox Christians who held a discussion in Moscow in late 1986 expressly to examine whether or not the religious phenomena of the past decade deserved that label. A tape recording of their conversation was sent to the West. What follows is a portion of that discussion.

" I f "religious renaissance" is no more than a slogan meaning a general growth of religiosity and of the numbers of believers and church folk in the country, as well as an evolution in public attitudes from indifference to sympathy for and interest in the church and religious experience, then the answer here is unquestionable. There is a religious renaissance in Russia.

The religious renaissance reflects a certain profound improvement in the consciousness of the whole of contemporary Soviet society. Its obvious fruits are the overfilled churches, the unprecedented growth of Protestant congregations, and persecuted groups of Orthodox and Baptist youth, and so forth. And this by no means exhausts the present and future experience of the phenomenon we are surveying. . . .

But if one turns away from these indicators toward what is really important, namely the spiritual, then what will the answer be?

In the first place, it is difficult to say that there is a renaissance merely because churches in the cities are over-filled, considering that there are very few functioning churches; this is not a sign of rebirth, but it is the norm. I have been in very many cities of Russia and can testify that — primarily, of course, in district centers widely scattered geographically —there really are young folk in the church as well as the middle aged and children. Participation in rites of baptism of children, weddings, and funerals is especially massive. Unfortunately, it is true, these rites still have, as we know well, the character of something that is purely magical, superstitious, and sometimes even just a national tradition, which, of course, has nothing to do with Christianity and its sacraments.

And nevertheless when I see these people in the churches, what do I say? Do I say to myself that this is a religious renaissance? Of course not. Why should such a high name be given to it? This is people going to church. The people go to church. They should go to church. That is natural. We went a hundred years ago, and we go now, and we will be going a hundred years from now. It is possible to say only that there was in the history of our country a period when people were subjected to repression, the camps, and extermination because they went to church. Now that does not happen. For now, at least.

"Round Table about the Russian Orthodox Church," *Russkaia mysl* (Russian Thought) (published in Paris) April 17, 1987.

In the second place, of course there is a flow of new persons into the church in the 1980s. It still is continuing, more and more new people are coming, and all the time you learn about some one or five or eight persons joining. But to say that this is a massive flow, that for our 270 million this is a very significant and noteworthy phenomenon — that, of course, we cannot do. Unquestionably, all layers and parts and ethnic groups of our society are not being affected by this trend. Nor is there a very large group of pastors who can effectively and adequately serve them. . . .

In the third place, a religious renaissance is a phenomenon with which the society, state and rulers could not fail to reckon. However, this is not happening. . . .

Thus, I would suggest that we call the present process either a religious awakening, which has already been suggested by the other speaker, or a restoration of the status quo. After several decades of very cruel persecution, a certain status quo has been reestablished. As one priest said: "Well, they promised to destroy the social roots of religion, and they destroyed them. And just as soon as they ceased the persecution, the Christians reappeared and again filled the churches." And this is the truth.

"

The church leaders quoted above spoke of churches filled to capacity and a reawakening of interest in religion. Just how many religious believers are there in the Soviet Union?

In his advice to lecturers on atheism, Goldenberg stated that 10 percent of the population were believers. This is a frequently cited figure, but in the next excerpt, William Fletcher, an American scholar, questions its accuracy.

William C. Fletcher, *Soviet Believers* (Lawrence, KS: Regents Press of Kansas, 1981), pp. 201–211.

" The picture that emerges from a survey of Soviet sociology of religion provides useful insights into this important aspect of contemporary society in the U.S.S.R. The picture is not completely clear and sharply defined in all its aspects. Soviet sociological research is by no means free of problems; it is an imperfect tool. . . .

It is a grave misfortune for Soviet sociology of religion that the central problem of the number of believers in Soviet society has still not been resolved. The problem of who is and who is not religious is fundamental to any assessment of other parameters concerning the believing citizens, and until this critical issue is resolved, the potential value of other findings of the research is gravely reduced. . . .

The evidence seems fairly strong that religious belief tends to concentrate among the older people in society. Certainly this would seem to be the case among those who outwardly participate in religious

activities. . . . That belief in God is present (or that active disbelief is absent) among some young people is indubitable; how many of the contemporary youth belong to this category cannot be estimated. . . .

Soviet research also seems to be fairly persuasive in asserting that the majority of religious believers are women. Certainly in the churches, and quite possible absolutely, women believers are more numerous, outnumbering male believers by perhaps three or four to one. . . .

Icons would seem to be exceedingly popular in traditionally Orthodox areas; the great majority of the homes contain icons whether or not the people who live there consider themselves to be believers. When churches are available religious believers apparently attend them fairly regularly, although a significant percentage attend only occasionally. The inadequate number of functioning churches complicates the picture, however. . . .

Religious holidays are widely observed in Soviet society, even among nonbelievers. Strict observance of the various fasting requirements, however, is relatively infrequent. Among the sacraments, baptism is still widely practiced; even nominal unbelievers have the rite performed on their children. [Religious] marriage, by contrast, is rather less popular; civil ceremonies suffice in the great majority of cases. Religious funerals, however, are the most tenacious of the religious rites: a very high percentage of the funerals in the U.S.S.R. are still religious, whether the ceremony is conducted directly or by correspondence. . . .

Returning now to the central problem of the size of the religious sector of the population, it is apparent that Soviet researchers have not yet achieved general agreement among themselves in defining who is

Soviet research indicates that female believers outnumber male believers by three or four to one.

Furnished by the Moscow Patriarchate, Courtesy of J. Martin Bailey.

and who is not religious. Attempts to achieve some sort of behavioral criteria have not been persuasive nor widely accepted. . . . The most general conclusion of Soviet sociologists is that 15 to 20% of the population is religious; as will become apparent below, this figure is unrealistic. While it may be comforting to those who are seeking to confirm the predictions of Marxism, it can only be maintained by a completely uncritical acceptance of some — but by no means all — of the data presented by Soviet sociology of religion, without examination or analysis.

When the great mass of the data is brought together and reviewed, figures below 10% for the number of believers in the U.S.S.R. would not seem to be realistic, for there are too many studies that indicate a higher incidence of religiousness. Conversely, in the Russian areas, figures as high as 50% may seem improbable. Perhaps the best estimate might suggest that in these parts of the country, 25% to 35% of the population continues to be religious.

At first glance, this estimate may seem high. . . . The several large-scale studies consistently yield figures higher than 25%, sometimes higher than 30%. In the Penza study, in which more than 30,000 Soviet citizens were surveyed, it was found that 28.4% were religious. The largest project reported to date, in the Voronezh region, despite its many inadequacies in design and execution, nevertheless indicated that no fewer than 22.4% were classifiable as believers and that an additional 27.8% could be classified as nonreligious but not unbelievers (whatever that may mean; obviously, the possibility must remain that some citizens who believe in God were included in this category). Thus, an aggregate

> "If 45 percent of the population is indeed religious, there must be some 115 million believers in the U.S.S.R."

RUSSIAN GRANDMOTHERS —
"THE BACKBONE OF THE CHURCH"

Dana L. Robert, "Grandmothers and the Millennium of Russian Christianity," *Christian Century*, December 24–31, 1986, pp. 1175f.

"The Russian churches are full of Christians of all ages, but the majority of believers we met at services were elderly women. Like the widows of old, these women are the backbone of the church, keeping it alive through their sacrificial offering, prayers and physical services such as cleaning the buildings and planting flowers. When somebody asked a Russian priest whether it was healthy for the church to be composed of so many aged women, he replied with a story: "In the early days of communism," he said, "many churches were blown up and the priests, monks, and nuns were executed. Lenin argued that once the grandmothers died nobody would remember that there had been a church in Russia. But now Lenin is long dead, and the church is still full of grandmothers who were children when he was alive. As long as the Russian church has its grandmothers, it will survive."

As the millenium of Chris-

estimate of 30% does not seem to be unreasonably high; indeed, lower estimates become increasingly difficult to justify on the basis of the data presented by Soviet sociological research.

But this figure applies only to the predominantly Russian areas. . . .

In non-Russian areas the level of religiousness is much higher than in the Russian areas. An estimate that 60% or more of these people remain religious would seem to be fairly credible. Admittedly, several difficulties are inherent in any estimate such as this. First, the estimate may seem high for the Ukrainians and Belorussians . . . the actual figure for these areas is probably higher than the 30% estimated for the Russian nationality, although it might be debated vigorously whether it in fact is so high as 60%. However, in other areas, 60% may be an unrealistically low figure. Among the Muslim nationalities, who constitute nearly 15% of the population, religion and culture are so intimately identified that it may be quite unrealistic to suggest that more than a fraction are nonreligious in any meaningful way. . . .

Combining these two estimates — 30% for the Russian half of the population, 60% for the rest — yields a composite figure of 45% for the religious sector of the Soviet population. This may seem unexpectedly high; but not all Soviet sociologists would necessarily be surprised by it. V.D. Kobetskii, for example, although he also acknowledges the received estimate of 15 to 20%, remarks that "During the years of Soviet rule, the level of religiousness has declined by approximately 50%." He does not elaborate further. However, if the conventional wisdom is accepted that 90% or more of the population of the Russian Empire used to be religious (and he does cite Lunacharskii's statement that in the 1920s, a decade

tianity in Russia approaches, it is the faith of the Russian grandmothers that shakes the foundations of Soviet atheism. In the 1950s, Nikita Khrushchev initiated a massive crackdown on Christianity, arresting Christians and closing and dynamiting churches. But Leonid Brezhnev's mother was a Christian, and rumor has it that his easing of pressures on the church and his restoration of some church buildings was for her sake.

Until today's reality, the best that the Russian Orthodox Church can do is to preserve itself for the future. By negotiating for the reopening of churches, quietly training priests in the countryside, cherishing every scrap of religious literature, and working for peace, the church prepares for a better day when religious freedom may return to Russia. But in terms of prospects for the near future, nobody seems to know yet whether Mikhail Gorbachev had a Christian grandmother [although it is reliably reported that his mother attends church regularly, and he himself has reminisced about attending church as a child].

"

after atheism has been proclaimed as the official ideology, 80% of the Soviet people were religious), Kobetskii's remark would coincide very well with the 45% estimated here.

... if 45% of the population is indeed religious, there must be some 115 million believers in the U.S.S.R. **"**

It would be of interest to know how the level of religiousness in Soviet society compares with that of other countries. Unfortunately, the available data do not permit precise comparisons because of the inadequacies of sociological research. General indicators suggest that religious behavior in the Soviet Union is significantly greater than it is in Western Europe, while it is probably less than that in North America. Information from the British Gallup organization for 1986 reports that in Western European countries, weekly church attendance varies from a low of 3 percent in Denmark to 12 percent in France and 14 percent in England. The American figure is 43 percent. When Fletcher estimates that perhaps as much as 45 percent of the Soviet population is religious, he is not saying that that many people attend religious services weekly. But until more careful studies can be performed, it seems that the suggestion that Soviet people are more religious than Western Europeans should be accepted.

The following reports from Soviet sociologists are at variance with Fletcher's conclusions. Again the 10 percent figure is given, although it may be meant to apply only to the Russian part of the population. However, there are discrepancies in the figures; taken together they point to substantially more than 10 percent involved in some way in religious activity. It is interesting that the reports try — both fairly unsuccessfully — to discover why so many Soviet citizens continue to cling to their religions.

A. N. Alekseev, *Formirovanie* **"** *nauchno-ateisticheskikh ubezhdenii* (Formation of Scientific Atheist Convictions) (Moscow: Vysshaia shkola, 1986), pp. 27–28.

n our country there are believers, including young ones. Results of research have shown that among believers, young people under thirty years of age constitute 3 percent, people from thirty to sixty, 27 percent, and those over sixty, 70 percent. As we see, even today there are youth among believers. It is true, there are only 3 percent; nevertheless they do exist. We must not forget about this. Besides, it is necessary to remember that those believers who are thirty years old, and even forty or fifty, grew up and were educated in the years of Soviet rule.

Further, researchers are examining why religious vestiges are maintained in the consciousness of some people, who encourages the development of religiousness in youth, and how they do it. Here there are three factors which can be identified: family, fanatical believers, including the clergy who actively conduct religious propaganda, and religious propaganda which comes from abroad. Sociological data show that among urban dwelling workers, 5 percent are Orthodox believers; 27 percent of the collective farmers, 27.5 percent of homemakers, and 28 percent of retired persons are believers; while fewer than 1 percent of white collar workers are.

According to data from sociological research, around 90 percent of the adult urban population is nonbelieving. In the villages this percentage is somewhat lower. It is estimated that the nonreligious among the adult population is 70 to 80 percent and active believers constitute 8 to 10 percent.

"

Antireligious writers in the Soviet Union conventionally give a low estimate — one that does not jibe with much of the evidence. In the following interview of a researcher for the Young Communist League

HISTORIC HOMELANDS OF SOVIET RELIGIONS

The boundaries of this map are those of the present-day U.S.S.R. The map shows the dominant religions of the areas within the country before the twentieth century. Large areas of the far north and Siberia were sparsely settled by populations who practiced tribal and animistic religions.

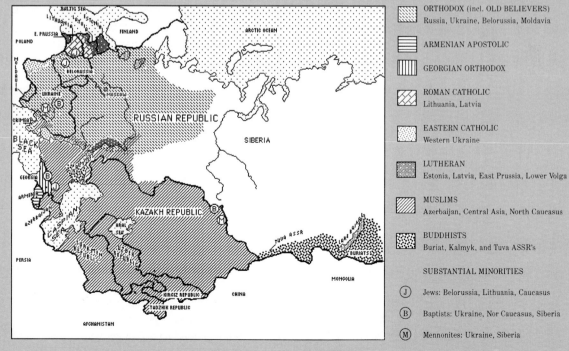

ORTHODOX (incl. OLD BELIEVERS)
Russia, Ukraine, Belorussia, Moldavia

ARMENIAN APOSTOLIC

GEORGIAN ORTHODOX

ROMAN CATHOLIC
Lithuania, Latvia

EASTERN CATHOLIC
Western Ukraine

LUTHERAN
Estonia, Latvia, East Prussia, Lower Volga

MUSLIMS
Azerbaijan, Central Asia, North Caucasus

BUDDHISTS
Buriat, Kalmyk, and Tuva ASSR's

SUBSTANTIAL MINORITIES

(J) Jews: Belorussia, Lithuania, Caucasus

(B) Baptists: Ukraine, Nor Caucasus, Siberia

(M) Mennonites: Ukraine, Siberia

Compiled by the author.

(Komsomol) there is a hint that the low estimates may be inaccurate. The researcher starts out by repeating the conventional figures, but the interviewer leads him to point to information which suggests a higher estimate. Clearly many more than 8 to 10 percent of the population demonstrate some religious leanings merely in their interest in church rituals, religious literature, and religious objects.

"Research Has Shown," *Nauka i Religiia* (Science and Religion), August 1987, p. 11.

Question: Boris Ivanovich, are there many believers among young people nowadays?

Answer: According to our data (we questioned youth under thirty years of age), half as many as among older people, that is, from 2 to 5 percent. In recent years this indicator has neither grown nor declined. . . .

Q: How do young people view religious ceremonies and behaviors?

A: A large proportion of youth view them negatively, although 29.8 percent either have baptized their own child or have taken part in this ceremony. And one needs to remember that this even includes Komsomol workers. As regards the objects of religious rituals [such as icons], they are kept either for tradition's sake or as mementos or artistic valuables in the families of more than 72 percent of the workers and 62 percent of rural youth, in 75 percent of the rural intelligentsia, 95.6 percent of research institute workers, 90 percent of service workers, and 85 percent of engineers. In 17.4 percent of the families, these objects are used for religious purposes by the older generation.

Q: Do young people read religious and atheistic literature?

A: Seventy-three percent answered that they are not acquainted with religious literature. Atheistic literature is systematically read by only 4 percent, around 11 percent have read books and brochures on atheism, and approximately 53 percent have read articles in papers and magazines.

Q: Frequently one can hear the mutually contradictory opinion that in churches and prayer houses there are many young people or that only older folk attend. What does your research indicate about this?

A: Only 2 percent of our sample regularly attend churches, prayer houses, or mosques. About 28 percent attend rarely. Another 12 percent gave no answer. Fifty-eight percent never have gone to church. Consequently, both opinions are unsubstantiated extremes.

Q: You would agree, however, that a person who has never been to a church or prayer house would not refuse to answer a question about church attendance. It is more likely that the 12 percent giving no answer are people who do not want to talk about it. But then the figure becomes an impressive 42 percent.

A: Well, I think that the main point is not the number as much as the reasons for attending. The majority attend because of their interest in the cultural monuments or simply out of curiosity.

Q: Obviously, other people exert a lot of influence, in particular the family?

A: Yes, the family—that is the basic channel for passing religion on to the new generation. Forty-four percent of the sample have believers in their family, and 46 percent frequently do things with them outside of the home.

Q: And how do young people participate in propagating atheism?

A: The figures are as follows: 4.1 percent deliver lectures, 6.5 percent conduct discussions in their collective, 3.3 percent carry on individual work, 20.2 percent responded that in their daily life they speak out against religious prejudices. But now here's the bad thing: the largest percentage of educated youth, the engineers, scholars, and workers in scientific institutes actually do not participate in atheistic work. For example, only 0.9 percent of the scholars conduct discussions and 0.2 percent are involved in individual work. And among service workers, absolutely no one conducts individual work. . . .

Q: How do you evaluate atheistic work in the Komsomol organizations you have studied?

A: It is unsatisfactory. Thirty to 40 percent of those questioned were not able even to recall when there had been lectures, debates, or discussions in their collectives on this subject. Several times in the course of the past year atheistic lectures were attended by only 28.2 percent. However, even in those organizations where atheistic work is conducted, the work is done, as a rule, formally and superficially. Only an insignificant portion of those asked ventured an evaluation of it, and that was basically unsatisfactory. And what can one say when 65 percent of the believers questioned were members of the Komsomol?

Can one compare the numbers of "believers" in the Soviet Union to the number of "religious people" in Western Europe?

At present it is not possible to determine with precision just how many Soviet citizens are religious believers. Fletcher's estimate of 45 percent is probably the upper limit of a reasonable estimate. Christel Lane, British sociologist and author of *Christian Religion in the Soviet Union* (London: Allen and Unwin, 1978), examined the Soviet sociological literature using a method similar to Fletcher's, but more conservative. She arrived at what might be considered the lower limit. Her "rough general estimate" was that at present "30 to 35 percent of the total Soviet population are religious." Very likely, Soviet figures are an underestimation, and, even in the absence of precise statistics it is reasonable to conclude that many Soviet citizens are still religious.

THE GORBACHEV ERA

WHAT IT MEANS FOR RELIGION

Mikhail Gorbachev's election as general secretary of the Communist Party and his sponsorship of dynamic reform in the Soviet Union have added two Russian words to the English lexicon: *glasnost* and *perestroika*. These words are trademarks of a new era in the Soviet Union and thus the subject of intense interest in the United States. What do they mean? "Glasnost" is difficult to translate because no single word in English conveys its full meaning. It denotes both "openness" and "publicity" — talking in public about subjects that were taboo in earlier times. "Perestroika" literally means "restructuring," — organizing and carrying out tasks in a new way. Part of what glasnost and perestroika are intended to accomplish is shown in the title of a book by Secretary Gorbachev that introduces his program to Americans: *Perestroika — New Thinking*.

Gorbachev's reform program has naturally raised questions about whether (and how) "new thinking" would apply to religion. This chapter will attempt to answer such questions by examining some of the effects of glasnost and perestroika upon religion and ideological values.

As mentioned in the preceding chapter, during his first year and a half in office Gorbachev made no public statement specifically about religion. When he did speak, he called for a "decisive and uncompromising struggle against manifestations of religion." But the speech was downplayed by the news media and was reported only in Uzbekistan, where it was given, not countrywide. Nevertheless, some observers who recalled the time of Nikita Khrushchev were alarmed, for Khrushchev had also appeared as a reformer, and at the same time had launched a harsh attack on religion. To calm fears, anonymous Soviet sources soon gave assurances that no new restrictions on religion were planned. Gorbachev's statement, they claimed, was aimed specifically at Communist Party leaders from regions bordering on Afghanistan.

How do we evaluate the significance of the changes underway in the Soviet Union — will their impact on religious affairs be minimal or enormous?

Novosti from Sovfoto.

When Gorbachev explicitly declared his intentions for religion under perestroika in his address to the extraordinary party conference in June 1988, they sounded less threatening than his earlier statement. He made clear that he had no revisionist thoughts about the materialism of Marxist-Leninist ideology but also predicted changes in laws originating in the Stalinist era.

M. S. Gorbachev, "Concerning the Realization of the Decisions of the Twenty-Seventh Congress of the C.P.S.U. and the Tasks of Deepening Perestroika," *Izvestiia*, June 29, 1988, p. 4.

" want to deal with the important question of freedom of conscience. Attention to this matter is currently at a high point because of the millennial anniversary of the introduction of Christianity into Rus. We do not hide our opinion that the religious worldview is nonmaterialistic and nonscientific. But this is no reason to show disrespect for the spiritual world of believing people, and it certainly is no justification for the use of any kind of administrative pressure in order to confirm materialistic views.

Lenin's decree on the separation of the church from the state and school from the church, which was adopted seventy years ago, created new bases for a relationship among these institutions. It is well known that these relations have not always worked out in a normal way. But life itself and the course of history have united believers and nonbelievers as Soviet citizens and patriots in the years of the trials of the Great Patriotic War, and they have joined in the creation of our socialist society and in the struggle for peace.

All believers, irrespective of their religious denomination, are citizens of the U.S.S.R. with full rights. The overwhelming majority of them participated actively in our economic and social life and in performing the tasks of perestroika. The draft of the law on freedom of conscience which is now being prepared will be based on Leninist principles and will take into account the realities of the present. **"**

> **"We do not hide our opinion that the religious worldview is nonmaterialistic and nonscientific. But this is no reason to show disrespect for the spiritual world of believing people and it certainly is no justification for the use of any kind of administrative pressure in order to confirm materialistic views."**
> **Mikhail Gorbachev**

Since Gorbachev took office, Soviet leaders and journalists have begun talking about religion and values in new ways. Today they admit that the way religion was treated in the past was wrong; a few years ago the same leaders and journalists would have avoided the subject completely. Many speak about religion in a positive, sympathetic tone, in contrast to the cynicism and animosity of the past. Some discuss the role that religion could play in addressing contemporary social problems of the Soviet Union and even go so far as to suggest that for some problems, religion may offer more effective solutions than modern secularism. Glasnost has invigorated public discussion of values.

To be sure, in the past the Soviet press has occasionally admitted that in some places believers had been treated in ways not in accordance with laws or official policy. What is new today, however, are the suggestions that the policy itself was mistaken and the laws need to be changed.

Some Soviet citizens in positions of authority now maintain that since the mid-1920s the policies of successive regimes have contradicted Lenin's original intent and principles. Even Lenin's principles themselves have been questioned in a few recent cases — especially his repudiation of the value of a religious worldview.

The earliest clear signal that the official policy on religion might be reformed came from the chairman of the Council for Religious Affairs, Konstantin Kharchev. About three months before Gorbachev became general secretary, Kharchev replaced Vladimir Kurodov, whose claims that Soviet believers enjoyed full freedom to satisfy their religious needs appeared, and were critiqued, in the two previous chapters.

While traveling abroad, Kharchev began hinting in his public statements that religious policies were being rethought on the highest levels in keeping with the themes of Gorbachev's program. In late 1986, *The New York Times* reported an interview he granted while visiting New York. In that interview, which is excerpted below, Kharchev made the first official public prediction that the laws governing religious activity would be revised and pointed to evidence that a new policy was emerging. He also stated that 20 percent of Soviet citizens are believers. This is double the conventional figure but still probably an underestimation.

Often thought of only as the headquarters of the Soviet government, the Moscow Kremlin is actually an ancient citadel, sometimes described as an ecclesiastical citadel because of the numerous churches and chapels within its walls.

Courtesy of David Snelbecker.

Joseph Berger, "A School Gets Unlikely Visit by a Russian," *The New York Times*, October 30, 1986.

"In an hour long interview Thursday, Mr. Kharchev, 52 years old, a gregarious man who was smoking American cigarettes, said the "revolutionary process of democratization under way" under Mikhail S. Gorbachev would also affect religious life. . . . Mr. Kharchev said that under revised legislation, churches would be permitted to own property. He also said that religious leaders were appearing on radio and television, that more churches were open and encountered fewer tensions with the authorities and that 100,000 Bibles would be published there next year.

He said the official attitude toward religion had changed. In the 1960s, he said, the official view was that religion would vanish, but this prognosis did not turn out to be true. Authorities now realize, he said, that they must work realistically with religion in a country where 20 percent of the people are regarded as "believers."

"For the first time in the Soviet Union," Mr. Kharchev, a nonbeliever, said, "the believer is being portrayed as a positive person, as a good person, as a person with high moral qualities.""

A year later, during another trip to the United States, Kharchev spoke more directly about past conflicts between religion and the Soviet state, saying that "officials had 'digressed' from Lenin and treated churchmen rudely." He indicated that he wanted a return to the "original version" of the policies of Lenin. What is meant is unclear, because Lenin's legacy is ambiguous, including both vehement contempt for religion and pragmatic concessions for believers. Kharchev tended to accent Lenin's

"For the first time in the Soviet Union, a believer is being portrayed as a positive person, as a good person, as a person with high moral qualities."

October 1986, Konstantin Kharchev, Chairman of the Council for Religious Affairs of the U.S.S.R.
AP/Wide World Photos.

concessions, not his contempt when he spoke of atheists and religious believers as equally entitled to propagate their ideas. In the constitution that Lenin's government issued in 1918, equal rights were given to both groups, but, when Stalin consolidated his control in the late 1920s, the right to "religious propaganda" was deleted from the constitution.

In late 1987, the Soviet media, especially the popular press, began to give wide coverage to Kharchev's new thinking. This wide dissemination of his ideas suggested that the changes he hinted at should be taken seriously and might become a reality. In the following excerpt from a 1987 interview published in *Science and Religion*, Kharchev adds to his list of specific religious activities that were permitted in Lenin's day but later forbidden by Stalin's policies. These include charitable activities by religious organizations, the right of conscientious objection from military service for individual believers, and extensive publishing of religious literature.

"The deciding role in the normalization of relations between state and church was played by the carefully developed policy of the Soviet state. Having abolished the reactionary [tsarist] legislation, the new state gave the church the real opportunity to concentrate its efforts on satisfying the religious needs of believers. At the same time, when believers themselves were engaged in the solution of social problems within the boundaries of religious associations, such initiatives received approval and support. There were cases . . . where [Protestant] sects aided starving people and when individual members of the clergy voluntarily went into hospitals for cholera and other contagious diseases, working not only as spiritual pastors but also as aides to physicians. Church papers and magazines were published throughout the country.

Showing an awareness of religious convictions, Soviet legislation provided for the possibility of exemption of believers from compulsory military service by substituting for it, as they said at the time, service on the medical front.

In a word, Leninist norms determining the mutual relations between state and church and their practical application in principle excluded any kind of war with the believers and clergy because of their religious convictions. . . .

The party and state frequently have condemned decisively such a "war against religion" as a violation of socialist legality, civic rights and freedoms, and Leninist principles with respect to religion and believers. Our Council [on Religious Affairs] tries to correct such violations when it learns of them. In conditions of expanding perestroika, democratization, and glasnost such anomalies will be eradicated more quickly. . . . It is obvious that an improvement of the legislation on religion itself is needed. "

"Guarantees of Freedom," *Nauka i religiia* (Science and Religion), November 1987, pp. 21–23.

Kharchev continued to promote Lenin's strategy on religion in a article marking the seventieth anniversary of Lenin's law on the separation of church and state. The topics which he touched on include exemption from military service and the religious education of children. His repeated references to conscientious objection may mean that this right will soon be restored. He repeated the charges that Stalin's policy departed from Lenin's, that violations of Leninist principles have continued in recent years, and that, consequently, new legislation on religion must be written to replace that of the Stalinist era which makes these violations possible.

K. Kharchev, "Affirming Freedom of Conscience," *Izvestiia*, January 27, 1988, p. 3.

"The decree [of January 1918] removed all legal debilities connected with a person's religion. . . . Concern for democracy and respect for the feelings of believers appeared in other articles of the decree as well. It granted the possibility of substituting one civic obligation for another in connection with religious beliefs. This norm was extended even to cases of exemption from military service. And adherents, for example, of the [pacifist Protestant sects such as the] Dukhobors, Mennonites, Molokans, and several other sects were assigned to alternative service instead of to the army and in war time they were put into special rear and frontline service units. . . .

We must say a few special words about the separation of the school from the church. Both the Russian Orthodox Church and other religious organizations opposed this provision of the decree. They accused the Soviet power of intruding into the "national soul" and "Christian conscience," which were not subject to state regulation. There were many collective appeals from believers demanding that the prohibition on the teaching of the "law of God" in schools be rescinded. . . .

The state had to explain patiently that state, public, and private educational institutions where subjects of general education are taught had to be freed from the influence of religion and the church.

At the same time the decree provided that citizens could teach and be taught religion in a private manner. Religious doctrine could be taught in special educational institutions, and parents themselves could decide to teach or not to teach religion to their children within the family and to invite or not to invite clergy to do this.

In other words, the decree accounted, in equal measure, for the interests of both believers and atheists. . . .

Of course, it would be incorrect not also to see where there have been failures.

Negative phenomena of the thirties—the cult of personality, violation of legality, tyranny and repression — had a negative effect upon the conduct of policy regarding religion, churches, and believers. Measures that were arbitrary, administrative, voluntaristic, and restrictive were supported and justified. As a result there was massive and unjustifiable closing of prayer buildings, tyranny in respect to clergy, and neglect of the legal rights of believers and their religious feelings. Today it is impossible to recall these things without grief. In the years of stagnation [i.e., under Brezhnev] there was a gap between the real religious situation and the lacquered public depiction of it. . . .

In the conditions of democratization the issue of the functioning of the church in socialist society has been clarified and a number of obstructions have been removed from the path to guaranteeing genuine freedom of conscience for all citizens. The participation of religious organizations in the struggle for peace and in the movement for preserving our historical-cultural heritage has notably increased. Cooperation between the church and public organizations in our country and with progressive movements abroad have been expanded. This has a favorable effect upon the attitudes of both believing and nonbelieving citizens and helps them to overcome mutual distrust and prejudices.

Nevertheless there is still a need to carry out practical improvements in the application of the principles and the provisions of the decree and in the regulations which are based upon it. This is especially the case for local officials, some of whom oppose the new thinking and complain about "concessions" to the church. Others, unable to deal with believers on their own, await orders from above for each situation, and by doing this they create "red tape" over simple questions. This causes believers to send complaints to Moscow. In just the past year, for example, more than three thousand complaints reached the Council on Religious Affairs. For many years there have been problems with the registration of religious associations in Lvov, Ternopol, Grodno, Kuliabsk, Perm, and Leningrad oblasts and in a number of districts of Moldavia. In Arkalyk, Kazakh S.S.R., despite the legal protests of believers, the mosque remains locked up. In Archangel and Sverdlovsk oblasts the ringing of church bells is prohibited. In Krasnodar territory obstacles are being put in the way of construction and repair of religious buildings. **"**

As unprecedented as it is to hear the chairman of the Council on Religious Affairs talking about mistreatment of religious groups by officials and unfair publicity about religious believers, it is even more surprising to find one of the top bishops of the Orthodox Church speaking in similarly critical tones. Ever since Acting Patriarch Sergius issued his proclamation in 1927, bishops have studiously refrained from any suggestion that the Communist state persecutes religion. Even while the church suffered under Khrushchev's campaign, church officials covered up the antireligious violence endured by believers. But in the interview below, which appeared in *Moscow News* in September 1987, the Metropolitan of Leningrad broke with past practices and raised the sensitive subjects of illegal actions of local officials against churches and the need for restructuring the working relationship between church and state.

RELIGION AND THE LAW

Several hints have appeared recently that a change in the laws regulating religion is imminent; one very strong one is an article in the official magazine of the Orthodox Church laying out the legal provisions affecting religion. Significantly, some of these provisions directly contradict the laws published in the past. For example, the new provisions give religious societies "rights of juridical persons." This suggests that laws have been changed, but the changes have not yet been officially announced. American readers may be surprised by such a situation; however, it is not unusual in the Soviet Union for laws to be in effect before they are published.

"The Rights and Obligations of Religious Believers," *Journal of the Moscow Patriarchate*, no. 1 (1986), p. 80.

"**THE RIGHTS AND OBLIGATIONS OF RELIGIOUS SOCIETIES**

A religious society is formed in order to satisfy jointly religious needs and is an association of believing citizens (founding members of the society), who are of age, no less than 20 in number and reside in one district. A religious society may commence its work after it has been registered at the appropriate state bodies. This is necessary for the legality of the religious society to be recognized from the moment of registration. Moreover the registration signifies that a religious society takes upon itself the obligation of observing the U.S.S.R. Constitution and the Soviet laws.

For administering the internal affairs of a religious society and for economic management, the meeting of the founding members must elect an executive body and an auditing commission. The executive body handles finances, signs contracts and may act as a plaintiff or defendant in civil, labor and other lawsuits in which a religious society may be involved.

A religious society may invite officiants of its cult and openly hold religious services and prayer meetings in a house of worship, which may be attended by the believing citizens of any age, and perform religious rites. If the religious rites and processions have to be held outside the premises of the house of worship the permission of the Executive Committee must be obtained. Permission is not necessary if the religious rite or ceremony is a part of the religious service and takes place round the house of worship and does not violate public order or traffic rules. With the permission of the Executive Committee religious rites may be performed in the homes of citizens. Religious rites may be performed without the sanction of the Executive Committee in case of grave illness — in hospitals, in the homes for the aged and invalids, and in prisons; in case of death — at home, the cemetery or crematory. The believing citizens, including children of ten and over, may be voluntary participants in religious rites. In the case of children religious rites are performed with the consent of their parents. Religious rites have no legal force.

A religious society enjoys the rights of juridical persons and as such may, if need arises, build or purchase, with its own money and according with the law, necessary premises; acquire means of transport, church requisites, and objects of religious cult with right of ownership. The purchase by a religious society of a building for its needs is legalized by a notarized seal. The building thus acquired becomes the property of the religious society.

A religious society has a right to take a lease on property or premises. An agreement may be made with the Executive Committee for the use by a religious society of a special house of worship free of charge. For prayer meetings, a religious society may make use of other premises leased from individuals or the executive committees of a district or city Soviet of People's Deputies. A religious society may own only one house of worship.

If the house of worship, living quarters and other premises happen to be state property leased to a religious society, government insurance must be paid by the society. Furthermore, the religious society must guarantee the safety of the given property; in case of loss or damage the society will be liable. The real estate or property owned by a religious society may be insured if it so desires.

A religious society has its own monetary funds accumulated from donations and collections made in the house of worship, the sale of objects of cult and the performance of religious rites. These are free of tax. The money is spent on the upkeep of the houses of worship and other property of the cult, on the wages of the servants of the cult and religious centers, as well as of workers and employees.

Possessing monetary funds, religious societies have the right to employ, on a permanent or temporary basis, workers and employees on contracts drawn up with or without trade union participation. Wages are determined by agreement with the religious societies but they must not be lower than the government rates of corresponding workers in state institutions or enterprises. Persons working for religious societies on contract drawn with the participation of a trade union are protected by labor laws. Moreover, terms of contracts drawn up by religious societies without the participation of a trade union must not in any way contradict the existing labor legislation. If they do, the contract is considered invalid.

"

"There are No Insoluble Contradictions!" *Moscow News*, September 27–October 4, 1987, p. 13.

" *uestion:* What determines, in your opinion, relations between the Russian Orthodox Church and the State today?

Answer: In my view there are no insoluble problems in these relations, and no irreconcilable contradictions. But there are questions awaiting solution. . . .

It is particularly sad when, sometimes, at a local level, and running counter to the basic principles of our socialist state of the people, they are treated as "second-rate" people and looked at with a certain suspicion and watchfulness. Quite often, local bodies violate the existing legislation on cults to the detriment of believers. The more there are such cases, the easier it is for Western propaganda "to get hold" of them and use them in their interests. Therefore, I think that the first thing to do is to fulfil promptly the existing legislation on cults.

However, it must be stressed that the operating Resolution on Religious Associations, regulating relations between the Church and the state, was adopted in 1929, and underwent only minor changes in 1975. It was adopted at a time when the events of revolutionary and the first postrevolutionary years were still fresh in people's memory, when the representatives of the Church and believers did not always take the correct stand. And this was reflected in the legislation. **"**

"It is particularly sad when, sometimes, at a local level, and running counter to the basic principles of our socialist state of the people, they [believers] are treated as 'second-rate' people and looked at with a certain suspicion and watchfulness."

September 1987, Metropolitan Alexis of Leningrad and Novgorod
Sovfoto.

The public airing in *Moscow News* of a specific case in which a church was mistreated provides a clear manifestation of glasnost. An outspoken advocate of perestroika, this newspaper ran an article in August 1987, about a problem that had been festering for twenty-five years. The article, an expose of the administrative abuse of power, intended to spur changes in the way local congregations, such as those in Kirov, are handled by officials.

Difficulties for Orthodox believers in the city of Kirov arose during the Khrushchev antireligious campaign. For some unknown reason, in Kirov and the surrounding district, local officials were especially aggressive in harassing religion. They refused to authorize enough meeting space for believers. They closed one Orthodox church, leaving only one other in a city of 400,000. They refused to allow even one church in some towns. Moreover, local officials were supported in their arbitrariness by the local commissioner of the Council of Religious Affairs, the representative of the central government whose very job it is to assure that local officials apply the law correctly.

Alexander Nezhny, "Law and Conscience," *Moscow News*, August 23–30, 1987, p. 13.

" ld views, especially those that have ossified into dogmas, often have absolute power over people. The times are changing, society is straining to form new convictions and is trying to live in conditions of democratism and openness. . . . But old views, dogmas, and some secret yearnings for the recent past,

. . . where views that even slightly differed from those of officials were branded as dissent and where the immutability of the law was conveniently substituted by "political expediency," still persist. . . .

Before 1962, Kirov had two Russian Orthodox Church communities, two churches—St. Fyodor and St. Serafim. In 1962, in line with the then official policy that we should enter communism (which was believed to be close at hand) without religious people, or at least with a minimal quantity of such, St. Fyodor Church was closed and its parish dispersed. . . . Almost ever since, [the believers] have been trying to get back what they had been denied—the second religious community. . . . On July 15, the faithful of the city of Kirov sent to the Procurator General of the U.S.S.R. a cable of complaint—the 42nd such complaint addressed to Moscow. . . . Why on earth shouldn't Ivan Martynov, a war veteran who worked 36 years as a fitter at the Mayak factory, fight for his rights guaranteed by the Constitution? And Gennady Yolkin, 42, working for the Lepse factory? And foreman Viktor Shchelchkov? and Anastasiya Nesterenko, an old-age pensioner who only recently was a senior engineer at a factory in Kirov? Full-fledged citizens of this country, they feel hurt when someone tries to hoodwink them, to intimidate, to drive them into a blind alley. In former times, they would have kept silent, but they speak up today. Said Nesterenko with emotion: "Just think, we are advanced in years, have worked in production for 40 years or so, we have decorations, think about us! Don't we have the right to go to church?"

Kirov has more than 400,000 residents. It has, as I've said, one church. (To compare: Moscow has 44 Russian Orthodox churches, Kostroma with a population of nearly 300,000 has six.) The religious people of Kirov and the city officials are locked in a heated argument. Believers are unanimous that, especially in winter, on holidays and at weekends, the church is filled to capacity. "You can't raise your hand to make the sign of the cross," complained Yekaterina Noskova, a seamstress who worked 30 years. . . .

The most profound idea of the perestroika process, if you wish, is that we would only be able to take the country's economy out of its precrisis condition when observance of laws and unconditional observance of human rights, including the right to freedom of conscience, become an absolute norm of our life. . . . It is the job of the Council for Religious Affairs and its commissioners in the localities to see to it that these relations are in line with the Constitution. A commissioner's job is to put right all the infractions of law by either the local officials or the local church. But the greatest trouble with A. Shalaginov [commissioner of the Council for Religious Affairs for the Kirov Region] is that for nine years he has been doing a job he is unsuited for and, as happens in such cases, he bungles it. He does not, to put it mildly, accept the church with all his heart; he thinks that religious people are very unpleasant, and priests — repulsive. He, for instance, is supposed to meet the justified requests made over many years by religious people in the town of

What are some of the religious issues now being debated that were once considered too controversial to be discussed openly?

An important part of Orthodox worship since the sixteenth century, bell ringing has been intermittently outlawed during the twentieth century and continues to be forbidden in some cities despite Kharchev's description of such a prohibition as an "absurdity."

Sovfoto.

Vyatskiye Poyany about having their religious community registered. Instead he opposes them. He is duty bound to make L. Pechatkina, Secretary of the City Executive Committee of the town of Malmyzh, who only harasses both the churchgoers and their priest, Alexei Sukhikh, obey law and order. Instead, he seems to watch this harassment with glee. He was supposed to at least try and explain to the executive committees in Kirov and the region that the grounds on which they refuse the registration of a second religious community in Kirov hold no water from the legal point. Instead, he resolutely supports the local officials. "

The author of this report from Kirov apparently hopes that substantial changes in the official treatment of religion will be made. Indeed, significant changes have already occurred under Gorbachev, showing that glasnost can be credited with tangible results.

In anticipation of the millennial celebration of the baptism of Rus, the government returned to the Orthodox Church three monasteries of great historical significance: the Optina Pustyn, which was vividly depicted in Dostoevsky's novel, *The Brothers Karamazov,* the Tolga Monastery of Yaroslavl, and the most ancient monastery on Soviet soil, the Cave Monastery of Kiev. The Tolga Monastery will designate part of its space as a nursing home for elderly clergymen. Orthodox leaders see government authorization of the nursing home as a hopeful sign that eventually churches will regain the right—which was withdrawn in 1929 —to operate charitable services. Metropolitan Filaret of Minsk reported in May 1988 that more than fifty Orthodox churches had been reopened recently. For the first time in several decades, various Orthodox congregations around the country have received permission to build new buildings. The plans for the new church in Murmansk include a nursing home to be run by the parish.

In 1988, the Orthodox Church received permission to print 100,000 copies of the Bible, and the Evangelical Christians–Baptists received permission to import 100,000 Russian Bibles, 10,000 German Bibles, and 8,000 Moldavian Bibles. This addition to the supply of Bibles will be the largest increment in a one-year period in all of Russian history. The synagogue in Moscow received permission to import 5,000 Hebrew Torahs.

The number of Jews allowed to emigrate has increased sharply. Whereas 51,000 Jews left the Soviet Union in 1979 and 21,000 in 1980, emigration was severely restricted from 1981 to 1986, but in 1987 the number jumped to 8,011 and that rate was maintained through the first half of 1988. Official permission was given for a Jewish *yeshiva* (rabbinic school) to be opened in Moscow, possibly in affiliation with Moscow State University, and provisions were made to ship kosher food to Moscow from Hungary and the United States.

The number of persons in prison for activities connected with the practice of religion dropped from 411 in early 1986 to 225 in April 1988. About one-third of that number are Muslims and Hare Krishnas, and of the remaining two-thirds, about thirty are Jehovah's Witnesses who refuse to perform military service, and three dozen are dissident Baptists.

In 1987, the Seventh-Day Adventists opened a seminary in Moscow. The new institution is the only Protestant theological school legally functioning in the country. Obtaining permission for the seminary was a significant development for the Adventists, who have led an uncertain existence since their central denominational structure was legally dissolved during the Khrushchev antireligious campaign.

In another even more significant development, negotiations on the legalization of the Ukrainian Catholic Church began in the summer of 1988 in Helsinki. This church, which includes more than three million believers, has been outlawed since 1946. Success in these negotiations will be very difficult to achieve because the Orthodox Church considers the Ukrainian Catholics as rightfully a part of its community.

In a dramatic gesture, Mikhail Gorbachev received a delegation of Orthodox metropolitans led by Patriarch Pimen on April 29, 1988, in the Kremlin. This meeting recalled the only other audience granted to the head of the church by a Communist leader: Stalin's reception of Metropolitan Sergius during World War II, which led to the sudden improvement in the church's fortunes. By this action, Gorbachev explicitly identified himself and his program with the changing attitudes and actions affecting religion. Gorbachev's remarks to the patriarch included the following statements which were televised across the country:

"Meeting of General Secretary of the C.C. of the C.P.S.U. Gorbachev with Pimen, Patriarch of Moscow and All Russia, and members of the Synod of the Russian Orthodox Church," *Izvestiia*, May 1, 1988, p. 1.

" The mistakes that were made in the treatment of the church and believers in the 1930s and subsequent years are being rectified. . . . More active participation of religious leaders in the work of public [charities] like the Culture Fund, the Lenin Children's Fund, the Motherland Society, and others has become possible. In response to the believers' requests, the Soviet state has transferred to church administration the Monastery of St. Daniel in Moscow, the historic Optina Pustyn in Kaluga Province, and the Tolga Monastery in Yaroslavl Province.

The new law of freedom of conscience that is being drafted will reflect the interests of religious organizations. All these things are the real fruits of new approaches to state-church relations in conditions of perestroika and democratization of Soviet society. We are now restoring in full the Leninist principles regarding relations with religion, the church, and believers. "

In a startling repudiation of the Stalinist policy on religion, Gorbachev told the patriarch that the church should not confine itself to strictly religious activity. "The church cannot distance itself," he declared, "from the complex problems that disturb humanity or from the changes taking place in society."

These obvious changes in official words and deeds have not been free from controversy. It is impossible for a radically new political program to be introduced without opposition. Some Soviet citizens believe that there was nothing wrong with the former state of affairs and that the government should not make it easy for religious organizations to thrive. Others believe that some changes are needed but are not sure what those changes should be. The following transcript of a discussion was printed in *Science and Religion*, the most popular atheist publication in the U.S.S.R. The editorial comment accompanying this

In what is believed to be the first meeting of its kind since Stalin met with Metropolitans Sergius, Alexis, and Nikolai in 1943, General Secretary Gorbachev and Patriarch Pimen met in April 1988 as part of the millennium celebration.

Novosti from Sovfoto.

article noted that "the forms and methods of atheistic education are in need of comprehensive perestroika" and suggested that readers should critically evaluate the opinions expressed by the discussants. "The principal way to achieve perestroika is to have glasnost, that is, a free discussion of the painful problems of social development. Therefore we have given to each of the participants in this 'round table' the opportunity to express his point of view." The tentativeness of such a comment suggests that the "atheist establishment" is quite uncertain about what changes might be in store.

This discussion took place at Moscow's Institute of Scientific Atheism. The participants — relatively influential figures in local Communist Party affairs — acknowledged that believers have sometimes been discriminated against in employment and that congregations have suffered from administrative measures, and they recognized that some of the antireligious measures of the past have produced results contrary to what was desired. What they said shows that they are rethinking their opinions about religion and puzzling over what the official approach to it should be.

"What Prevents Us," *Nauka i religiia* (Science and Religion) October 1987, pp. 20–21.

"Savchenko:* Does it not concern you that our "roundtable" is late by at least one year? Economics, art, literature, the school, health care, the Komsomol — perestroika is going on everywhere. As regards atheist education, I shall not be mistaken if I say that in the two and a half years after the memorable April [1985] Plenum of the C.C. C.P.S.U. [when Gorbachev's program was inaugurated], it has not experienced very many notable changes.

It is obvious that this is the reason that the journal has come to our place in order to hear opinions on this problem. . . .

Zadorozhnaia: I should note that sometimes consideration also is given to the religious situation in the region, to church rituals, the size and number of sects, and the like.

Savchenko: The figures on baptisms, church weddings, and funerals do not give a complete picture of religiousness. Perhaps we are dealing with some fad or enthusiasm? . . . We need other data about the dynamics of religiousness, special and regular investigations of a social character. And we conduct them very rarely and only episodically. Almost always in an amateurish and unprofessional manner. I do not consider this reliable. . . .

Zadorozhnaia: And in time it produces results which are the opposite of what we are trying to get. I have seen this happen: I go to the manager of a factory of a certain worker. Let's say a competent specialist. After two months this person comes to me at the city committee with a complaint. He has been fired. I call up the factory; the manager answers: "Apparently you did not know that he is a believer. Because of him I will be called to all sorts of conferences and they will complain that I have a sectarian in the collective. I have no troubles if I don't have him." And where did this kind of reaction come from? You and I are the ones who have "formed" this kind of manager. And I must say that I do not know of a single case when a manager was punished for violation of the legislation on religion [which forbids discrimination against people on the basis of religious beliefs].

Savchenko: Unfortunately, that story is typical. But if we look at its consequences then we shall see that things are sadder and more tragic. The one who has been unfairly fired feels that he is suffering for his faith, and this causes that faith to grow stronger and he finds in it his only hope and support. Looking at him and understanding the unfairness of what has been done, many people whose own convictions are not strong begin to sympathize with him.

Some places officials do not want to register religious congregations. The struggle becomes one of life and death. The sectarians receive a kind of martyr's aura as if they were some sort of saints. And who needs that?

Embulaeva: Formalism is an inescapable result when the educational work of a region is judged only by figures. In general I oppose sorting out atheistic education into columns. We should evaluate it not by figures, the number of lectures or club sessions, nor even by the indices of religiousness, but according to the only reliable and accurate criterion: what kind of person are we producing — a good worker, a community-minded citizen, a good family person, a patriot? Atheistic education is not a separate department alongside labor or patriotic or moral education. You don't train a person in parts! There must be a complex approach, unifying all aspects of educational work. Formalism has eaten its way into the very methods of atheistic work. We have taken refuge in mass measures too much. The individual approach requires creativity and, I would say, a certain sacrifice on the part of the propagandist. He must devote some of his free time to the believer.

Zadorozhnaia: Of course, the individual approach requires more effort and energy. And, you know, it would be no sin if we learned a bit from the preachers.

Savchenko: Indeed, they know how to reach the heart. I recall a case that happened in one region of the territory. In a sermon, the head of the Baptist society said: yesterday there was a wedding of the daughter of the secretary of the factory's Communist Party committee. They drank so many bottles of vodka and champagne! That's atheists' behavior — drunkenness. And he finished the sermon this way: tomorrow we'll be chopping firewood for a certain sister. And everyone went off to work; nobody shirked. The call for sobriety and moral purity, working together, and a personal example finds a response in the heart. I do not know whether you can call this an individual or mass approach, but the important thing is that it is effective.

Ulmasov: It seems to me that we have reached a new turn in the conversation: we should recognize finally that we can learn a lot from the church. People object: what is this? they are the opponents! But I think that there is no shame in learning how to approach a person. In general, it is necessary to know exactly the strategy and tactics of the struggle for a person. And in this matter religion has enormous and long experience. . . .

Zadorozhnaia: I am disturbed that our negative attitude toward the religious worldview sometimes is transferred to the believing person. But he is just as much a Soviet citizen as the rest.

Savchenko: I feel that many people are questioning and want to say something like the following: today the strategy of relations with the church is changing. In many respects we are working for the same purposes. We are working alongside believers, let's say, in the international arena in the struggle for peace and for a just international order and against the threat of nuclear catastrophe and the ecological crisis. It seems that in many aspects of education, in particular in the moral, we are also able to have common goals, for example, in the realization of the moral commandments such as "thou shalt not kill," "thou shalt not steal," "thou shalt not commit adultery." Of course there are essential differences in the premises of the moral norms, and we cannot ignore them.

Or let's take the attitude toward labor. While noting that the church teaches that one should work, we emphasize that it puts in first place not labor for the good of society but labor as worship. All of this is true. But it is impossible to deny the other: for some people who accept moral truths only in a religious form, such a motivation for labor works rather persuasively. And if we want to mobilize the labor of each Soviet person, upon which in the final analysis the acceleration of the socioeconomic development of the country depends, we cannot fail to take account of this reality.

It is possible that my thoughts will seem to somebody to be treason, but it seems to me that while we must conduct a polemic with church organizations about their worldview; we must also consolidate those points where our views essentially coincide. I think that this corresponds to the general spirit of perestroika in the country which will point us to a sober and realistic approach.

When individuals speak of going "back to Leninist principles," to what are they referring?

Soviet leaders are now beginning to show respect for the tremendous religious devotion that continues to move many Soviet citizens.

SIPA Press.

As the preceding discussion demonstrates, the image of religious believers, as portrayed in the media, has changed substantially during the Gorbachev period. No longer are believers depicted only as ignorant, fanatical, socially deviant, or even criminal and politically subversive. Instead, the media seem willing to acknowledge the human value and possible contribution to society of religious people.

In the following excerpt, the director of the Institute of Scientific Atheism examines how the ideological work of the atheist establishment is affected by this new image of the believer.

"Perestroika of atheist work requires a review of a number of schemes and habitual stereotypes which are not based upon reality but which have gained a foothold in scientific atheism. . . .

[According to our Marxist theory] religion will disappear to the degree that socialism itself develops. . . . This is a complex and contradictory process which is difficult and requires time. Overcoming religion in this perspective is not a goal to be achieved today but is a matter for the distant future.

Believers undoubtedly are experiencing the effects of the socialist form of life, of our ideology, and of the Communist system of values. In their consciousness and activity they do not see themselves as different from the whole Soviet people. They live for its interests. They support the domestic and foreign policy of the party and state and measures for perestroika. Evidence for this comes from numerous instances of rewarding believers for conscientious labor and fulfillment of military obligations with state medals, prizes, and awards of honor. In their congregations believers declare their loyalty to the socialist system and to Soviet legislation. . . .

We never can agree with religion in its basic worldview notions. There is not and cannot be any common position, or a compromise, between materialism and idealism in the answers to questions about the nature of the world and about what constitutes fundamental reality — matter or consciousness. However, one's worldview is not confined to the solution of the basic questions of philosophy. . . . There are also questions which are quite concrete — about good and evil in their historical and social forms, about war and peace, about humanity, etc. In this area believers and nonbelievers can and do find a common language. Believing citizens of our society, along with nonbelievers, comprehend and adopt socialist ideals and values. Life itself trains them in the spirit of Marxism-Leninism and gives socialist content to their consciousness, even when they remain religious. . . .

We do not equate religion with clerical anti-Communism and we see the possibility of cooperation with religious circles in the joint struggle for peace and social progress. Our political relations with believers and

V. Garadzha, "To the Level of Life's Demands," *Nauka i religiia* (Science and Religion), January 1988, pp. 10–12.

In his painting "The Return of the Prodigal Son," officially recognized artist Ilya Glazunov uses religious themes to portray the Russian "home," thus underscoring the importance of religion in the Russian cultural tradition.

Soviet Life.

religious organizations include useful dialogue and cooperation. Being atheists, we can and must find a common language with believers, and we must reach mutual understanding with them in the approach to the cardinal problems of the contemporary world. In the resolution of these problems, that which divides believers and atheists turns out to be less important by comparison with that which unites. And it is precisely because we want to strengthen such mutual understanding and cooperation that we are decisive opponents of those who seek means of setting believers in opposition to nonbelievers and sowing discord between them on religious grounds.

"

This new, positive perspective which sees religion as a potential ally of Communism in solving society's problems is provoking a lot of discussion at present. One of its outspoken advocates is Dmitry Likhachev, a highly respected specialist in old Russian culture, who was exiled in the 1920s for participating in underground study groups on Orthodoxy.

This interview was printed in the *Literature Gazette,* another newspaper which has stepped forward as a strong proponent of Gorbachev's program. The gazette's discussion is representative of a large number of articles that have appeared in Soviet magazines and newspapers in recent years on whether the Communist worldview, necessarily atheistic, can provide a sufficient motive force for ethical behavior. According to Communist Party dogma it can, but today some people are calling dogma on this point into question, to the dismay of the more conventionally minded Communists.

While Likhachev rejects the idea that a return to religion would solve the ethical problems of Soviet society, he does express greater appreciation for religion than has normally been found in Soviet antireligious writing.

nterviewer: Reflecting along with you on the moral problems of our society and on the causes of spiritual vacuum, falsehood, corruption, and dishonor, readers — and there are many of them — assert that in an earlier epoch the church opposed evil and that it has the experience of moral training, and that what you are advocating is already contained in religious morality.

Likhachev: Morality is a part of human nature. Its norms are eternally established. Really, what's the alternative to the command, "Thou shalt not kill"? What is the opposite: "Kill"? And the command: "Thou shalt not steal"? Or, "Thou shalt not bear false witness"?

This is one side of the question. And here is the second. I receive many letters which tell me about atheist propaganda: it frequently creates in our citizens attitudes of hostility toward believers and the church. Faith is considered a sign of ignorance, although it should be said that hostility toward believers comes from ignorance, from ignorance of history of the church and history in general. I also received in response to [an earlier article] some letters advocating contempt for believers and clergy. This is not only the fruit of ignorance but also the absence of another spirit — the spirit of democracy.

Some of our people have the opinion that monasteries were hotbeds of obscurantism. But who copied the books? Who introduced new systems of agriculture? . . . Who made new varieties of fruit? Even in Ancient Rus they studied problems of genetics and selection — in the monasteries. They knew about 300 varieties of apples. And this is not to say anything about aesthetics — aesthetics of church singing, aesthetics of eccle-

D. S. Likhachev, "From Repentance to Action," *Literaturnaia gazetta* (Literature Gazette), September 9, 1987, p. 2.

ILYA GLAZUNOV'S RELIGIOUS ART

Ilya Glazunov, among the most celebrated painters now active in the Soviet Union, is very controversial because of his explicit use of religious themes. This interview explores his thinking about art.

Marina Khachaturova, "Unraveling the Mystery of the Soul," *Soviet Life,* February 1987, pp. 48–50.

Question: Why do you reject modern art?

Answer: . . . National culture gives people the strength to weather the storms and calamities of history. Artists draw their inspiration from that inexhaustible source. In Russian culture I discovered the world of the icon. The Russian icon has completely fascinated me, like many others, with its profound content expressed through color, melodious line, form and outline, which convey the spiritual essence of a phenomenon: crude materialism is dissolved in a definite philosophical interpretation. After visiting Moscow, French artist Henri Matisse, a man so far removed from Russian culture, said all modern artists should study the icon . . . .

Q: Why do you consider your painting *The Return of the Prodigal Son* to be one of your major works?

A: I used the well-known biblical theme of a son leaving his father's house. After squandering everything he had and after being reduced to eating with swine, the son remembers he has a father and a home. By father and home I mean the self-awareness and the spiritual culture of the people. That's why I put Andrei

siastical language, painting, architecture, which we now honor and which always were at the highest level. It is impossible to close one's eyes to all of this. And besides, we know what role the church played in the history of Russia. We can mention that in the period of feudal division, it worked for unity and against civil strife; it inspired the fight against foreign invaders. We speak about the victory of Dmitry Donskoy at the battle of Kulikovo but we are silent about Sergius of Radonezh, the inspirer of this victory, who, as the church says, "promised to Grand Prince Dmitry the conquest of numerous sons of Hagar who intended to devastate Russia with flame and sword." And who spoke against the harshness in the evil time of Ivan the Terrible? Metropolitan Filip, who fearlessly denounced the cruel ruler.

And speaking about the contemporary church, especially today on the eve of the millennium of the baptism of Rus, it is necessary to emphasize: we stand for full, real separation of the church from the state. Our state must be really nonreligious, it must not interfere in the affairs of the church. And of course likewise the church also must not interfere in the affairs of the state. The Council for Religious Affairs must see to this. Unfortunately, in the recent past the council interfered

Rublyov, St. Sergius of Radonezh, Rachmaninoff, Scriabin and the great defenders of the land in my picture. My painting is about being true to one's roots. If the roots of a tree dry up or are chipped off, the tree dies. Everyone, every country has a national culture, and all people, all nations should be encouraged to cherish it.

Q: The value of preserving relics of the past — a theme that occupies such an important place in your life — is very apparent in your *Prodigal Son.* Was that your purpose?
A: There's nothing more terrible for artists than to see beauty trampled on. Soviet artists are working to preserve the cultural monuments of Moscow and many other towns in the country because these monuments belong to all of humanity, not just to us. . . . Our architects failed to carry on the traditions of the great Russian architecture, and they are to blame for the destruction of many of our cultural relics of antiquity. . . .

Q: Why is Dostoyevsky your favorite writer?
A: Dostoyevsky is a kindred spirit to those who try to find the answers to the "cursed question" of human life. He is our constant companion in our search for the meaning of life, our understanding of good and evil and our quest to reveal the mysteries of the human spirit.

"

in church affairs, and it did so very actively. It is necessary to guarantee to the church the right to publish essential quantities of books which the believers need: Bibles, church calendars, and devotional and other church literature.

"

Likhachev, with his affirmation of the ethical value of religion, has joined in the public debate on the role of religion in society. The opposing point of view is illustrated by the next excerpt, in which a teacher at Moscow State University rejects the idea that religion is a useful ally of the Communist Party and Soviet state in working on social problems.

"

For a long time, a conciliatory and sometimes even apologetic attitude toward religion and idealistic philosophy has been regarded in some circles of the intelligentsia as "taking a broad view" and "civic boldness." The religious orientation of culture has come to be regarded in these circles as a means of humanizing society and increasing its spiritual potential. . . . In reading certain works of belles lettres and public-affairs writing, one can detect

Z. Tashurizina, "Just How is Religion 'Useful'?" *Komsomolskaia pravda,* April 10, 1987, in *Current Digest of Soviet Press,* vol. 39, no. 19, p. 10.

that their authors do not have a scientific notion about religion, that they are interpreting it very broadly, without perceiving its specific character or, consequently, its essence. Elementary mistakes are made. Thus, religion is confused with other forms of social consciousness: morality, art, philosophy, politics. But, as is known, religion is not morality and not politics.

But there are also deeper reasons why some cultural figures turn to religion. The unfavorable social atmosphere of the 1970s and the early 1980s played a significant role here: the violation of the principle of social justice, the growth of private-ownership and dependent sentiments, the gap between words and deeds, and the increasing impact of the consumption-minded stratum on public and spiritual life. Some people have begun to accuse the "official doctrine" — i.e., Marxism — of being the culprit here. However, in these people's opinion religion is an ideology "unsullied" by negative phenomena. In search of ways of overcoming negative phenomena, of ways of enhancing morality, some cultural figures have turned to religion.

Paradoxically, antisocialist morality has been perceived not as a result of deviations from socialism but as a consequence of the loss of religiousness and the spread of materialism and atheism among the working people in the post-October period. . . .

There is often talk to the effect that atheism has created a moral vacuum in people's souls. Atheism is accused not only of amoralism but also of destroying artistic monuments. Certain writers, with Olympian indifference, have ignored a great many extremely interesting studies and popular works in the field of scientific atheism and have begun to accuse it of narrow mindedness and "ironclad" dogmatism and even of replacing enlightenment with administrative fiat.

It is interesting that the past few decades have seen almost no artistic works embodying images of the freethinkers and atheists of the past. On the contrary, more often than not characters from the Bible and the Koran or clergymen, as well as monks, are put forth as moral examples. Religious holidays and ceremonies have frequently been propagandized in the press, in movies, and on television.

Strangely enough, during the current period of perestroika, some writers are starting to compete with one another, as it were: who will go farther in advocating religious or abstract-humanist views? It has become fashionable to switch from the idea of social transformation to the idea of "spiritual transformation. . . ." During this period, a desire has been observed to present religious norms of morality and religious ideals as common to all mankind and to impart a religious nature to simple norms of morality that are common to all mankind. It is even said that we, present-day Soviet people, are still living according to the Ten Commandments. . . . It's time to remove the halo of civic boldness from attempts to propagandize religious ideas in Soviet culture.

"

Professor Tashurizina did not identify by name any member of the creative intelligentsia that she considers to be guilty of sympathy for religion. But what she was talking about is illustrated in the next excerpt from an article by someone on the Likhachev side of the debate: Yevgeny Yevtushenko, a highly popular Soviet poet who achieved international fame in the early 1960s when his work was used to support Khrushchev's de-Stalinization program. His most famous poems were "Babi Yar," which attacked anti-Semitism in the Soviet Union, and the anti-Stalinist, "The Heirs of Stalin." Although there has remained about him a suggestion of opposition to the ruling establishment, Yevtushenko has not sided with the political dissenters. In favor with the authorities, he has been able to travel abroad frequently as a representative of Soviet culture and today may be functioning as a quasi-official spokesperson for reformers in the highest circles of the party. In his article Yevtushenko defends religion as a part of the national heritage of culture which, he says, is the ultimate source of morality.

This choir class at the Leningrad Ecclesiastical Academy illustrates one way the church circumvents state restrictions on youth meetings and thus includes young people in church activities.

From *Orthodox Church in Russia*,
Courtesy of USSR Embassy, Washington, DC.

Like Likhachev and Kharchev, Yevtushenko openly refers to the discrimination which religion has endured under Soviet conditions. He hints at the shortage of religious literature and goes even further in suggesting that atheism enjoys an unfair advantage in the ideological battle.

Yevgeny Yevtushenko, "The Source of Morality is Culture," *Komsomolskaia pravda,* December 10, 1986, in *Current Digest of Soviet Press,* vol. 38, no. 52, pp. 2–4.

"The source of morality is culture. But religion cannot be dismissed from the historical experience of morality, for its history is inseparable from history as such."

Soviet poet Yevgeny Yevtushenko

The source of morality is culture. But religion cannot be dismissed from the historical experience — both positive and negative — of morality, for its history is inseparable from history as such. Reflections on religion, even though they are not in the nature of straightforward exposes, should not be interpreted derisively as "flirting with God." Lenin's phrase was devastatingly exact, but it was said at a particular time and was aimed at a particular target, and it is inappropriate to transfer it to today, readdressing it to our leading writers. . . .

Let's at least remember that at the time of the Roman Empire Christianity played an unquestionably progressive role. It was no accident that the bearers of the ideas "Thou shalt not kill" and "Love thy neighbor as thyself" were torn to pieces by the emperor's lions. . . .

Our country's Constitution speaks clearly and precisely about freedom of religion. In our country church and state are separate, and that is as it should be. But nowhere in our laws is it written that atheism and the state are inseparable. Our socialist state is a union of Communists and non-Party people, believers and atheists. Atheism is a voluntary phenomenon, not one that is forcibly imposed. Atheism should be one of the manifestations of the freedoms of our society, as religion is, and it should not involve coercion. . . .

The Bible is a great cultural monument. To this day, I don't understand why state publishing houses have published the Koran but not the Bible. Without knowing the Bible, our young people cannot understand many things in Pushkin, Gogol, Dostoyevsky, and Tolstoy. . . . The socialist world view has absorbed all the moral searching of human thought in the name of man, including the best of what Christian morality contains. . . .

Atheism in itself is not a source of morality. The source of morality is culture.

Yevtushenko correctly credited Lenin with the phrase "flirting with God," but, by using that phrase Yevtushenko also meant to call to mind a much talked about recent article in which a well-established philosopher clearly enunciated the anti-Likhachev side of the debate, as may be seen in the following excerpt.

The author, Ivan Kryvelev, criticizes accepted Soviet writers who suggest that answers to the current ethical crisis may be found in religion rather than atheism.

"**R**eligion has always claimed a monopoly in the field of ethics. Without faith, it asserts, there is no morality. This would seem to be a matter of the remote past. But it's not. Recently, statements whose authors support these claims either openly or in a thinly veiled way have been encountered with increasing frequency. . . .

Let us recall that Lenin . . . resolutely rejected any manifestations of "flirting with God," which he characterized as "an unutterable abomination," applying this description generally to "any religious idea, any idea about any sort of god."

To reject principles and consistent atheism is to reject the very foundations of the scientific-materialist world view. And to leave morality to the domain of religion — isn't that a form of flirting with God? . . .

In this connection, it is impossible to overlook certain statements made by V. Astafyev in the magazine *Nash sovremennik* (Our Contemporary). He asks: "What has become of us? Who has thrust us into an abyss of evil and woe, and why? Who has extinguished the light of goodness in our soul? Who has blown out the lamp of our consciousness and thrown it into the dark, deep pit in which we are groping and seeking the bottom, seeking a support and some kind of guiding light to the future? What use do we have for the light that leads to the fires of hell?" The writer movingly recalls the time when "we lived with a light in our soul, a light that had been acquired long before us by doers of great deeds (Moses, Christ, Mohammed, Buddha? — I. Kryvelev) and had been lit for us so that we would not wander in the darkness, not dash our faces into trees in the forest or collide with one another in the world, not scratch out each other's eyes, not break our neighbor's bones." This paradisiacal time has receded into the past; it has been "stolen from us and nothing given in its place, which has given rise to unbelief, to a universal disbelief in everything." What can be done, the author asks in despair? "To whom can we pray? Who can we ask to forgive us?" And he recalls: "After all, we once knew and have still not forgotten how to forgive even our enemies.". . .

Reading such a thing in the Soviet press is more than strange. And not only because of the plainly expressed tendency of flirting with God, but also because what we see are extremely flagrant examples of forgetting the commonly known facts of history and the present day — facts, moreover, that have been illuminated and theoretically interpreted by Marxism and that, by virtue of their obviousness, have not been disputed for a long time. . . .

I. Kryvelev, "Flirting with God," *Komsomolskaia pravda*, July 30, 1986, in *Current Digest of Soviet Press*, vol. 38, no. 47, pp. 4–5.

"GOD-SEEKING"

Atheism and Religion: Questions and Answers is an annual Russian language publication designed to give an official response to current questions dealing with atheist education. As is indicated in the text, Soviet officialdom has expressed considerable concern about "God-seeking" behaviors on the part of Soviet youth, especially among those with a university education.

Ateizm i religiia: Voprosy i otvety (Atheism and Religion: Questions and Answers) (Moscow: Izdatelstvo politicheskoi literatury, 1985), pp. 138–142.

" **Q**uestion: What significance does Lenin's criticism of God-seeking and God-building have for the contemporary ideological struggle?

Answer: The defeat of the revolution of 1905 and the subsequent onset of political reaction reinvigorated religious and mystical ideas among the intelligentsia. In the article, "Our Liquidators," Lenin wrote: "It is not accidental but a kind of necessity that all of our reactionaries in general and liberal reactionaries in particular have pounced upon religion." Ideological reaction among the intelligentsia took on a religious literary and philosophical orientation which received the name "God-seeking." The idea of the God-seekers found most clear expression in the collection *Landmarks* (Vekhi) published by the Constitutional Democrats and in the works of Dmitry Merezhkovsky, Ziniada Gippius, Vasily Rozanov, N.M. Minsky, the former Marxists Sergei Bulgakov and Nicholas Berdiaev, the works of the decadent poets, and the words of philosophers who were promoting the ideas of the mystic Vladimir Soloviev. God-seekers worked from the premise that there is a God and it is only necessary to "find" him. Every person can find God in his own soul, in a mystical experience of unification with God.

Opposing the ideas of materialism, scientific socialism and atheism and trying to neutralize their effect on the progressive part of the intelligentsia and the working class, God-seekers figured that all social movements, if they want to achieve success, must be guided by religious principles and the ideal of god-manhood. They called the Russian people the "God-bearing people," and they considered that a profound religiousness was a part of their essential character. The God-seekers spoke about the need to develop a "new religious consciousness" which should be introduced into the "dark religious elemental nature of the Russian people" and since they considered that only a religious community could save Russia they summoned the intelligentsia to unite with the Russian Orthodox Church. . . . Lenin subjected the ideas of God-seekers to sharp criticism, calling their views "ideological garbage."

"The writers of *Landmarks* are helping the advanced bourgeoisie to find a new ideological stick, a spiritual stick," he wrote. . . .

The idea of god, Lenin emphasized, has never "linked the personality with society" but has always "bound the oppressed classes by faith in the divinity of the oppressors." Lenin wrote that in contemporary bourgeois society, "the people and workers are stupefied by the idea of a purified, spiritual, fabricated little deity." He emphasized the special danger of refined forms of religion, "which preach the creation and fabrication of little deities," and he sharply condemned all attempts of toying or "flirting" with the idea of God. . . .

In connection with the approach of the millennium of the introduction of Christianity into Rus, the bourgeois religious propaganda and religious centers are spinning out a campaign whose goal is to distort the true role of religion and the church in the history of Russia. They are puffing up the myth about the true religiousness of the Russian people and the close link of the cultures of Russians, Ukrainians, and other peoples of our country with religion, extolling religious writers and thinkers and trying to ignite interest in God-seeking and the works of Merezhkovsky, Berdiaev, Bulgakov, and Vladimir Soloviev. . . .

On the other hand, representatives of religious organizations in the U.S.S.R. are trying to formulate a "new religious consciousness" and create a new type of believer. And in the works of several Soviet writers religious terms and symbols as well as mystical plots sometimes are used unnecessarily and unjustifiably. At the June (1983) plenum of the CC CPSU [Central Committee of the Communist Party] it was noted that God-seeking themes of the idealization of the patriarchal way of life were creeping into certain works. All of these phenomena require principled criticism. And here the party approach and methodological principles of the struggle with God-seeking worked out by Lenin provide invaluable help.

"

The best and loftiest minds in the history of mankind have selflessly fought against the ecclesiastical intoxicant. A noble and heroic tradition of freethinking and atheism has been established.

We Communists have received that tradition and developed it. Our atheism is founded on the scientific world view, and it is as unshakable as that world view. Morality not only is not contradictory to it, it is organically inherent to it. This is a nonreligious morality that necessarily presupposes conscientiousness, justice, and spirituality, in the best and loftiest sense of these words. **"**

Are religion and atheism viewed as equally rich sources for social values in the Soviet Union today?

Kryvelev deals here with "God-seeking," a highly significant feature of the "religious" aspect of Soviet society — interpreted broadly to encompass values and beliefs. The name was used even before the revolution to identify the spiritual and philosophical quests of intellectuals at the end of the last century, including Nicolas Berdiaev, whose discussion of the Russian religious tradition concludes an earlier chapter. Lenin harshly criticized "God-seeking" (see box, pp. 198–199).

The conflict between "God-seeking" and the goals of Soviet atheist education is elucidated in the following excerpt from *Critical Problems of the Theory and Practice of Scientific Atheism*. The author cites a June 1983 speech made by Konstantin Chernenko in which the party secretary complained "that 'God-seeking' motifs and idealization of the patriarchal order" were creeping into books and films.

M. P. Novikov and F. G. Ovsienko, eds., *Aktual'nye problemy teorii i praktiki nauchnogo ateizma* (Critical Problems of the Theory and Practice of Scientific Atheism) (Moscow: Moscow University, 1985), pp. 50ff.

" For the majority of our young people, attempts to gain an understanding of the complex problems of life and of the spiritual culture are conducted characteristically from a materialist point of view. However, it is not always the case that young people's discussions about these questions are based upon knowledge of scientific atheism. One of the causes of this is an unsystematic and superficial comprehension of a great array of cultural information, including religious information, which leads sometimes to an outright defense of religion.

Another cause is the presence of "God-seeking motifs" in a number of works of Soviet literature, which were criticized at the June 1983 plenum of the Central Committee of the Communist Party. "God-seeking motifs," which are sometimes sprinkled into the really powerful artistic works of our culture, nevertheless exert an undesirable influence upon the formation of the scientific-materialistic worldview of youth. Their forms are rather diverse: attempts to reevaluate our cultural heritage which highlight a conservative, reactionary line in culture and treat it as if it were fruitful; emphasis upon the religious elements in the cultural tradition; idealization of church figures, including those who hunted out heretics and condemned them to be burned (for example, Josef of

Volotsk); identification of the national culture with religion; emphasizing ideas of eternal humanity, pure spirituality, absolute good; disregard for the revolutionary democrats, etc. And although "God-seeking motifs" are criticized and condemned by the more progressive leaders of culture in our country, they continue to occur in various areas of culture — in fiction, literary criticism, painting, etc., creating substantial difficulties for atheistic education. One must not forget that all productions of the Soviet printing houses are taken by our youth as having high quality and providing trustworthy guidance for thought and conduct. **"**

In his article on flirting with God, Kryvelev accused one of the most popular Soviet writers of the past ten years, Chinghiz Aitmatov, of promoting "God-seeking" in his novel, *Plakha* (The Executioner's Block). According to an American critic, this novel, which appeared in the second half of 1986, can be read as "the most representative text of the Gorbachev thaw in the sense that it both incorporates most of the relevant themes and has served frequently as occasion for their discussion among intellectuals" (Katerina Clark, "The Executioner's block: A Novel of the Thaw," *Times Literary Supplement*, June 26, 1987, p. 696). This assessment accords with another by a Soviet literary critic who said: "Aitmatov's novel reflects the intensive moral searching of our days, searching which is an indispensable condition of perestroika." ("A Novel's Paradoxes, or Paradoxes of Perception," *Literaturnaya gazeta* (Literature Gazette), October 15, 1986, p. 4.)

The chief atheist journal, *Science and Religion,* carried an unusually long discussion of this novel — further demonstrating that the novel has significance for the Soviet religious question. The discussion was introduced with these words: "In recent times there have appeared many brilliant, significant literary works which have excited readers. But, really, not one has evoked such heated discussion as Aitmatov's novel *Plakha*."

The author of *Plakha* comes from Kirghizia, a traditionally Muslim nation, but he declares straightforwardly that he is an atheist. However, his protagonist is a Christian named after the Hebrew prophet, Obadiah (Avdii in Russian). Aitmatov's choice of a protagonist, he said, was "no accident." He continued, "The Christian religion provides a very powerful vehicle in the figure of Jesus Christ. The Islamic religion, in which I am included by virtue of my origin, has no such figure. Mohammed was not a martyr. He experienced difficult, agonizing days, but as for being crucified for an idea and forgiving people for it forever — there is none of that. Jesus Christ provides me with an occasion to say something from my innermost being to present-day man. Therefore, I, an atheist, encountered him on my creative path. This explains my choice of a protagonist, and the fact that Avdii Kallistratov is exactly

"Aitmatov's novel reflects the intensive moral searching of our days, searching which is an indispensable condition of perestroika."
Soviet literary critic

who he is" (Irina Rishina, "The Price is Life," *Literaturnaya gazeta* (Literature Gazette) August 13, 1987, in *Current Digest of Soviet Press*, vol. 38, no. 49, p. 5).

The son of an Orthodox priest, Advii enters the seminary not in quest of a church career but of God. The God he seeks, however, is not the God of the church, and Avdii is expelled because of his unorthodox views. But he does not abandon his faith. He wants to lead society to the solution of its problems by way of a universal acceptance of God. In his spiritual quest, Avdii interprets the Gospels in a new way that leads him to proclaim the coming of a messiah who will bring peace and justice. The struggle against current problems in society is portrayed in Avdii's infiltration of the Soviet drug culture. On assignment as a reporter for a Komsomol newspaper he is crucified by drug dealers.

Plakha caused quite a stir, as shown in the following excerpts from a roundtable discussion printed in *Science and Religion* involving several scholars in the fields of literature, philosophy, and scientific atheism. The participants show that they are unsettled by the popularity of the novel, and they try to discover what that popularity says about the needs of Soviet people.

"Until Heaven Vanishes," *Nauka i religiia* (Science and Religion), September 1987, pp. 21–26.

Question: What is the cause of such a broad, mass reaction to *Plakha*?

Romanov: Aitmatov has raised the urgent, painful questions of worldwide scope and spoken about them with the ruthless frankness with which people discuss them in our society and the contemporary world. This resonance of the pain of human social needs and the power of the emotional and artistic impact has struck a vital chord.

Anninskii: Of course, the fundamental reason is that the problems are current. Although the fabric of the novel is weak in places.

Kochetov: I agree. Aitmatov's novel attracts because of the reality of the moral, ecological, and philosophical questions which are treated with special relentlessness, nakedly, without gloss. But I think that one of the chief reasons for such broad reader interest is the very fact of the treatment of Christianity — the character of such a treatment.

Romanov: Well, that would be too simple. After all Aitmatov is not alone in using religious themes.

Question: Alexei Nikolaevich, you spoke about the character of the treatment of the religious theme. What do you have in mind?

Kochetov: The writer declared that he is an atheist. . . . However the question arises: Is it really worth propagating the ideas of Christianity in order to demonstrate that the people of our planet have become aware of the inescapable consequences of nuclear catastrophe? In our struggle for peace is it necessary to appeal to religion? Do we really need the rudiments of religious doctrines which have long ago been worn out and overcome? The author comes to the conclusion that the self-destruction of humanity is the result of its sinfulness, that is, its "guilt" before God! Is there any difference here from the doctrines of contemporary "fundamentalists" who conclude from the Apocalypse that nuclear catastrophe is unavoidable and undermine the struggle for peace?

Zolotusskii: I think that the use of the Christ theme is connected with the discussion of values that is broadly developed in our literature. Humanity has a tradition of such discussion and we do, too, in our country. Take any great Russian writer. Can there be a single vital problem without a dispute about whether God exists and whether everything is permitted or not? . . .

Romanov: It seems to me that Aitmatov's treatment of the language of Christianity and its symbolism emphasizes that the problems which torment his heroes reach beyond the bounds of the problems of nations, beyond the Muslim world, beyond the world in which a materialistic worldview is affirmed. They have a thousand-year-old history, and therefore there is a thousand-year-old experience for their understanding, interpretation, and attempts at practical solutions. . . . In using biblical subjects he is using images that have been widely dispersed in world public opinion and which have strong emotional hues. Isn't it enough to argue from science? Apparently not. . . .

Question: The use of biblical images and subjects is understandable. But isn't it possible to see such use as a popularization of religious doctrines which have been repudiated by history?

Zolotusskii: I could not agree with that. Aitmatov's Jesus of Nazareth is not the Son of God, not a god-man, but a twentieth century figure. He is a reformer, a revolutionary, a liberal, and a fighter for nuclear disarmament. He has visions of the atomic apocalypse. But what in the New Testament is the work of God or the Devil is, in Aitmatov's novel, the work of man. The problem of God in Aitmatov is not posed simply — it is resolved as the problem of social justice. . . .

Kochetov: I see in *Plakha* a retelling of the Christian doctrine of sin as a result of people's loss of their "divine essence" and their rejection of the saving mission of Christ, the Son of God — a retelling from a frankly theological position. There is an attempt to identify with atheism the problems against which we are struggling today — egoism, materialism, indifference to real social evils, and vulgarity. . . . The essence of the novel's religion is faith in the reality of the supernatural and a conviction that all nature and man are dependent upon it. Aitmatov himself builds his novel on an exaltation of the saving mission of Christ, the Son of God. . . .

"

The large number of publications with religious themes and great public interest in wrestling with spiritual questions show that glasnost has changed the ideological atmosphere of Soviet society. Signs that

THE EXECUTIONER'S BLOCK

In this excerpt of *Plakha,* the protagonist is murdered by a criminal gang whose leader is portrayed as a neo-Stalinist thug. The incident, from which the novel gets its name, contains explicitly drawn religious images. See the text for a discussion of the significance of this novel in the new atmosphere of open exploration of religious questions.

Chingiz Aitmatov, *Plakha* (The Executioner's Block) (Moscow: Molodaia gvardiia, 1987), pp. 200–203.

"Avdii lost consciousness; he fell under their legs and they began to kick him with their boots. Avdii's last thought was of Inga: What will become of her? Surely no one can love her as I can.

He had lost all hearing; everything faded from sight and for some reason a gray she-wolf appeared before him. It was the very same one which had sprung over him in that hot summer on the steppe. . . .

"Save me, wolf," Avdii suddenly blurted out.

For some reason he felt intuitively that the wolves, Akbara and Tashchainar, would shortly come to their lair which humans were occupying this night. . . . But again the wolves had to retreat into the steppe. Tortured, restless, they withdrew into the dark, into which their eyes peered. . . .

And the trial, the kangaroo court, continued. The roaring-drunk hunters did not notice that the accused, Avdii Kallistratov, could barely stand when he swung his fists back at them.

"Come on, stand up, parson," they prodded him with kicks and obscenity, first Mishash, then Kepa, but Avdii simply groaned quietly. Breaking into a rage, Ober-Kandalov seized Avdii, crumpled like a sack, picked him up by the collar, and spit out a stream of words which themselves got him madder:

"You swine, you've decided to scare us with God, to put the fear of God in us, to ram him down our throats, you stinking skunk! You won't frighten us with God, you can't do it, you bitch. And who do you think you are? We are doing the state's business here, and you are fighting the plan, you bitch, fighting the district, — you're some kind of swine, an enemy of the people, an enemy of the people and the state. And there is no place on earth for enemies, wreckers, and saboteurs! That's what Stalin said: 'He who is not with us is against us.' We must destroy the enemies of the people! Give them no quarter! . . . And you church rat, what are you up to? Sabotage! You wrecked the mission! You tried to make monks out of us. But I'll choke you, bastard, like an enemy of the people and they'll thank me for it because you are an agent of imperialism, skunk. You think that Stalin is no more, so there is no justice for you? Preacher boy, you're kneeling now. I have you in my power — curse your God or else it's the end for you, such a swine!"

Avdii couldn't keep his balance. He fell. They picked him up.

"Speak up, skunk," Ober-Kandalov bawled. "Renounce God! Say that there is no God."

"There is a God," Avdii moaned weakly.

"That's the way it is!" Mishash began to yell as if a burning coal had struck him. "I already said that you're speaking up for him, but he has left you now just to get even!"

Panting from rage, Ober-Kandalov again shook Avdii by the collar.

"Come on, padre, we'll put on a show for you that you'll never forget! Drag him over to that tree, we'll string him up, we'll hang the skunk!" Ober-Kandalov shouted. "We'll build a fire around his legs. Let him burn!"

They dragged Avdii quickly over to the scrub ringing the hollow.

"Bring the ropes!" Ober-Kandalov ordered Kepa.

He dashed to the cab.

"Hey you there! Uziukbai, big shot, get your ass over here, and you, whatcha standing around for? Hurry up! Heave to! If you don't I won't even let you smell the booze," Ober-Kandalov threatened the sots, and they broke their necks to string up the doomed Avdii.

The hooligan game suddenly took a horrible turn. The ugly farce was about to turn into lynch justice.

"The only thing that's wrong is we don't have a cross and nails in this god-forsaken steppe! Such a pity!" Mishash lamented, breaking a twig off the scrub with a snap. "That would really be

something — to crucify him!"

"It's no matter, we'll do it with ropes! It won't be any worse than hanging on nails," Ober-Kandalov found a way out of the situation. "We'll crucify him by his hands and feet, like a frog; tie him up so that he can't wiggle. Let him hang 'til morning; let him think about whether there is a God or not! I shall conduct such educational measures with him that he'll remember for sure all the rest of his life, the black collared rot! I never trained such types in the army! Well, get him, guys; grab him! String him up there on the branch, higher! Tie his hand there; his foot there!"

Everything happened so suddenly that Avdii was not able to fight back. Tied to the scrub, bound hand and foot with ropes, he hanged there, like a fresh pelt hung out to dry. Avdii still heard the cursing and the voices, but they seemed so far away. The sufferings sapped all of his strength. In his stomach, by the liver, was an unbearable throb, and it was as if something gave way in his waist under the pain. His strength slowly ebbed away. And it did not even concern him that the drunks vainly tried to set fire around his feet. Nothing more mattered to him. . . .

The lights flared up, the engine groaned, and the truck slowly crawled across the steppe. Darkness closed in. Quiet all around. And Avdii remained, bound to the tree, alone in the whole world. His chest burned, his insides throbbed, beclouding

his mind with pain. Consciousness left him, like slipping under a wave.

"My island on the Oka. Who will save you, Teacher?" his last thought broke forth like a flame and died away.

Then that final river drew near. Before his dying gaze appeared a great sea, an endless, continuous watery surface without edge or limit. The water seethed noiselessly and over it came a silent white wave like a blizzard over the field, out of nowhere. But barely visible on the edge of that noiseless sea the faint figure of a man vaguely descried — and Avdii recognize that man, Deacon Kallistratov, his father. And suddenly Avdii could hear his very own adolescent voice — the voice read aloud for father his favorite prayer. . . .

glasnost and perestroika might produce favorable changes for the religious situation, however, should be interpreted with caution. In the next three excerpts, observers express doubts about where the reforms may be leading. The first one, from the Commission on Security and Cooperation in Europe, suggests that a renewed openness to traditional Russian religious and cultural values may bring with it a revival of the repression of non-Christian religions that existed before the revolution.

"A New Wave of Soviet Anti-Semitism?" *CSCE Digest*, October 1987, p. 2.

The leader of Pamyat — a group that claims more than 20,000 Muscovite members — Dimitri Vasiliev believes that Russians must dominate all Soviet nationalities and that Jews are "masterminding" the systematic destruction of Russian culture.

Reuters/Bettmann Newsphoto.

" Has glasnost ironically unleashed a new wave of anti-Semitism in the Soviet Union?

At least some Soviet and Western Jewish leaders fear it has, and former Soviet political prisoner and Jewish refusenik Natan Sharansky believes that the Soviet Government is actually fostering it. What they are referring to is the public emergence of "Pamyat," the Memory Society, whose Russian nationalist positions have in many cases taken on anti-Semitic overtones. . . . Signs of its growing anti-Semitism became apparent at a meeting in December 1985, when one member delivered a speech featuring excerpts from the notorious anti-Semitic document, *The Protocols of the Elders of Zion.* . . .

Soviet officials have condemned Pamyat. [Former Moscow Party leader Boris] Yeltsin, who had met with Pamyat members after their May demonstration, later described them as "dangerous people" who "are not openly combatting democratization and glasnost, but . . . going after phantoms, like Freemasons and Zionists. They claim to want to preserve the country's legacy. In fact, though, it is democracy they are attacking."

The Soviet press has also attacked Pamyat, calling its actions divisive and its members deluded. *Moscow News* accused the society of "disseminating absurd fictions." *Komsomolskaia Pravda,* which has written about Pamyat's anti-Semitism, reported that it has received more than 300 letters denouncing the organization. *Sovetskaya Kultura* has asked why Pamyat is allowed to exist, and who provides it with funding and premises for its meetings. . . .

Sharansky argues that "Soviet officials have only criticized [Pamyat] in very mild and restrained language." In a September interview with the *Washington Times*, Sharansky charged that for Pamyat "to flourish the way it has, it had to be permitted by Gorbachev. Without his approval, they could not carry on." Others point to the fact that Pamyat has been allowed to hold demonstrations while public protests by Jewish refuseniks have been broken up by authorities. "

Another note of skepticism about the prospects for real change for the better is sounded by Kirill Golovin, an Orthodox believer. In an article written in late 1986, Golovin states that, in spite of slight improvements here and there in its fortunes, religion cannot be genuinely free so long as atheism remains officially approved and retains its control of the levers of power. In his view, the era of glasnost has merely introduced more clever and effective ways for atheism to keep its stranglehold on religion.

"Have there been any changes for the better in the attitude of the Soviet regime to the millions of Orthodox on the eve of the approaching great holiday, the millennium of the baptism of Rus? . . . In the [Brezhnev] years of seeming stability there began a "religious awakening" which, despite its restricted scope and contradictory character, rather strongly disturbed the functionaries. . . . They were forced by all of this, not to revise the developing policy in relation to the Orthodox Church (it was effective because it was cruel, and why abandon it when there is no need?), but to adjust it somewhat in the direction of more flexibility and formal variety. The adjustment was begun recently and, it seems, is still not finished.

Although the chief principle of this policy, based as before on the frank words of Lenin that "all ideas about any kind of god are the most unthinkable abomination," remained apparently unchanged, it was enriched by several contemporary nuances. Orthodox people, for example, were divided into the loyal Soviet majority and a few "religious extremists, aides, and stooges of imperialism." Loyal believers should be treated kindly but without concession, respectfully but without indulgence, understanding that they are citizens; "extremists" should be treated as clear and dangerous enemies, who must be identified and immediately isolated at all costs. The boundary between both categories is drawn very conditionally: in the capital it is one thing and in the provinces another, more hostile and arbitrary. Although, for example, in Tambov the appearance of a new person in church is a signal for special attention from the K.G.B., in the capital their concern is aroused only by a long-lasting Orthodox study-circle and influential activist. For this reason in the provinces it is now possible only to worship, while public religious activity (within definite bounds) can be conducted in a few chief cities only. . . .

Although the abandoned and half-destroyed churches are still standing in loneliness in the villages and cities, just try to tear them down now: the outcry and dismay will be inescapable. . . . Although public consciousness, which is being freed from the long antichurch fog is still a long way from the idea of opening the churches for services rather than simply preserving them, it undoubtedly is developing in a direction which is beneficial for Orthodoxy, since it is gradually coming to understand what its values and traditions have meant for the whole nation and its future. . . .

The inveterate state atheists have been trying to combat this ever-

Kirill Golovin, "The Dawn is at Hand," *Russkaia mysl* (Russian Thought) (published in Paris), March 27, 1987, pp. 6–7.

Closed as a place of worship for almost sixty years — authorities converted it into a reform school, sold its bells, plastered over its frescoes, and turned its Holy Trinity Cathedral into a recreation center — the Danilovsky Monastery, the oldest in Moscow, was returned to the church in 1983 and will serve as the new headquarters for the Russian Orthodox Church (right and facing page).

Courtesy of Evelyne Musser (right).
Melanie Stetson Freeman/*The Christian Science Monitor* (facing page).

increasing process of self-consciousness. In July of this year, Doctor of Philosophy Kryvelev struck out with a club in *Komsomolskaia pravda* against this growing "sedition," reprimanding Rasputin, Astafiev, and Aitmatov. It is not difficult to imagine what consequences this outcry would have brought thirty years ago; but now it only ignites interest in the readers. . . . The militant ardor of state atheism has faded and the staunch cadres have died out; there is not the former drive, energy and influence, and even the simple-minded intellectual is disgusted by it. However, we will not forget that it remains as before the most important and the capstone element of the ruling ideology, and therefore it is mobilizing its reserves in preparation for the jubilee of the baptism. . . .

In the time of the celebration of this jubilee propagandists will obviously not fail to mention how many Orthodox churches and prayer houses have been opened in recent years (since 1977, 33) naturally forgetting to say how many of them were closed simultaneously. It is no secret that the local authorities, especially in the provinces, use any available reason in order to restrict or liquidate the places of worship, which they hate. For opening a new church, as a rule, exceptional local or political circumstances are required. . . . Christ's institution remains a

> **"Christ's institution remains a foreign body in the socialist state and the essence of church activity runs counter to the chief ideas of this state."**
> Kirill Galovin, member of Russian Orthodox Church

foreign body in the socialist state and the essence of church activity runs counter to the chief ideas of this state. . . .

Taking into account the change in public opinion, and especially the pressure from the outside, today's atheists are using the old method of the carrot and the stick. In February 1986, one of the founders of the religious youth seminars, Valery Poresh of Leningrad, was freed from prison without his giving any sign of repentance, and presently Alexander Ogorodnikov, the other founder, finished his term. The poetess Irina Ratushinskaia was released. But almost right away a librarian in Kiev, Protsenko, was sentenced to three years. They gave to the church some judicial indulgence by legalizing existing practice [Note: this is apparently a reference to a new interpretation of the law on religious associations — see box], but then they charged an old priest, Father Joseph, from a remote parish in Novgorod District, with "possession of firearms."

Considering these facts, one can only conclude that even under the new general secretary the attitude of the authorities to Orthodoxy, despite the correction which has occurred, has not changed in principle; it has only been embellished demagogically as has happened in other areas. It is rumored that at a Kremlin reception, Gorbachev asked the Orthodox Church to help the party raise the moral level of the people. If this desire is sincere, then why not permit the opening of more churches for this goal and resurrect the Temperance Society which existed in Russia before the revolution? But no. Partocracy continues to hold the old atheist dogma and the earlier forms of treatment of religion.

Thus the illusion being spread . . . that the Communists have no other recourse than finally to make peace with the church and, having achieved a concordat with it, to give it more freedom in the life of society seems naive. Communists will not voluntarily give up a bit of their power over people's minds. **"**

A number of those expressing doubts about the real value of perestroika in religion believe that generalized improvements in the "atmosphere" for religion cannot produce genuine freedom of religion so long as the legal and administrative systems that the revolution brought about remain in place. The following open letter, addressed to the heads of the Soviet state and the Communist Party, was signed by people from several Christian denominations — Orthodox, Protestant, and Catholic — including Alexander Ogorodnikov, founder of the Christian seminars mentioned in the previous chapter. The signers enumerate the major structural changes which they believe must be made if perestroika and glasnost are to lead to more than change in the atmosphere. Their specific concern is for the Orthodox Church, but as they themselves suggest, their proposals would apply to other religions as well.

To the President of the Presidium of the Supreme Soviet U.S.S.R., A.A. Gromyko, and

Member of the Presidium of the Supreme Soviet, General Secretary of C.C. C.P.S.U., M.S. Gorbachev:

In our time in which important changes in the public life of our country are occurring, the problem of the position of the Christian Church becomes a critical matter of principle. . . . Unfortunately, at present the situation is complicated because the church is deprived in practice of the possibility of taking any real part in the life of the nation. While it is legally separated from the state, the church really turns out to be separated from society as well. The leading and directing force of Soviet society, according to article 6 of the constitution of the U.S.S.R., is the Communist Party of the Soviet Union, which is atheist in its ideology. Thus it is only with great difficulty that the church, the spiritual leader of believers, is able to fulfill its most important and proper functions. . . .

We seek concrete changes in the legislation on religion and cults. The following are necessary:

1. Grant to the church and religious associations the status of juridical person;

2. Abolish the decree on nationalization of all church property. This must be expressed in the return, gratis, to the church and to religious associations of all property and valuables which historically have belonged to them: buildings and associated structures, church vessels, relics, icons and other objects belonging to the church, and also books of Holy Scripture and religious-philosophical literature;

3. Change article 52 of the constitution of the U.S.S.R. in such a way that it declares the equality of rights of both antireligious and religious propaganda and of religious and antireligious organizations;

4. Abolish the resolution of April 8, 1929 on religious associations in which all charitable activity of the church and religious associations was forbidden. Permit the creation within the church of charitable organizations which have the purpose of giving material aid to the needy from voluntary contributions and do not hinder the free collection of contributions for charitable purposes. Permit and guarantee in practice visitation by clergy of prisons and hospitals upon request of believers and their relatives as well as upon the personal initiative of the clergy. Do not prohibit religious rites in prisons and hospitals; do not deny the right of prisoners in places of confinement to wear crosses and other religious symbols under their clothing and to have religious literature. Permit them to make confession and to have spiritual counsel with priests;

5. Give the church full freedom in the performance of religious proclamation and dissemination of religious teaching, including outside of the places appointed for worship services. Give the church the possibility of using mass media and of freely distributing its publica-

"An Open Appeal of a Group of Christians of Various Confessions," *Russkaia mysl* (Russian Thought) (published in Paris), September 18, 1987, p. 7.

tions, including those which are produced by contract with the state. Permit the creation of independent religious publishing houses and presses; do not hinder the publication and dissemination of independent bulletins about religious life in the U.S.S.R. Permit the creation of open public libraries and reading rooms for religious literature;

6. Do not hinder the activity of the church in the area of education and training, including such training for minor children. Permit the church to organize public Sunday schools and other religious educational institutions for children with the agreement of the children themselves and their parents. All believers, including children, should have the right to be absent from places of work or study on days of the great religious holidays, as is the case in almost all countries of the world;

7. Give to the church and to religious associations the rights of public organizations in the U.S.S.R., including the right to nominate deputies for local and central governmental bodies, the right to own and dispose of property and other means. Grant a wider possibility for the church and religious associations to participate in the public life of the country, and in particular permit their participation in the work of administrative commissions of the executive committees, medical institutions, temperance societies, and other public and Soviet organizations;

8. Guarantee in the new legislation the independence of religious organizations and the noninterference of the state in the affairs of the church. Protect the church from discriminatory taxation and emphasize the principles of voluntary participation of the church in state funds, which is frequently violated in practice;

9. Do not impede the development of free contacts of the church and believers with international religious centers and with individual believers abroad. Guarantee the unhindered enjoyment of the right to make pilgrimages to holy places outside of the Soviet Union. Permit believers free emigration from the U.S.S.R. for religious convictions;

10. Understanding the needs of other denominations, the members of the Russian Orthodox Church insist that all citizens who are not able to bear arms because of their religious convictions should be granted the option of alternative service in place of obligatory service in the Soviet Army. We recognize that many of our requests here pertain not only to the Russian Orthodox Church but also to other confessions;

11. Do not impede the activity of Bible societies on the territory of the U.S.S.R. Give legal guarantees of such activity;

We trust that our suggestions will be reviewed by you attentively and benevolently, and we will receive an answer to them in accordance with legally established procedure;

[This letter was signed in Moscow, by thirty-eight persons: seventeen identified themselves as Orthodox — six from Moscow, two from Leningrad, four from Riga, two from Minsk, one from Rovno, one from Astrakhan, and one from Arkhangelsk; eight identified themselves as

Catholic; one was from the Armenian Apostolic Church; eleven identified themselves as members of a group called "Regeneration and Renewal of the Evangelical Church of Latvia," eight of whom were associated with a theological seminary.]

If all these suggested legislative changes were enacted, the entire mechanism for state control of religion would be dismantled. The writer's vision is grandiose, even utopian. While influential persons have certainly hinted that glasnost and perestroika will bring new opportunities for religion, they have never suggested that a fundamental

Many Jews have seized glasnost as an opportunity to protest the denial of their right to emigrate.
AP/World Wide Press.

In a rare display of high-level state respect for the importance of religion, General Secretary Gorbachev's wife Raisa attended a June 1988 millennium celebration with Soviet and foreign churchmen.

AP/Wide World Photos.

restructuring would take place. Indeed, control of the church by the state has been a Russian tradition for one thousand years; there has never been a time in Russia when there was freedom of religion as it is understood in the West. Moreover, those who determine official policy toward religion still subscribe to ideological atheism. Chairman Kharchev himself declared: "Religious consciousness will disappear with the coming of pure Communism. But that won't be soon: maybe a hundred years, maybe a thousand" (William Teska, "Glasnost and Religion," *The Witness*, February, 1988, p. 7).

Nevertheless, it may be significant that Gorbachev refers to the new law being prepared as a "law on freedom of conscience." This language suggests that the law in preparation is not merely an amendment of the old Stalinist law "on religious associations," which is the most objectionable to religious people because it requires registration of churches and outlaws many activities which religious organizations seek to carry out. If the old law basically remains in place, the hopes of the letter writers will be frustrated completely, but, if the old law is replaced with a new one, some of their hopes may be realized. It also seems significant that Gorbachev has chosen to use again the original title of Lenin's law: "On Freedom of Conscience." (The law's title was changed shortly to "Decree on the Separation of the Church from the State and the School from the Church.") By using Lenin's original title, Gorbachev may be signaling that the new law will implement Leninist principles.

Many questions remain about what effect Gorbachev's leadership will eventually have on religion. One important one is whether Gorbachev can retain his hold on his office. Opposition to all his reforms is well entrenched because they threaten many established interests. Now that Gorbachev has committed himself to substantial improvements in the official treatment of religion, it is conceivable that his opponents may use that issue alone as a battleground on which to defeat his entire reform program.

In the past, the religion issue has fallen victim to Soviet political factionalism. Some observers claim that Khrushchev's antireligious campaign was a concession to dogmatic hardliners in order to secure their approval of his reforms; people who hold to this interpretation wonder whether Gorbachev might be compelled to make a similar tradeoff. But a full generation of people have come of age between Khrushchev and Gorbachev, and the idea that religion must be accorded respect—for pragmatic reasons if nothing else—is now recognized by a substantial number of leaders in Soviet society.

Despite these doubts and fears, the period of glasnost and perestroika has already cleared some hurdles. First, important people have admitted categorically that some of the practices and policies of the past violated the rights of religious believers and contradicted the professed principles of the Soviet system. Second, clear demands for change have been aired openly, some practical changes have been made, and others are promised. Third, influential figures in the Soviet cultural community have expressed an appreciative view of religion and have identified themselves as advocates of change. Whatever may happen to the Gorbachev program, a simple return to the way things were in the past does not now seem possible.

"There has never been a time in Russia when there was freedom of religion as it is understood in the West."

Is "freedom of religion" an absolute, a condition that can be objectively measured everywhere — or does it mean different things to different people at different times?

CONCLUSION

Russian rulers, tsars as well as Communist Party secretaries, have tried for centuries to stamp out the religious faiths adhered to by substantial portions of their people. But these beleaguered targets of religious oppression have tenaciously held to their faiths despite repeated antireligious campaigns, pogroms, restrictive laws, executions, and the desecration of houses of worship.

Government efforts to impose religious uniformity began with Prince Vladimir. As soon as he adopted Orthodoxy as the state religion, he embarked on a program of uprooting the traditional religious practices of indigenous Slavic tribes. Remnants of paganism nonetheless survived for several centuries and were finally not so much eliminated as assimilated into Russian religious life.

As Moscow extended its political authority, especially after 1500, it incorporated more and more people of diverse religions — Islam, Catholicism, Protestantism, Judaism, and Buddhism. And as Russian society was influenced by other cultures, especially Western European, diversity of religious expression began to emerge among the Russians themselves in the form of Old Belief, native Russian mysticism, and Protestantism.

To try to impose uniformity upon this increasingly heterogenous population, rulers like Ivan the Terrible, Alexis Romanov, Peter the Great, Nicholas I, Alexander III, and Nicholas II utilized the immense power of the state in combination with the power of Orthodoxy, wedded as it was to the state. The activities of non-Orthodox religions were thus almost always severely circumscribed and often directly suppressed. Jews were hounded out of the empire; Muslims were forcibly converted to Orthodoxy; Old Believers were burned at the stake; Eastern Rite Catholics had their children taken away to be raised as Orthodox; Baptists were exiled to Siberia and the Caucasus.

∎ **217**

The revolution altered this general pattern only slightly; but the details were different. After 1917, the ruling Communist Party, aggressively committed to atheism and expecting the disappearance of religion, applied restraints on all organized religions. Synagogues, mosques, and churches were closed by the tens of thousands and equal numbers of clergymen of all faiths were liquidated. Children attended classes led by teachers trained and required to nurture atheistic thinking.

The question of whether this traditional Russian pattern of authoritarianism may be fading under General Secretary Mikhail Gorbachev cannot yet be answered. If he does break the pattern and end the centuries-old official suppression of religious activity, this break may prove to be among the most significant achievements of his restructuring program — a truly revolutionary departure from past practices. It will also constitute a strikingly ironic, tacit recognition of the failure of the first Communist state to achieve one of its primary and oft-articulated goals: the eradication of religion. Conceived as a complete and pure ideology — a system of belief, like Orthodoxy, purporting to have all the answers — Communism has often emulated the practices of the religions it has sought to eliminate. Quasi-religious Communist pageants, hymns, rituals, and a code of conduct have been created to supplant religion. Paradoxically, they may have strengthened the determination of believers to abide by their faiths.

The state's effort to quash religion in the Soviet Union has not fully succeeded; millions of Soviet citizens are still believers. On the other hand, the efforts of believers to eliminate state control and repression have also not fully succeeded; restrictions and regulations continue to limit the practice of religion in the Soviet Union. After seventy years of Communism, and one thousand years since the baptism of Vladimir, the changes taking place in the last two decades of the twentieth century may well be decisive in determining the future relationship between religion and ideology in the Soviet Union.

The complex and often contradictory nature of this relationship is captured in the final excerpt. The following poem, as well as the author's description of the inspiration for it, was written by Eugenia Ginzburg while she was in a Soviet prison. The wife of a senior party official, and a Communist herself, Ginzburg was a victim of Stalin's massive purge of the party five decades ago.

CONCLUSION Eugenia Semyonovna Ginzburg, *Journey into the Whirlwind* (New York: Harcourt, Brace & World, 1967), pp. 229–230.

" **W**e happened to read some lines about the destiny of the Jewish people, their stubbornness and vitality, and the ancient greeting: "Next year in Jerusalem!" I took this as the theme of the New Year verses Julia [another prisoner] had asked me for:

And again, like gray-haired Jews,
We shall cry out eagerly
With voices cracked and weak:
Next year in Jerusalem!

Clinking our prison mugs
We shall drain them dry —
There is no sweeter wine
Than the wine of hope!

Comrade, be of good cheer,
Our prison food is not manna from heaven
But, like the gray-haired Jews,
We believe in the Promised Land.

We may be poor and persecuted,
But on New Year's Eve
We'll cry:
Next year in Jerusalem.

So at last New Year's Eve arrived — our first in prison. We were confident that before the year was out we should be "in Jerusalem" and fell asleep dreaming sweetly of the months to come. Next year in Jerusalem! 〞

READER'S GUIDE

INTRODUCTION

This guide is a companion to *Keeping the Faiths*, the second book in a series published by the Committee for National Security and entitled *Beyond the Kremlin*. It is designed for use by a wide range of people: some who are using only one volume (and doing so alone), others who belong to a community group that plans to discuss each volume, and still others who will organize small community discussion groups. This guide does not tell you how to read or what to conclude from your reading. It is designed to amplify and complement this particular book.

Section one of this guide provides questions that may be useful for you to think about while reading the materials and afterward. Questions that are especially appropriate for beginning and focusing discussions are marked with an asterisk (*).

Section two lists phone numbers of organizations and institutions you can call for answers to brief questions about the Soviet Union and U.S.-Soviet relations.

Sections three and four offer guidance for people who want to follow up their reading of these materials by either participating in a discussion group (section three) or undertaking some other type of educational project (section four). The section on discussion groups outlines how they work (from defining the purpose of such groups to wrapping up a meeting), identifies some common problems, and offers a set of models for structuring and running discussion groups. Although the educational projects described in section four can be undertaken by members of a discussion group, they are also activities that individuals can pursue on their own.

The Guide concludes with a short annotated reading list of books, periodicals, and videos.

■ **221**

F. Hibon/Sygma.

> "It is better to know some of the questions than all of the answers."
>
> **James Thurber**

I. QUESTIONS

You might want to ponder certain general questions such as the following:

- What do I think of religion in the Soviet Union?
- How and why have I formed these impressions?
- Do I know any Russians or other Soviets?
- How are political ideology and religious belief related in the United States?

As you read, reflect upon, or discuss each section of this book, you might focus on some of the following more specific questions. (As noted above, questions followed by an asterisk may be especially useful in focusing a group discussion.)

Religious Tradition

- What do the very beginnings of Orthodoxy in tenth century Kiev reveal about early Russian society and its values?
- In what ways are the revered saints of Russia different from the saints worshiped by Christians in the West?
- How did Orthodoxy contribute to the Russians' historic sense that their nation had a special role to play in the world?*
- What is the enduring political significance of Patriarch Nikon's seventeenth century decree altering Orthodox religious practices?
- What was the impact of Russian expansion on religion? And conversely, how did Orthodoxy view state expansion?
- What were the most significant aspects of Orthodox belief in Russia—and how had church-state relations evolved—before the 1917 revolution?

Competing Faiths

- What has been the impact of Communist ideology on religion in the U.S.S.R. since 1917 — what has changed, what has endured, what has flourished?
- How could Orthodoxy or any religion sustain itself in the profoundly inhospitable circumstances of the new Communist regime?
- In what ways did the treatment of different faiths vary in the early years of the Soviet state?*
- Do the various approaches to religion adopted by the Soviet state under Lenin and Stalin reveal the existence of fundamentally different attitudes toward religion, or are they simply different political tactics?
- In what ways have international relations restricted or enlarged the ability of Soviet citizens to practice their religious beliefs?

Religious Life

- How do people of faith in the Soviet Union practice their beliefs?
- Do Soviet authorities see their own statements about freedom of conscience as hypocritical in light of repeated official antireligious statements?

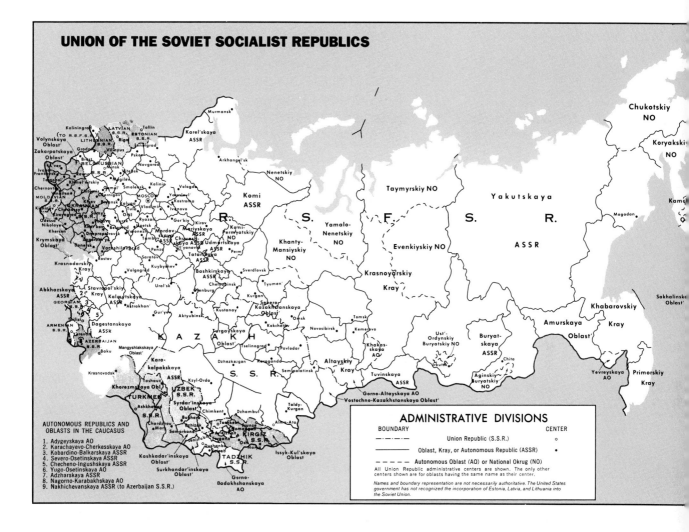

UNION OF THE SOVIET SOCIALIST REPUBLICS

AUTONOMOUS REPUBLICS AND
OBLASTS IN THE CAUCASUS

1. Adygeyskaya AO
2. Karachayevo-Cherkesskaya AO
3. Kabardino-Balkarskaya ASSR
4. Severo-Osetinskaya ASSR
5. Checheno-Ingushskaya ASSR
6. Yugo-Osetinskaya AO
7. Adzharskaya ASSR
8. Nagorno-Karabakhskaya AO
9. Nakhichevanskaya ASSR (to Azerbaijan S.S.R.)

ADMINISTRATIVE DIVISIONS

BOUNDARY		CENTER
—·—·—	Union Republic (S.S.R.)	◉
————	Oblast, Kray, or Autonomous Republic (ASSR)	•
— — — —	Autonomous Oblast (AO) or National Okrug (NO)	

All Union Republic administrative centers are shown. The only other
centers shown are for oblasts having the same name as their center.

Names and boundary representation are not necessarily authoritative. The United States
government has not recognized the incorporation of Estonia, Latvia, and Lithuania into
the Soviet Union.

■ To what extent are disagreements among Westerners about the state of religious freedom in the Soviet Union disputes about facts, or disputes about values?

■ How do Soviet officials explain the persistence of religion in the Soviet Union?

■ When used to describe the status of religion in the Soviet Union, what is meant by "renaissance"?

■ Can one compare the numbers of "believers" in the Soviet Union to the number of "religious people" in Western Europe?

The Gorbachev Era

■ How do we evaluate the significance of the changes underway in the Soviet Union — will their impact on religious affairs be minimal or enormous?

■ What are some of the religious issues now being debated that were once considered too controversial to be discussed openly? *

- When individuals speak of going "back to Leninist principles" to what are they referring?
- Are religion and atheism viewed today as equally rich sources for social values in the Soviet Union?
- Is "freedom of religion" an absolute, a condition that can be objectively measured everywhere — or does it mean different things to different people at different times?

CONCLUSION

- Has my understanding of religious affairs in the Soviet Union been altered by reading *Keeping the Faiths*?
- Which of my views have been reinforced and which have been called into question?
- What are some of the insights I have gained?
- What are some of the ways religious issues significantly influence U.S.-Soviet relations?

II. TELEPHONE REFERENCE SOURCES

The telephone permits access to a vast range of information. The following organizations, or their libraries, may be able to provide you with answers to short questions on the Soviet Union or U.S.-Soviet relations.

American Sources

■ Access: (202) 785-6630
■ American Association for the Advancement of Slavic Studies: (415) 723-9668
■ The Committee for National Security: (202) 745-2450
■ Department of State, Office of Soviet Affairs: (202) 647-3738
■ Harriman Institute for Advanced Study of the Soviet Union, Columbia University: (212) 280-4623
■ Institute for Soviet American Relations: (202) 387-3034
■ Kennan Institute for Advanced Russian Studies, Smithsonian Institution Libraries: (202) 287-3105
■ Library of Congress, Telephone Reference Service: (202) 287-6500
■ New York Public Library, Telephone Reference Service: (212) 340-0847; Slavic and Soviet Collection: (212) 930-0714
■ Russian and East European Center, University of Illinois: (217) 333-6012
■ Your local library may also have a telephone reference service.

Soviet Sources

■ Embassy of the Union of Soviet Socialist Republics (hours: 9–12, 3–4:30): (202) 628-7551
■ Consulate General of the Union of Soviet Socialist Republics: (415) 922-6642

"Mr. Watson, come here, I want you."
Alexander Graham Bell (speaking the first words transmitted via telephone).

III. EDUCATIONAL PROJECTS
A. Discussion Groups

To continue educating yourself and to begin educating others about the Soviet Union, consider joining an existing community group that might set aside time for interested people to discuss this book. If you are not interested in a discussion group, you might consult the list of other educational projects in part B of this section.

Whether you are a participant in a group or someone organizing or leading a discussion group, it is important to remember that such groups can be used and structured in many different ways. There is not a clearly right or wrong method. Various organizations in your community may run discussion groups in different ways. For example, the local World Affairs Council might run monthly discussion groups as a follow-up for a regular program of presentations at a local high school. A local church or temple may have a smaller and more informal group without a regular speaker. The places where groups meet can also vary widely. In addition to schools and meeting halls, local businesses might provide a conference room and refreshments for regular morning or evening discussion groups.

If you cannot find a local group with which you feel comfortable, you might consider starting a discussion group consisting of people you regularly spend time with anyway. If you commute to work with the same group of people every day, why not turn the 30- or 90-minute ride into a discussion of materials from the *Beyond the Kremlin*? A monthly or weekly luncheon dedicated to discussing the series might also suit some people's schedules.

The actual structure of discussion groups is also quite flexible. Some groups may meet only once; others will have a series of meetings. Each person can read his or her copy of the entire book, or teams can be responsible for presenting a summary of particular parts of the volume to the larger group. Visitors might be invited to speak to certain groups at every meeting, every other meeting, or only at the first and last meeting.

The following nine suggestions and questions may be useful to consider regardless of the structure of your particular group and even if you are already a member of an established group.

1. *Focus:*
Without an articulated focus, discussions tend to wander and people can be left frustrated and confused. When possible, the focus for each future meeting should be discussed and determined at the end of the preceding meeting. Each member of the group, particularly new individuals, should have a clear understanding of the basic issue or question to be discussed. In addition, factual materials from the book should be discussed and summarized at the outset of the meeting. This is particularly important because at any given meeting some members may not have had time to prepare fully.

The asterisked (*) questions at the beginning of this guide can be used to help focus a discussion. The following section entitled "Questions and Answers" illustrates the range of answers that may be offered by members of a discussion group.

2. *Questions and Answers:*

A wide range of views may be voiced in response to discussion questions. The sample below refers to a single question, the third in section four: "To what extent are disagreements among Westerners about the state of religious freedom in the Soviet Union disputes about facts, or disputes about values?"

- "It's not about values or images, it's about facts; some people just don't want to see them."
- "Endless debates about numbers of refuseniks, numbers of believers, numbers of churches obscure the real issues — issues rooted in our own personal beliefs, fears, and hopes."
- "Freedom of religion simply does not exist in the Soviet Union; that fact is simple and indisputable."
- "People who visit one church in Moscow and then say — as if it were a fact — that religious worship in the Soviet Union is free and open are irresponsible."
- "What tends to be overlooked in these disputes is that the state of religious freedom in the Soviet Union varies — from time to time and religion to religion."
- "No one has a monopoly on the facts; the disputes obviously involve facts as well as personal values."
- "The most important point is not the source of these disputes, but that Americans can argue about religious freedom in the Soviet Union; Soviets can't."

Not all of these sample answers respond directly to the question posed; some are also phrased aggressively. This is to be expected. Individual members of a group will interpret questions differently. Although a freewheeling discussion may be helpful initially to encourage open discussion, each member of the group should be aware of the need to maintain a focus — to help bring the discussion back to the specific question being discussed. One way to refocus a confusing discussion might be to rephrase the discussion question. For example: "Let's try to look at this controversial issue from a slightly different perspective. Rather than trying to determine definitively what is happening now, let's discuss what should be happening. When government officials develop our policy regarding religious issues in the U.S.S.R., what should they take into account: facts alone, values alone, or a combination of both?"

3. *Leadership:*

Decide at your first meeting whether the group wants a designated discussion leader. Groups that have operated without leaders when talking about other issues or books might want to consider having one for this book. Determine the discussion leader's responsibilities (for instance, guiding the discussion, arranging meeting times, and posing and answering questions).

After a leader is selected, he or she should plan to go through this guide carefully and to prepare for each meeting by elaborating on the points made here. Try to anticipate the discussion by mentally "walking through" the entire meeting before it actually takes place. What questions are likely to be asked? What conflicts might occur? How will the meeting end? What issues are likely to be interesting but frustrating or distracting?

4. *Goal:*

Is the group primarily educational or social in its purpose? Are the group meetings designed to complement or lead to some other type of activity?

5. *Meeting Specifics and Atmosphere:*
- Where should meetings be held?
- If one of the aims of the group is to involve new people in discussions of U.S.-Soviet relations, how will they be notified of the group's meetings — by a phone network or announcements in the local paper?
- Should food be served — drinks, snacks, a meal?
- How many people should be in the group — 5–10 or 15–25 people?
- Should the group meet for 45 minutes, 2 hours, or some other amount of time? Should it meet weekly, biweekly, or monthly?
- Should the group be made up of politically like-minded people, or is a diverse group preferable?

6. *Wrap-Up:*

Determining how to bring meetings to a satisfactory close is difficult. An agreed-upon time limit eases this problem, but someone still needs to summarize the discussion, noting agreements, disagreements, and unresolved questions. One person might be selected at the start of each meeting to be responsible for wrap-up.

Discussions aimed at understanding the relationships between religion and ideology in the Soviet Union are likely to provoke further questions and curiosity about many aspects of the Soviet Union. Expect that questions, rather than hard-and-fast conclusions, will result from discussion group meetings. (Some of these questions might be answered by undertaking some of the educational projects suggested below in part B.)

7. *Potential Problems:*

Successful group relations are very important but difficult to ensure, especially for an informal group. You should probably anticipate the following:
- *Attrition:* Throughout the weeks or months that the group meets,

people will periodically drop out.

■ *Scheduling:* Most people already have full calendars; becoming accustomed to new obligations takes time and commitment.

■ *"Hot spots":* Certain aspects of the Soviet Union and U.S.-Soviet relations are particularly explosive; these will inevitably arise and need to be dealt with. It helps to be aware of some of them and to think about why they are so sensitive. This is especially true if any members of your group have recently traveled to the Soviet Union or emigrated to America. Each member of a group will probably have his or her sensitive issues that may be raised during discussions. Some of these may prompt discussion about the following "hot spots":

■ Immorality of the Soviet regime.
■ Excessive influence of the American Jewish lobby.
■ Naivete of American church groups.
■ Blinding anticommunism that denies the power of Russian religious tradition.
■ Insignificant changes in Soviet tactics regarding believers.
■ Obvious revolutionary nature of Gorbachev's changes.

The "hot spots" just cited were intentionally phrased in a provocative manner, in judgmental and emotional language. Potentially tense situations can often be defused by choosing words that show respect even if they are critical. Topics such as these should not be avoided; they do need to be discussed and will almost certainly arise at some point during the group's meetings. Handling such discussions may be difficult, however, and will tax the diplomatic skills of experienced discussion leaders. A few tips may be helpful:

■ Don't cut people off; let them say in their own words what they feel.
■ Admit to disagreements when they occur; aim for tolerance and understanding of diverse views, not consensus.
■ Acknowledge people's fears and doubts; seek to understand, not to dispel them.
■ Encourage people not simply to restate their views but to share with the group why they hold certain views.
■ Invite group members to respond to all views; if they disagree, encourage them to offer an alternative.

8. *"Why Am I Doing This?":*
There will probably come a time when each member of a group will grapple with this question. It is not an easy one, and it generally requires a reassessment of individual or group goals. Groups and members change over time. Some groups may move in directions that alienate certain members. Certain members may undergo experiences that alter their interest or ability to participate. After a few meetings, group time should probably be set aside to discuss both the structure and direction of future meetings, and what has been accomplished so far.

9. *The Pontificator Vs. the Silent One:*
As the saying goes, "there is one in every crowd." Unless your group is chosen quite selectively, there are bound to be members with varied (and sometimes conflicting) styles, mannerisms, and attitudes. If there is one rule that applies to members of small community groups as well as to negotiators for the superpowers, it is that dealing with people who are different from ourselves is difficult but worthwhile. Patience, tolerance, and sensitivity to the needs and fears of others is essential to meaningful discussions.

The final part of this section of the guide provides three models for how discussion groups might be organized and planned.

Model 1: Complementing Ongoing Activities

Organizers	Community organizations, civic groups, clubs
Frequency	Monthly, first Monday, 7:30 p.m.
Pace and responsibility	Members read one chapter a month
Focus	Topic addressed by guest speaker — summarized at outset of meeting
Leadership	Chairperson, sponsoring group
Goal	Education and outreach
Size/location	25–30, classroom
Potential problems	Poor speaker
Wrap-up	Two-hour firm limit for meeting

Model 2: Increasing Awareness among Friends

Organizers	Groups of commuters, neighbors
Frequency	Weekly, Wednesday, 8:15 a.m.
Format	During morning commute
Pace and responsibility	Teams describe chapters to group, two meetings per chapter
Focus	Asterisked questions from Reader's Guide
Leadership	Organizer
Goal	Educational use of spare time
Size/location	6 per bus, car, or train
Potential problems	Lack of time, distractions
Wrap-up	Arrival at destination

Model 3: Acquiring In-Depth Knowledge of the U.S.S.R.

Organizers	Travel groups, adult education classes, and others
Frequency	Weekly, during month prior to trip
Format	Pot-luck dinner
Pace and responsibility	Members read one chapter a week
Focus	Questions chosen by group members at planning meeting
Leadership	No single leader
Goal	Preparation for trip
Size/location	8–10, neighbors; apartments or houses
Potential problems	Lack of a leader
Wrap-up	By designated person at each meeting

B. Additional Projects

1. Develop a "Sister Congregation" project with the help of local religious organizations so you can communicate directly with groups in the U.S.S.R. Consider working through the Soviet and American embassies as well as national religious and ecumenical organizations.

2. Compare the annotated reading list at the end of this guide to the card catalog of books available in local public and school libraries. Make suggestions for new purchases or give missing books as gifts.

3. Organize a series of interdenominational meetings within your community to discuss the importance of religion in U.S.-Soviet relations.

4. Offer to provide local libraries or religious institutions with a regularly updated file of articles on religion in the Soviet Union.

5. Organize a small group of friends to monitor congressional debates about issues relating to religion in the U.S.S.R. — such as the Jackson-Vanik amendment.

6. Contact the Committee for National Security and indicate your willingness either to give the *Beyond the Kremlin* series to a local library or school as a gift, or to help with the distribution of the series in your community.

7. Offer to provide speakers on the Soviet Union to groups of friends, neighbors, colleagues, or classes.

8. Distribute *Beyond the Kremlin* to readers and organize a regular discussion group (see the earlier section on discussion groups).

9. Plan a local, regional, or national conference on U.S.-Soviet relations (see *Organizing a Conference on National Security*, published by the Committee for National Security).

10. Review or critique this book and other publications on the Soviet Union for a local newspaper, newsletter, or nonprofit organization.

11. Plan an interdenominational trip to the Soviet Union and provide preparatory educational materials to participants.

IV. ANNOTATED BIBLIOGRAPHY
The Russian Religious Tradition

Bailey, J. Martin, *One Thousand Years: Stories from the History of Christianity in the U.S.S.R.* (New York: Friendship Press, 1987), 61 pages. Popularly written spiritual biographies of seven Russian Christians, including one Orthodox metropolitan and one Baptist from the second half of the twentieth century.

Baron, Salo Wittmayer, *The Russian Jew under Tsars and Soviets* (New York: Macmillan, 1976), 468 pages. Originally published in 1964, this is an authoritative history of the Jews from tsarist times until the era of Khrushchev.

Belliustin, Ioann S., *Description of the Clergy of Rural Russia: The Memoir of a Nineteenth-Century Parish Priest,* trans. by Gregory L. Freeze (Ithaca, NY: Cornell University Press, 1985), 214 pages. A bitter critique of the Russian church by an outspoken priest who died in 1890. This critique was originally published in 1858 in France since it could not be published legally in Russia. The long introduction written by Gregory Freeze contains a good description of the Orthodox Church as the state church of the nineteenth century.

Bennigsen, Alexandre and Chantal Lemercier-Quelquejay, *Islam in the Soviet Union* (New York: Praeger, 1967), 272 pages. The first sixty pages of this book give an insightful history of Muslims in Russia before the revolution. The rest of the book is a helpful treatment of Soviet policy toward Islam.

Berdyaev, Nicolas, *The Origin of Russian Communism* (Ann Arbor, MI: University of Michigan Press, 1969), 191 pages. Originally published in 1937, this essay attempts to demonstrate that Soviet Communism is a traditionally Russian religious phenomenon in a distorted form.

Billington, James, *The Icon and the Axe: An Interpretive History of Russian Culture* (New York: Random House, 1970), 786 pages. A detailed discussion of the intellectual history of Russia from pre-Christian Kiev through the Khrushchev era in which the influence of various religious currents figures prominently.

Bolshakoff, Sergius, *Russian Mystics* (Kalamazoo: Cistercian Publications, 1980), 303 pages. A clear exposition of the history of Russian monasticism, with separate chapters devoted to the lives of especially important monks, including Nil of Sora, Tikhon of Zadonsk, Seraphim of Sarov, Ignatius Brianchaninov, and Paisy Velichkovsky.

Brandenberg, Hans, *The Meek and the Mighty: The Emergence of the Evangelical Movement in Russia* (New York: Columbia University Press, 1977), 210 pages. A study of the rise of the Baptists in Russia in the nineteenth century.

Fedotov, George P., ed., *A Treasury of Russian Spirituality* (New York: Sheed and Ward, 1950), 501 pages. A collection of classic texts of Russian Orthodox religious literature, including lives of Saints Theodosius of the

"Books are the treasured wealth of the world."
Henry David Thoreau

Caves, Sergius of Radonezh, Nil of Sora, Tikhon of Zadonsk, and Seraphim of Sarov, and devotional writings on prayer and self-examination.

Klier, John D., *Russia Gathers Her Jews: The Origins of the "Jewish Question" in Russia, 1772–1825* (Dekalb, IL: Northern Illinois University Press, 1986), 236 pages. A clear, scholarly history of the state's treatment of Jews when they were incorporated into the empire for the first time as a result of Russian expansion into Polish territory.

Leskov, Nikolai S., *The Cathedral Folk* (Westport, CT: Hyperion, 1986), 439 pages. This brilliant and entertaining novel shows Russian religion from an eyewitness and participant perspective. Originally published in 1872, it portrays the parish life of Orthodox clergy and laypeople.

Meyendorff, John, *The Orthodox Church* (Crestwood, NY: St. Vladimir's Seminary Press, 1981), 258 pages. A history of Eastern Orthodoxy from the Roman Empire to the present. Chapters 6 and 7 present an excellent survey of the history of the Russian Orthodox Church from 988 to the Khrushchev era. This is an exceptionally helpful introduction to Orthodoxy for the non-Orthodox reader.

Miliukov, Paul, *Outlines of Russian Culture, Vol. I. Religion and the Church in Russia* (New York: Barnes, 1972), 220 pages. Written by the leader of the liberal democrats in Russia at the time of the revolution, this history of Russian Christianity from 988 to the 1920s gives more attention to the non-Orthodox movements of dissent against the church than to the church itself.

Ouspensky, Leonide, *Theology of the Icon* (Crestwood, NY: St. Vladimir's Seminary Press, 1978), 232 pages. A sophisticated treatment of the place and meaning of icons in the Eastern Orthodox tradition written by a Russian theologian.

Steeves, Paul D., ed., *The Modern Encyclopedia of Religions of Russia and the Soviet Union* (Gulf Breeze, FL: Academic International Press, 1988). A multi-volume reference work containing information on all aspects of religious activity in the societies included within the boundaries of the Russian empire and the U.S.S.R.

Thompson, Ewa M., *Understanding Russia: The Holy Fool in Russian Culture* (Lanham, MD: University Press of America, 1987), 229 pages. A scholarly study of Russian holy men who behaved like mad men and who were called "fools for the sake of Christ." The study expounds character traits of the Russian people in the light of their regard for these strange persons.

Zernov, Nicolas, *The Russian Religious Renaissance of the Twentieth Century* (New York: Harper & Row, 1963), 410 pages. An exposition of the emergence of interest in Orthodoxy among Russian intellectuals just after the turn of the century, with special attention to four leading Marxists who converted to Christianity, Peter Struve, Sergius Bulgakov, Nicolas Berdiaev, and Simon Frank.

Religion and Revolution

Alexeev, Wassilij and Theofanis G. Stavrou, *The Great Revival: The Russian Church under German Occupation* (Minneapolis: Burgess, 1976), 229 pages. An account of the reopening of churches, closed during the Stalinist attack upon religion in the 1930s, in the western regions of the U.S.S.R. between 1941 and 1944.

Anti-Semitism in the Soviet Union: Its Roots and Consequences, 3 vols. (Jerusalem, 1979–1983). Collections of papers delivered at international conferences by scholars and recent Jewish emigrants. Volume 3 includes reprints of material of an anti-Semitic nature from the Soviet Union.

Beeson, Trevor, *Discretion and Valour: Religious Conditions in Russia and Eastern Europe* (Philadelphia: Fortress, 1982), 416 pages. A slightly revised version of a 1974 study, about forty percent of this book deals with the history of church-state relations in the Soviet Union. It contains much factual material about the Orthodox and other Christian religions; the treatment of Judaism and Islam is sketchy.

Bennigsen, Alexandre and Marie Broxup, *The Islamic Threat to the Soviet State* (New York: St. Martin's, 1983), 170 pages. A handy introduction to the history of Muslims under both tsarist and Soviet rule, with a reference to the international context in which Soviet policy toward Muslims developed.

Bennigsen, Alexandre and S. Enders Wimbush, *Muslims of the Soviet Empire: A Guide* (Bloomington: Indiana University Press, 1986), 308 pages. A reference book that provides a broad variety of information about the Islamic population of the Soviet Union.

Bociurkiw, Bohdan, *Ukrainian Churches under Soviet Rule: Two Case Studies* (Cambridge, MA: Harvard University Ukrainian Studies, 1984), 60 pages. Scholarly treatment of two churches that exist illegally in the Soviet Union, the Ukrainian Orthodox Church and the Ukrainian Catholic Church.

Buss, Gerald, *The Bear's Hug: Religious Believers in the Soviet State, 1917–1986.* (Grand Rapids: Eerdmans, 1986), 224 pages. A reliable summary of basic information about church-state relations from a generally anti-Soviet perspective.

Dunn, Dennis J., *The Catholic Church and the Soviet Government: 1939–1949* (New York: Columbia University Press, 1977), 267 pages. A detailed scholarly account, with special attention to the Kremlin's policy toward the Vatican.

Dunn, Dennis J., ed., *Religion and Modernization in the Soviet Union* (Boulder, CO: Westview Press, 1977), 414 pages. Twelve scholarly articles, five of which deal with religion under Soviet rule in general and others which deal separately with Judaism, Islam, Protestantism, Russian Orthodoxy, Ukrainian Orthodoxy, and Latin Rite Catholicism.

Fletcher, William C., *Soviet Charismatics: The Pentecostals in the U.S.S.R.* (New York: Peter Lang Publishers, 1985), 287 pages. A dispassionate treatment of legal and illegal Pentecostal groups.

Fletcher, William C., *A Study in Survival: The Church in Russia, 1927–1943* (New York: Macmillan, 1965), 168 pages. A scholarly study of the development of the strategy of Metropolitan Sergius for coping with the antireligious policy of the Soviet regime.

Kolarz, Walter, *Religion in the Soviet Union* (New York: St. Martin's, 1966), 518 pages. Written in 1960, this is the most thorough work ever published on all religions of the U.S.S.R., and even though it is over twenty years old its historical material is of undiminished value.

Korey, William, *The Soviet Cage: Anti-Semitism in Russia* (New York: Viking, 1973), 369 pages. A survey of anti-Semitism in the Soviet Union by a specialist in Soviet Jewish affairs.

Levin, Nora, *The Jews in the Soviet Union: A History from 1917 to the Present*, 2 vols. (New York: New York University Press, 1988), 864 pages. The most thoroughly researched study of Jews in the U.S.S.R. to date.

Marshall, Richard H., ed., *Aspects of Religion in the Soviet Union, 1917–1967* (Chicago: University of Chicago Press, 1971), 489 pages. A collection of scholarly articles that serves to supplement and update the material in Kolarz's *Religion in the Soviet Union*, listed above.

Parsons, Howard L., *Christianity Today in the U.S.S.R.* (New York: International Publishers, 1987), 187 pages. This book contains long excerpts from conversations and publications by leaders of the Russian Orthodox, Armenian, Latvian Catholic, Baltic Lutheran, and Baptist churches and several scientific atheist scholars. Its sympathy for the U.S.S.R. is a counterpoint to the hostility of the Buss's *The Bear's Hug*, listed above.

Pospielovsky, Dimitry, *The Russian Church under the Soviet Regime, 1917–1982*, 2 vols. (Crestwood, NY: St. Vladimir's Seminary Press, 1984), 535 pages. A well-researched account of the response of the Russian Orthodox Church to the antireligious policies of the state.

Pospielovsky, Dimitry V., *A History of Marxist-Leninist Atheism and Soviet Anti-Religious Policies* (New York: St. Martin's, 1987), 200 pages, and *Anti-Religious Campaigns and Prosecutions* (New York: St. Martin's, 1988), 256 pages. The first two volumes of a three volume intensive study of the atheist establishment in the Soviet Union. The projected third volume is entitled *Soviet Studies on the Church and the Believer's Response to Atheism*.

Powell, David E., *Antireligious Propaganda in the Soviet Union* (Cambridge, MA: MIT Press, 1975), 206 pages. A history of organized antireligious activity from its beginnings with the League of Militant Atheists in the 1920s.

Rothenberg, Joshua, *The Jewish Religion in the Soviet Union* (New York: Ktav Publishing House, 1971), 242 pages. After a chapter discussing the Soviet laws on religion and their impact on Judaism in particular, the author describes how various forms of Jewish religious practice are carried out under Soviet conditions.

Sawatsky, Walter, *Soviet Evangelicals Since World War II* (Scottdale, PA: Herald, 1981), 527 pages. Excellent scholarly study of the history of the Evangelical Christians–Baptists congregations since the creation of the officially recognized Protestant union; includes a substantial survey of the history of Protestant evangelicalism from its beginning in the mid-nineteenth century.

Thrower, James, *Marxist-Leninist "Scientific Atheism" and the Study of Religion and Atheism in the U.S.S.R.* (Berlin: Mouton, 1983), 500 pages. Critical analysis by a philosopher of the attempt by Soviet atheists to develop a rational refutation of religious belief.

Toews, John B., *Czars, Soviets and Mennonites* (Newton, KS: Faith and Life Press, 1982), 221 pages. Historical account of the Mennonite experience in Imperial Russia and the U.S.S.R., including information on Mennonite emigration.

Religion in Contemporary Soviet Society

Altshuler, Mordechai, *Soviet Jewry Since the Second World War: Population and Social Structure* (Westport, CT: Greenwood Press, 1987), 278 pages. A thorough statistical study and handy reference.

Bennigsen, Alexandre and S. Enders Wimbush, *Mystics and Commissars: Sufism in the Soviet Union* (Berkeley: University of California Press, 1985), 195 pages. Valuable study of political and religious resistance that expresses itself in underground Islamic activity.

Bourdeaux, Michael, *Risen Indeed: Lessons in Faith from the U.S.S.R.* (Crestwood, NY: St. Vladimir's Seminary Press, 1983), 113 pages. A semi-devotional and inspirational collection of accounts of Russians living out their piety in adverse circumstances.

Braeker, Hans, "Buddhism in the Soviet Union: Annihilation or Survival?" *Religion in Communist Lands*, vol. 11, no. 1 (Spring 1983), pp. 36–48. Virtually the only reliable information about Buddhism in the Soviet Union available in English.

Critchlow, James, "Islam and Nationalism in Soviet Central Asia" in Pedro Ramet, ed., *Religion and Nationalism in Soviet and East European Politics* (Durham, NC: Duke University Press, 1984), pp. 104–120. Examines the continued vitality of Islam in supporting national identity among traditionally Muslim ethnic groups.

Dudko, Dmitry, *Our Hope* (Crestwood, NY: St. Vladimir's Seminary Press, 1977), 292 pages. A faith statement by an Orthodox priest who provided theological direction to the intellectuals who were rediscovering Orthodoxy in the religious renaissance of the 1970s.

Ellis, Jane, *The Russian Orthodox Church: A Contemporary History* (Bloomington, IN: Indiana University Press, 1986), 540 pages. The most exhaustive study of the internal life of the church available in English, with chapters on the Orthodox clergy, bishops, monks, parishes, and theological education. Part 2 contains a thorough analysis of the literature of the Orthodox religious renaissance of the 1970s.

Fletcher, William C., *Soviet Believers: The Religious Sector of the Population* (Lawrence, KS: Regents Press of Kansas, 1981), 259 pages. A critical analysis of studies of religion reported by sociologists in the Soviet Union.

Kojevnikov, Alyona, "Religious Renaissance in the Russian Orthodox Church: Fact or Fiction?" *Journal of Church and State*, vol. 28 (Autumn 1986), pp. 459–474. Documentation of the renewal of interest in Orthodoxy on the part of formerly nonreligious intellectuals.

Pankhurst, Jerry, "Religion and Atheism in the U.S.S.R." in Sacks, Michael P. and Jerry G. Pankhurst, *Understanding Soviet Society* (Winchester, MA: Allen and Unwin, 1988), 320 pages. A sociological model for describing the way in which religion has survived under the policies of the Communist Party state.

Pospielovsky, Dimitry, "Intelligentsia and Religion: Aspects of Religious Revival in the Contemporary Soviet Union. The Orthodox Church" in Dennis J. Dunn, ed., *Religion and Communist Society* (Berkeley, CA: Berkeley Slavic Specialties, 1983), pp. 11–44. A well-documented study of conversions to Orthodoxy in the 1970s.

Soviet Jewish Affairs, vol. 15, no. 1 (1985). This issue contains a number of scholarly articles presented at a conference on Soviet policies affecting national groups and religion. The following articles are especially noteworthy: Philip Walters, "Soviet Policy on Religion," pp. 72–78; John A. Armstrong, "Soviet Nationalities Policies," pp. 57–71; Zvi Gitelman, "The Abridgement of the Rights of Jews in the Fields of Nationality, Culture, and Religion," pp. 79–87; and Helene Carrere d'Encausse, "The Islamic Minorities," pp. 88–95.

Steeves, Paul D., "Amendment of Soviet Law Concerning Religious Groups," *Journal of Church and State*, vol. 19, no. 1 (1977), pp. 37–52. Analyzes the practical effects of the system of Soviet legislation governing religious activities.

The Gorbachev Era

Broun, Janice, "Still Waiting for the Millennium. The Churches and Soviet 'Glasnost,'" *Commonweal*, October 23, 1987, pp. 592–595. A list of both the gains and frustrations of the glasnost era in 1987.

Commission on Security and Cooperation in Europe, *Reform and Human Rights: The Gorbachev Record* (Washington: U.S. Government Printing Office, 1988), 89 pages. A summary of important developments through the spring of 1988 produced by the American "Helsinki Commission."

Levin, Nora, "American Jewish Concern for Soviet Jews," *Occasional Papers on Religion in Eastern Europe*, vol. 8, no. 1 (February 1988), pp. 1–10. Reflections on the support Americans have given to Soviet Jews, including reference to Gorbachev's policies on Jewish emigration.

Soviet Life, July 1988, pp. 39–65. This Soviet magazine produced for foreign readers marked the millennium celebration with impressive pictures and a variety of human-interest articles dealing with Orthodox, Old Believers, and Baptists.

Steeves, Paul D., "The June Plenum and the Post-Brezhnev Antireligious Campaign," *Journal of Church and State*, vol. 28 (Autumn 1986), pp. 439–458. Discusses the political background of the approach to religion adopted in Gorbachev's reform program.

Periodicals

Regular information about religion in the Soviet Union can be found in the following periodical publications.

Keston News Service (bi-weekly), *Frontier Magazine* (bi-monthly), and *Religion in Communist Lands* (three issues per year) from Keston, USA, P.O. Box 1310, Framingham, MA 01701.

Religion in Communist Dominated Areas (quarterly), published by Research Center for Religion and Human Rights in Closed Societies, 475 Riverside Drive, New York, NY 10115.

CAREE Communicator and Occasional Papers on Religion in Eastern Europe, published by Christians Associated for Relationships with Eastern Europe, 475 Riverside Drive, New York, NY 10015.

Light in the East News (bi-monthly) published by Light in the East, 184 Mars Hill Road N.W., Powder Springs, GA 30073.

Journal of the Moscow Patriarchate and *Muslims of the Soviet East* are English publications produced in the Soviet Union, available by subscription through Imported Publications, 320 W. Ohio St., Chicago, IL 60610.

Newsbank (bi-weekly), from National Conference on Soviet Jewry, 10 East 40th Street, Suite 907, New York, NY 10016.

Videotapes

The following videos present the religious situation in the Soviet Union as of the mid-1980s.

A Glimpse of Heaven: Easter in the Soviet Union, 58 minutes, 1985. Produced by the Canadian Broadcasting Company, this film depicts a visit to the Soviet Union made by a delegation of Canadians in April 1985. It touches on issues of religious freedom, Jewish emigration, and peace.

Candle in the Wind, 58 minutes, 1984. Produced by Pacem Partnership of San Bernadino. Treats the difficulties in relationships between the state and Muslims, Jews, and Christians.

The Church of the Russians, 2 parts, 57 minutes each, 1985. Produced cooperatively by the National Broadcasting Company and the National Council of Churches, this description of the Russian Orthodox Church caused considerable controversy in the West because of its optimistic portrayal of the vitality of the church.

Primary Sources

Primary sources for the history of ideology and religion in the Soviet Union.

Lenin, Vladimir Ilich, *Collected Works,* 25 vols. (Moscow: Progress Publishers, 1964).

Stalin, Josef, *Works,* 13 vols. (Moscow: Progress Publishers, 1953–1955).

Kuroedov, V.A. and A.S. Pankratov, *Zakonodatel'stvo o religioznykh kul'takh* (Moscow: Iuridicheskaia literatura, 1971).

Vernadsky, George, et al., *A Source Book for Russian History,* 3 vols. (New Haven: Yale University Press, 1972).

Kommunisticheskaia partiia sovetskogo soiuza v rezoliutsiiakh i resheniiakh s"ezdov, konferentsii i plenumov TsK (Communist Party of the Soviet Union in Resolutions and Decisions of Congresses, Conferences, and Plenums of the Central Committee), 14 vols. (Moscow: Izdatel'stvo politicheskoi literatury, 1970–1987).